Christianity and Contemporary Politics

Christianity and Contemporary Politics

The Conditions and Possibilities of Faithful Witness

Luke Bretherton

WILEY-BLACKWELL

A John Wiley & Sons, Ltd., Publication

This edition first published 2010
© 2010 Luke Bretherton

Blackwell Publishing was acquired by John Wiley & Sons in February 2007. Blackwell's publishing program has been merged with Wiley's global Scientific, Technical, and Medical business to form Wiley-Blackwell.

Registered Office
John Wiley & Sons Ltd, The Atrium, Southern Gate, Chichester, West Sussex, PO19 8SQ, United Kingdom

Editorial Offices
350 Main Street, Malden, MA 02148-5020, USA
9600 Garsington Road, Oxford, OX4 2DQ, UK
The Atrium, Southern Gate, Chichester, West Sussex, PO19 8SQ, UK

For details of our global editorial offices, for customer services, and for information about how to apply for permission to reuse the copyright material in this book please see our website at www.wiley.com/wiley-blackwell.

The right of Luke Bretherton to be identified as the author of this work has been asserted in accordance with the UK Copyright, Designs and Patents Act 1988.

Wiley also publishes its books in a variety of electronic formats. Some content that appears in print may not be available in electronic books.

Designations used by companies to distinguish their products are often claimed as trademarks. All brand names and product names used in this book are trade names, service marks, trademarks or registered trademarks of their respective owners. The publisher is not associated with any product or vendor mentioned in this book. This publication is designed to provide accurate and authoritative information in regard to the subject matter covered. It is sold on the understanding that the publisher is not engaged in rendering professional services. If professional advice or other expert assistance is required, the services of a competent professional should be sought.

Library of Congress Cataloging-in-Publication Data

Bretherton, Luke.
  Christianity and contemporary politics : the conditions and possibilities of faithful witness / Luke Bretherton.
    p. cm.
  Includes bibliographical references (p.   ) and index.
  ISBN 978-1-4051-9968-1 (hardcover : alk. paper) – ISBN 978-1-4051-9969-8 (pbk. : alk. paper) 1. Christians–Political activity. 2. Christianity and politics. 3. Church and state. 4. Citizenship–Religious aspects. 5. Church work. I. Title.
  BR115.P7B675 2010
  261.7–dc22
                                                          2009029983

Set in 10/12.5pt Sabon by SPi Publisher Services, Pondicherry, India
Printed in Singapore by Ho Printing Singapore Pte Ltd

04   2014

For my mother and father

But seek the welfare of the city where I have sent you into exile, and pray to the Lord on its behalf, for in its welfare you will find your welfare. (Jeremiah 29.7)

Contents

Preface

This book emerges in large part out of reflecting on the neighborhood in which I grew up and close to which I still live. I grew up in the 1970s and 80s in West London. My neighborhood was variously described as North Kensington, Notting Hill, Ladbroke Grove, and Holland Park. Each term had a different social, economic, and political nuance. The first denoted an oppositional identity, with its unspoken assertion "I don't live in Chelsea"; the second made a claim for bohemian and literary color; the third for street solidarity and multicultural credibility; and the last accented class and good manners. As an insecure teenager I would make use of each of these descriptions so as to recalibrate my identity according to context and to whom I was talking. In addition to a sense of place, issues of class and ethnicity had to be negotiated: I was white and middle class in an area with a large Afro-Caribbean population. The Notting Hill Carnival went past the bottom of my street and in those days it was not perceived as a celebration of multicultural Britain but as a threat of violent disorder. The perception had some truth: there were a number of riots and murders and tensions always ran high. It was not until my late teens that I ventured down All Saints Road, a short walk from my house, as it was then the "frontline" between the Afro-Caribbean community and the police, and a white face was pointedly not welcome. But I had an additional identity that situated me as both an insider and an outsider simultaneously.

My parents are Evangelical Christians. To most of my school friends and neighbors, being this kind of Christian was a mark of weirdness and slightly suspect. For me, it meant that I felt I was supposed to disapprove of things everyone else seemed to find perfectly acceptable, namely sex, drugs, and rock 'n' roll. Yet while it marked me out from my social class, looking back, I realize that it brought me closer to the world around me. We worshiped at a local Anglican church where black and white, rich and poor, old and young came together Sunday by Sunday and many times in between. In 1963, through the church, my parents helped set up and run Latimer Housing

Association which provided good quality housing to low income families. It had been established as they began to see first hand the impact of the slum landlord Peter Rackman on members of their congregation. Rackman's henchmen would violently evict sitting tenants of properties he purchased (as they had statutory protection against high rent increases) and then pack the properties with recent immigrants. New tenants did not have the same protection under the law as the sitting tenants had possessed following the relaxation of rent controls by the Conservative government in 1957. This meant that they could be charged any amount Rackman wished. Most of the new tenants were Afro-Caribbeans who had no choice but to accept the high rents as it was difficult for them to obtain housing in London at the time because of racism. Notting Hill was the main area in which Rackman operated. In response to his activities a number of housing associations were initiated. They raised money from friends, jumble sales, and taking out loans in order to buy properties to refurbish and rent out. It was a form of community self-organization that only later on was helped and supported by state-led initiatives. For many years Latimer's office was the front half of our sitting room. I had to spend interminable amounts of time accompanying my parents to sort out various problems in the flats they administered, or waiting while my mother talked to some passer-by on the street about their rent situation.[1]

Two events drew all the different Christian denominations in the area together, including the large black majority Pentecostal church, Kensington Temple. The first was the communion services before Carnival where we would pray for peace and joy during the event. The second was the "Way of the Cross," a Good Friday stational liturgy that reenacted the Passion through the streets and culminated in staging the crucifixion in one of the large council housing estates. A particularly memorable one involved Cardinal Basil Hume, the then Catholic Archbishop of Westminster, leading a meditation surrounded by the tower blocks of the Lancaster West estate after David, who was black, had played the role of Jesus and hung on a cross in the middle of the estate. This was at a time of intense racial conflict and unrest.

It was the churches that were central to the civic life of my neighborhood and the vector through which the different and otherwise unrelated communities intersected. Differences were not denied or overcome but did, at the very least, come into relationship and a common world of action and shared responsibility was forged. My parents' relationship with Fr David Randall and Robin Tuck illustrates this. My parents were North Kensington Conservatives – a kind of Victorian civic conservatism that was very different to what my father viewed as the somewhat decadent, self-serving Conservatives who lived around Chelsea and South Kensington. Mrs Thatcher was a hero to him and he would fulminate against left-wing liberals who were, in his view, destroying the country. My parents are also very morally conservative. Fr Randall was a gay Anglo-Catholic and Christian Socialist priest who was much influenced by Liberation theology. Mr Tuck was an active member of the Liberal Party. Yet they all worked closely together in relation to the local Church of England primary school of which my mother is still a governor. Mr Tuck was the chair of governors, my mother the vice-chair, and it was Fr Randall's church to which the school was attached. When the school was destroyed in 1983 as result of a fire their relationship was crucial to building a new one and amalgamating the school with another local Church of England primary school, in order to create a stronger and better institution. Theirs was not simply a professional or civic relationship, but an ecclesial friendship that interlaced the public and private, *oikos* and *polis*, and common worship. As well as committee meetings and signing contracts, they enjoyed each other's hospitality and prayed and worshiped together.

The world I grew up in has been all but swept away by rising house prices, processes of gentrification, and the local impact of the City of London becoming the clearinghouse of global capitalism. There is little left of the conflicted yet common world that once existed. Notting Hill is now a homogenous if picturesque dormitory for plutocrats and their entourage. Most of its current immigrants are wealthy cosmopolitans from across the globe. Understandably they have little sense of place or involvement in the fabric of their neighborhood as they are only passing through. Of course, the irony is that when my parents moved into the area in 1961 they were the vanguard of these processes of gentrification. And gentrification has made the area safer, cleaner, and more prosperous.

What has all this to do with a book on Christianity and contemporary politics? Embedded in the home I grew up in was a particular understanding of the relationship between church, civil society, the market, and the state. In my parents' response to the world around them the market had a place but it must know its place. Vulnerable strangers were not to be treated as commodities to be exploited for monetary gain, but potential neighbors to be hosted. The state had a role but neither law nor central government was either the best or first place to turn to in order to address social, economic, and political problems. In the first instance neighborhoods could organize themselves to address issues of poverty or racial and religious conflict. One's identity, beliefs, and practices were to be hallowed and formed the deepest level of motivation, yet it was recognized that one's own primary community, be it based on religion, class, or ethnicity, was never all encompassing and never sufficient in itself to sustain a life of human flourishing. Rather, a shared life based around goods in common – for example, the good of education, health, or family – must be forged in order that the welfare of both you and your neighbor might be met. As the recent history of Notting Hill suggests, if the power of either the state or the market or of one particular community becomes too dominant, the fragile ecology that sustains a common world of action and responsibility amid difference and difficulty will collapse under the stress.

Luke Bretherton
Easter, 2009

Note

1   Latimer Housing Association was eventually merged with Octavia Hill Housing Association in 1985. My father is still a trustee.

Acknowledgments

I would like to thank Michael Banner, Stanley Hauerwas, Charles Mathewes, Joan Lockwood O'Donovan, Oliver O'Donovan, and Paul Janz for their comments on and critique of different aspects of this book; their insights were invaluable. I owe a huge debt to Maurice Glasman for the ongoing conversation, friendship, and perspective he has given me and without whom some of the key political insights could not have been developed. I am also greatly indebted to Neil Jamieson, Jonathan Lange, Jane Wills, Leo Penta, and all the many organizers and leaders of London Citizens and the Industrial Areas Foundation (IAF) for their trust, inspiration, and for opening out a world and a work to me that has provoked many of the reflections set out here. In relation to this I must thank the Arts and Humanities Research Council (AHRC) for the grant that sponsored some of the research for Chapter 2 and David Perry and the Great Cities Institute, University of Illinois in Chicago for their generous hospitality during my use of the IAF archive. The AHRC grant is related to a three-year qualitative, historical, and theoretical study of the relationship between the churches and community organizing. A particular word of thanks is owed to my immediate colleagues at King's College London, Alister McGrath, Andrew Walker, Pete Ward, and James Steven, all of whom have supported and enabled me to undertake this research in innumerable ways and whose conversation and encouragement have been key in its development. I would also like to thank my PhD students and the many students on the DMin and Theology, Politics, and Faith-Based Organizations MA who have interacted with various parts of this work. Their insights and responses, drawn as these students are from ongoing leadership in congregations and Christian ministries, have helped keep the work honest and engaged with their questions and struggles in negotiating faithfully the contemporary context. From another angle, I am grateful to John Casson and the participants in the Roundtable on Political Theology and Public Policy, which included representatives from nongovernmental organizations (NGOs), civil servants, politicians, and party activists, who kept asking how current debates among Christian theologians related to the policy issues they faced on a daily basis. I am not sure if this book goes any way to answering their question, but I hope it clears some of the ground. I must thank Ashley Meany for his prayerful support of this work. My greatest thanks go to my wife, Caroline, and my children, Gabriel and Isaac, for sustaining and abiding with me amid the vicissitudes of the writing process. Lastly, I would like to thank Rebecca Harkin and all those at Wiley-Blackwell who have contributed to the production of this book.

Parts of Chapter 1 have been taken, with revisions, from an article that appeared in *Political Theology*, volume 7, number 3 (2007) under the title of "A New Establishment? Theological Politics and the Emerging Shape of Church–State Relations." This is reprinted by permission of Equinox Publications Ltd.

Parts of Chapter 5 have been taken, with revisions, from an article that appeared in *Studies in Christian Ethics*, volume 19, number 1 (2006) under the title of "The Duty of Care to Refugees, Christian Cosmopolitanism, and the Hallowing of Bare Life." This is reprinted by permission of Sage Publications Ltd.

Introduction

This book is an attempt to make sense of, on the one hand, the intersection between Christianity, place, and identity, and on the other, the relationship between church, civil society, the market, and the state. Understanding the relationship between church, civil society, the market, and the state is vital for addressing the central questions that dominate contemporary politics, namely: What are the limits of the state? What are the limits of money? And what are the limits of community? These questions about the limits of the state, the market, and community are political questions because they relate directly to the just and generous ordering of a common life. For Christians, the challenge is whether there is a specifically Christian response to these questions or whether they can simply accept the responses derived from other, non-Christian ways of framing politics.

Churches today are presenting a variety of answers to these three questions. Some respond by letting the church be construed by the modern bureaucratic state as either one more interest group seeking a share of public money or just another constituency within civil society which can foster social cohesion and make up the deficiencies of the welfare state. The former reduces the church to a client of the state's patronage and the latter co-opts the church in a new form of establishment, one where the state sets the terms and conditions of, and thence controls, the relationship. Another response is for Christians to construe themselves as part of an identity politics. This entails reframing Christian political witness in terms of either multiculturalism – the church becoming just another minority identity group demanding recognition for its way of life as equally valid in relation to all others – or the rhetoric of rights – the church decomposing itself into a collective of rights-bearing individuals pursuing freedom of religious expression. A third response is to let Christianity be construed by the market as a product to be consumed or commodity to be bought and sold so that in the religious marketplace Christianity is simply another privatized lifestyle choice, interchangeable with or equivalent to any other. These three responses can be summarized as the dynamics of co-option, competition, and commodification.

Yet the above responses do not represent the sum total of how churches are answering the questions about the limits of the state, the market, and community. If the wider implication of the dynamics of co-option, competition, and commodification is that they let the church be shaped by conceptualizations and forces external to Christian belief and practice, then there are other forms of practice that attempt patterns of response which are congruent with Christianity. It is these practices that are the subject of this book, which is an attempt to discern ways in which, at a practical level, churches and individual Christians are responding faithfully to the questions about the limits of the state, the market, and community. The first chapter assesses the debate about the state funding of faith-based organizations and their contribution to the provision of social welfare services, both in the US and the UK. The chapter situates church–state relations within the context of wider debates about the contribution of religious actors and religious discourse to public life and assesses how non-theological discourses understand the limits of particular communities in relation to the state. The second chapter develops a constructive model for how different faith groups can work together at a local level. It does this through a theological analysis of broad-based community organizing as exemplified in the work of the Industrial Areas Foundation in the US and London Citizens in the UK. This second chapter outlines how different religious groups, through working together (and thence beyond the bounds of their particular communities), can establish limits to the state and the market. The third chapter addresses debates about asylum seekers and immigration as a case study of the contribution of churches to national politics and the question of how to value national identity. This chapter develops an account of Christian cosmopolitanism as an alternative to, on the one hand, overly protectionist visions of the nation-state, and on the other, abstract accounts of liberal cosmopolitanism that call for borderless states. The chapter sets out a case for, on the one hand, the importance of the nation-state as a territorially bounded arena of law and order, and on the other, of how the nation-state has only relative value. The chapter ends with an analysis of the US Sanctuary movement as an example of political action that embodies a Christian cosmopolitan vision in practice. The last chapter assesses the possibilities of Christian political witness under conditions of economic globalization. It does this through examining the involvement of Christians in "political consumerism," and in particular the Fair Trade movement, as a way of analyzing how Christians in the West can respond to their neighbors in more deprived and unstable parts of the world. The focus of this chapter is how a particular form of practice both values and tries to bring accountability to the globalized economy. At the same time, it sets out a "politics of ordinary time" that describes the responsibilities of ordinary political actors or citizens within their everyday life under conditions of globalization and how this intersects with Christian discipleship.

One way of conceptualizing the mixed response of the church to the questions about the limits of the state, the market, and community is via Augustine. My turn to Augustine is driven not only by the conceptual richness of the categories he developed but also because Augustine is a key figure both in the development of political thought and also in contemporary debates in political philosophy and theology. An additional reason to turn to Augustine is that historically we stand in a context analogous to his own. As Graham Ward notes: "Poised as [Augustine] was on the threshold between radical pluralism (which he called paganism) and the rise of Christendom, we stand on the other side of that history: at the end of Christendom and the re-emergence of radical (as distinct from liberal) pluralism."[1] As will become apparent, Augustine is a key conversation partner throughout the book and provides a common reference point for engagement with a number of other theologians and philosophers.

Augustine divides human societies in two: there is the city of God – which combines both the true church in this age and the New Jerusalem of the age to come – and Babylon or the earthly city.[2] Augustine characterizes the division not as a division *within* society but as a division *between* societies. These two cities are understood as two polities coexistent in one space and time: the time before Christ's return. Citizens of both cities seek peace; however, in the earthly city peace is achieved through the imposition of one's own will by the exercise of force, and is at once costly in its creation,[3] lacking in real justice,[4] and unstable in its existence.[5] For Augustine, the only true society and true peace exist in the city of God. Within Augustine's theology the visible church is as much part of Babylon, and thus directed to prideful ends, as any other part of a society and we should be suspicious of any attempt to identify one particular take on Christianity as somehow the embodiment of the New Jerusalem now. The visible church is always a field of wheat and tares, combining the earthly city and the city of God, and so cannot be separated until the last judgment. An Augustinian political vision identifies the first three responses outlined above – that is, letting the church be co-opted by the state, or situating itself in competition with other minority groups in society, or commodifying Christianity – as forms of pride. They are attempts to create a peace in the church and pursue justice for the church by prideful means.

Augustine's use of Babylon and Jerusalem as tropes draws on Jeremiah 29. The key passage in Jeremiah 29 states:

> Thus says the Lord of hosts, the God of Israel, to all the exiles whom I have sent into exile from Jerusalem to Babylon: Build houses and live in them; plant gardens and eat what they produce. Take wives and have sons and daughters; take wives for your sons, and give your daughters in marriage, that they may bear sons and daughters; multiply there, and do not decrease. But seek the welfare of the city where I have sent you into exile, and pray to the Lord on its behalf, for in its welfare you will find your welfare.[6]

For Augustine, Jeremiah 29 is an allegory of what it means to be a Christian in the earthly city while we wait, not for a return to Jerusalem, but the coming of the New Jerusalem. He writes:

> For, while the two cities [the city of God and the earthly city] are intermingled, we also make use of the peace of Babylon. We do so even though the People of God is delivered from Babylon by faith, so that it is only for a while that we are pilgrims in her midst. It is for this reason, therefore, that the apostle admonishes the Church to pray for kings and for all that are in authority, adding these words: "that we may live a quiet and tranquil life in all godliness and love." [1 Tim. 2.2] Again, when the prophet Jeremiah foretold the captivity which was to befall the ancient People of God, he bade them, by divine command, to go obediently into Babylon, thereby serving God even by their patient endurance, and he himself admonished them to pray for Babylon, saying "in the peace thereof shall ye have peace": the temporal peace which is for the time being shared by the good and the wicked alike.[7]

Augustine is recognizing that before Christ's return the godly and the wicked share a common world, a world in which the sheep and goats can only be separated by God at the last judgment. And that while the People of God are no longer bound by Babylon, until Christ's return, they share in and benefit from the peace and prosperity of Babylon, i.e., the prideful and sinful earthly city. Unlike the responses that fall prey to the dynamics of co-option, competition, and commodification, it is the contention of this book that practices such as Fair Trade or broad-based community organizing are ways in which the church pursues the peace of Babylon, all the time recognizing that this peace is a contingent, relative, and earthly peace. As a whole, the book attempts to hold up a mirror to the churches so they might discern patterns of faithful witness amid the earthly city and recognize when they are motivated more by pride or self-love than by love of God and neighbor.

The allegorical contrast between Jerusalem and Babylon is of course a central theme not only in Augustine but also in the Bible. In the New Testament it is seen most explicitly in Revelation. Despite the very negative portrayal of Babylon as representing the empire of the anti-Christ, Revelation does not counsel Christians to leave Babylon but to be faithful witnesses – martyrs – within Babylon so that all peoples might come to acknowledge and worship God.[8] Following Revelation, Augustine sees the Roman Empire as equivalent to Babylon – a strange, sinful, and evil place directed away from the love of God – but a place that nevertheless, Christians, for the moment, are called to serve God within and enjoy its peace. Augustine is in many ways doing no more than interpreting Paul's advice in Romans 13.1–7 – a passage that directly echoes Jeremiah 29 in its advice to a fearful, oppressed, and diaspora community gathered in a pagan city.[9] Paul advises the church in Rome to be subject to the governing authorities that, although pagan, nevertheless serve the purposes of God.

The challenge of Jeremiah 29 is to repentance and to relearning obedience to God.[10] However, the place and manner of this learning is somewhat counterintuitive: the Israelites were to learn obedience through pursuing the welfare of Babylon and through forming a common life with pagans and oppressors. Jeremiah's call to seek the welfare of Babylon comes to a defeated, subjugated, and marginal people struggling to make sense of what has happened to them.[11] In many ways that is the situation of Christians today: the church no longer has priority and Christians are not in control. The salience of Jeremiah 29 is its call to become part of the public life of the city and to reject the false prophets who perpetuate illusions of escape into a private world of gated communities, religious fantasies centered on Christ's imminent return, or daydreams of revolution; while at the same time, Jeremiah warns us not give way to a despairing fatalism that believes nothing will ever change.

What Jeremiah 29 alerts us to is how the place of exile is now the place where justice and faithfulness can be pursued and how Jerusalem – i.e., where we were most at home – has become a place of faithlessness, oppression, and corruption. In short, the Israelites are to learn in exile what they failed to learn in Jerusalem.[12] Instead of seeing suffering, dislocation, and domination as a reason to despair, the Israelites were invited by Jeremiah to see it as the context where God is most powerfully at work bringing new vision and being present in new ways (something made explicit in Jeremiah 24.1–10).[13] Following John Howard Yoder, this can be pushed further to suggest that Jeremiah is proposing exile in Babylon as a return to the true vocation of the People of God.[14] On Yoder's reading Jesus and the early church follow the Jeremianic pattern of not orienting themselves to the world politically or militarily so as to regain control or be in charge, but missiologically, so as to bear faithful witness.[15] Such a missiological orientation implies neither withdrawal nor subcultural resistance but, as exemplified in the stories of Joseph, Daniel, and Esther, entails combining active investment in Babylon's wellbeing with faithful particularity and obedience to God. On a Christological reading this can be put even more strongly and in the words of Yoder's suggestive translation of Jeremiah 29.7, it entails seeking "the salvation of the culture to which God has sent you."[16] On this account we discover at the heart of Easter the theo-logic of Jeremiah 29: that the way of the cross, the journey into exile, is the beginning of new life and new hope.[17] As will be seen, Jeremiah 29 is a leitmotif of this book and a key text for framing my account of Christian political witness in the contemporary context.

The Terms and Conditions of Political Life

The book offers a primarily theological analysis of the terms and conditions of political life in the contemporary context. However, it is helpful to situate and contrast this analysis at the outset with some other accounts drawn from political philosophy and social theory. There is a wide-ranging debate about the health and vibrancy of democratic life and patterns of civic association in Western liberal democracies. Some argue that what is seen is decline in political participation and the deracination of existing forms of solidarity that are central to maintaining social cohesion and political stability. Others argue that far from decline, what is occurring is the emergence of new forms of political participation and ways of acting together for the common good, ways that are more appropriate to contemporary political problems and patterns of life. For Christians this debate is of direct concern because, on the one hand, churches are and have been historically deeply immersed in the kinds of political association that are said to be declining. In addition, churches in themselves constitute an example of the kind of institution that is said to be under threat. On the other hand, churches are key catalysts and sponsors of emergent forms of political association. As will be seen in Chapter 4, the Fair Trade movement is but one of the most prominent examples of this. Theologically the above debate should be of concern because it directly relates to the conditions and possibilities of Christian witness amid the earthly city.

Four basic approaches can be identified to the question of whether solidarity and political participation in the West is declining or just adapting. First, there is the critique of contemporary political and social life that is pessimistic in outlook and sees the processes of modernization, and liberalism and capitalism in particular, as inherently diminishing the ability to pursue a common good and a just and generous society. The work of Alasdair MacIntyre and Sheldon Wolin are examples of such an approach.[18] The implication of such critiques is that we now live in a post-democratic market-state that has substituted mass, broad-based mobilizations of unions and political parties around substantive political visions for managerial and legal proceduralism divorced from any thick conception of the good. For MacIntyre, the remedy for this decline lies in building up thick communities of character formation that embody particular traditions of practice and visions of the good.[19] These thick communities of character foster the bonds of friendship and enable the rational deliberation that is a necessary precondition for the formation of a just and generous political order.

Second, there is a less stringent version of the first approach that is not directly critical of modernity per se. Its concern arises out of a desire to maintain and uphold modern liberal democratic regimes, but it does argue that there is an ongoing decline in social cohesion and long-established forms of civic association. For example, Robert Putnam tells a story of rise and fall, with a low point in America in the 1880s and a high point of political and civic engagement in the America of the 1950s. Putnam argues that since the 1950s "social capital" in all its forms has declined.[20] For Putnam and others, mass membership organizations, from trade unions and political parties to scouts and churches, socialize members into being more civic-minded and more oriented toward cooperation, trust, and reciprocity.[21] At the same time, such organizations help integrate citizens and the state into a common project.[22] Hence, it is argued, a decline in forms of civic and voluntary association affects the health of civil society, the stability of liberal democracies, and the ability to address intractable social problems such as urban deprivation.[23] Putnam, along with Theda Skocpol, is critical of emergent forms of political organization such as Greenpeace and what they see as the attendant "checkbook activism" and mail-order membership schemes.[24] In Putnam's view such organizations do not foster the kind of give and take and thicker forms of association that older forms of social capital did.[25]

A third account concurs with the first and second insofar as it agrees that there has been decline in both traditional institutions such as churches and modern bureaucratically mediated forms of solidarity such as political parties. However, it is not pessimistic because it sees the new forms of political and civic association and action that are emerging as supplementing and equivalent to older forms of solidarity (or what I will refer to has civic or public friendship). Anthony Giddens, Ulrich Beck, and Manuel Castells are key exponents of this third response.[26] For example, Ulrich Beck, as part of his broader account of "reflexive modernization" and the "risk society," argues that traditional collective and group-specific sources of meaning and identity are disintegrating, leading to a process of individualization and self-reflexivity in relation to social, economic, and political relationships.[27] However, instead of this leading to privatization, active reflection on society, social norms, and rules led to "new socio-cultural commonalities" and a "process of societalization."[28] In other words, new ways of relating and new large-scale forms of solidarity are emerging. These take the form of social movements, subcultures, and fluid political alliances that respond both to the increasing risks of the modernization process and the industrial and administrative interference in the realm of the personal.[29] Existing political institutions (for example, parliament) lose currency as people begin to construct their political and social lives differently and what was previously considered apolitical becomes highly politicized. In turn this leads to what Beck calls "sub-politics." Sub-politics is the de facto shaping and organization of political and social life by agents and organizations outside any formal political-administrative systems.[30] Sub-politics opens a space for new forms of direct political action by ordinary citizens in a global context.[31] It comes to mean for Beck "the shaping of society *from below*."[32] It has a number of consequences, one of which is that decision making is a much more contested and variegated process requiring multilateral negotiation. For Beck, sub-politics "sets politics free by changing the rules and boundaries of the political so that it becomes more open and susceptible to new linkages – as well as capable of being negotiated and reshaped."[33]

The fourth account again accepts that there is a shift in how people in the West are acting together politically. However, exponents of this account say that this is to be welcomed, neither constituting a decline in political engagement nor posing a threat to the health of liberal democracies. They argue that mass membership organizations and formal institutional patterns of political action may have been appropriate to the early stages of democratic development. However, a lack of trust and participation in such mechanisms is a sign of maturity indicative of higher education levels and greater and more widespread critical scrutiny. Pippa Norris argues that "indicators point more strongly towards the evolution, transformation, and reinvention of civic engagement than to its premature death."[34] Ronald Inglehart counters Putnam's pessimism by suggesting that the decline of prior modes of political association is part of a global and structural shift in values in Western societies. What he calls "survival" values of trust, obedience, and work commitment are being replaced by more self-expressive and what Inglehart calls "postmaterialist" values such as tolerance, freedom, and individual fulfillment. This may signal a change in how politics is done, but for Inglehart it represents a deepening of a commitment to democracy.[35]

A complementary but very different account can be found in some strands of post-Marxist thought.[36] For example, emergent forms of political association can be interpreted as part of a move to what Michael Hardt and Antonio Negri call "absolute democracy," and represent the most developed form of resistance to the dominant forms of economic and social production.[37] They state: "The future institutional structure of the new society is embedded in the affective, cooperative, and communicative relationships of social production. The networks of social production, in other words, provide an institutional logic capable of sustaining a new society."[38] Hardt and Negri claim, perhaps somewhat paradoxically, that:

> In the era of imperial sovereignty and biopolitical production, the balance has tipped such that the ruled now tend to be the exclusive producers of social organization. This does not mean that sovereignty immediately crumbles and the rulers lose all their power. It does mean that the rulers become ever more parasitical and that sovereignty becomes increasingly unnecessary. Correspondingly, the ruled become increasingly autonomous.[39]

Like Hardt and Negri, Luc Boltanski and Eve Chiapello, in their critique of the "new spirit of capitalism," see emergent forms of political association as representing both a critique and an outworking of the contemporary form of capitalism.[40] Boltanski and Chiapello argue that capitalism, in order to sustain and legitimize itself, absorbs and adapts to the criticisms that are made of it. Thus, for example, social democracy and the welfare state were adaptations to the critique of Marxism and Socialism.[41] Likewise, the critique of capitalism that emerged in the 1960s and 70s, which focused on the alienation and inauthenticity of the "mass society," and the monolithic, totalitarian conformity and huge size of the bureaucratic organization, have been incorporated into new patterns of management and business. The new spirit of capitalism, exemplified by the ethos and organizational structures of Microsoft and Ben and Jerry's, emphasizes fuzzy organizational boundaries with flat hierarchies, networks of people working in teams, innovation and creativity as part of a constant process of change, and personal flowering through the flexible world of multiple projects pursued by autonomous individuals. This new form of capitalism does bring new forms of oppression and injustice. However, on the basis of Boltanski and Chiapello's work, emergent forms of political association both embody the new "spirit" of capitalism and represent its critique.

All four accounts set out above are problematic when it comes to evaluating the condition of contemporary political life because they all misconstrue the relationship between emergent and existing forms of political and civic association.[42] The first two accounts preclude any symbiotic relationship between existing and emergent patterns of association. Likewise, in the third account, which attempts to relate existing and emergent forms constructively, there is an underlying assumption that what Beck and Giddens call "reflexive modernity" will inevitably result in the breakdown of traditional patterns of association and the emergence of more voluntaristic and individualized ones. Bureaucratic and institutionally mediated forms of association and older, "traditional" forms of solidarity are assumed to be relics of an age that is quickly passing. Thus the fourth account simply makes explicit what is implicit in the third account. Yet there is much evidence to suggest that emergent forms of political association both feed off and renew long-established patterns of political life and rely on and extend prior forms of social capital.[43] An additional factor that destabilizes the above accounts is that the historical development of patterns of political association is far less disjunctive than any of the above accounts allow. We are neither falling from a golden age nor are we locked into a historically deterministic process of inevitable change in one direction. As we shall see, there is a symbiotic relationship between what we might call "traditional" (e.g., churches), "modern" (e.g., political parties), and "emergent" (e.g., Greenpeace) patterns of civic and political association in the contemporary context. A sub-theme of this book is how churches integrate and mediate the relationship between different forms and levels of political action and how faithful political witness must reject overly deterministic declension or ascension narratives about the nature of political life. As will be delineated in Chapter 2, an Augustinian understanding of the relationship between politics, eschatology, and history provides a far more "realistic" basis for assessing the nature and direction of contemporary politics.

Religion and Postsecular Politics

Running alongside and cutting across debates about whether political participation in the West is declining or just adapting within the contemporary context are debates about the relationship between religion and politics. One term increasingly used to name the contemporary conditions and possibilities of the relationship between religion and politics is that of "postsecular." Part of the background to this term, as noted by one of its most prominent exponents, Jürgen Habermas, is a revision of the "secularization thesis."[44] The classic secularization thesis identifies modernization with secularization and sees secularization as an inevitable outcome of processes of modernization such as industrialization, urbanization, specialization, societalization (the shift from local to large-scale and increasingly complex patterns of social formation), and bureaucratization. Secularization names the process whereby, as Bryan Wilson puts it, "religious institutions, actions and consciousness, lose their social significance."[45] The secularization thesis posited a fundamental incompatibility between modernity and religious adherence. However, the empirical basis of the thesis has increasingly come into question, to the extent that Peter Berger, a former leading advocate of the secularization thesis, writes: "The world today, with some exceptions ... is as furiously religious as it ever was, and in some places more so than ever. This means that a whole body of literature by historians and social scientists loosely labelled 'secularization theory' is essential mistaken."[46] Confirming this evaluation, Rodney Stark argues that not only was the secularization thesis mistaken, it was based on false presuppositions about a previous "age of faith" that never existed, and was blind to the remarkable stability and, in places, increase of religious adherence since 1800 in Europe and elsewhere.[47] Debates about secularization are still ongoing, but what we can say is that a straightforward assumption that modernization leads to secularization is no longer tenable.

Since modernization is a worldwide process, advocates of secularization assumed that secularization would be a worldwide and uniform phenomenon. However, processes of modernization play out in different parts of the world in different ways depending on how they were transmitted (i.e., whether they were self-generated, as in Western Europe, imposed by colonialism, as in Africa, or imposed by elites, as in Japan and Turkey) and when they were transmitted (for example, it makes a difference if a society interacted with capitalism in its early stages or in its advanced stages of production). Thus, as Shmuel Eisenstadt argues, we must talk of "multiple modernities" all of which interact with religious belief and practice in different ways.[48] David Lyon and David Herbert both note that far from leading to a decline in the public significance of religion, processes of modernization can provoke and enable religious reinvigoration and an increase in its public significance.[49] Some, such as Grace Davie, now see Europe as the exception rather than the norm in terms of the relationship between religion and secularization.[50] However, as José Casanova points out, the most interesting thing about secularization in Europe is not whether it is an empirical reality, but that the secularization thesis was so internalized that both the non-religious and religious believers viewed it as normal. As Casanova puts it:

> We need to entertain seriously the proposition that secularization became a self-fulfilling prophecy in Europe, once large sectors of the population of Western

European societies, including the Christian churches, accepted the basic premises of the theory of secularization: that secularization is a teleological process of modern social change; that the more modern a society, the more secular it becomes; and that secularity is "a *sign of the times.*" If such a proposition is correct, then the secularization of Western European societies can be explained better in terms of the triumph of the knowledge regime of secularism than in terms of structural processes of socioeconomic development, such as urbanization, education, rationalization, and so on.[51]

The term "postsecular" has been deployed variously since the late 1990s as a way of coming to terms with the unfulfilled nature of the prophecy Casanova outlines. However, few of those who use the term question the assumption that drove the secularization thesis, namely, that secularity represents a decline, rather than the transformation, adaptation, or new developments in the social significance of religious belief and practice. Its use by Habermas to indicate the renewed visibility of religion in contemporary culture and the need for a model of law and politics in which religious arguments are not excluded still maintains that the secular, and in particular the secular state, is something that religious groups must conform or adapt to or be in conflict with.[52] This is made explicit in Wayne Hudson's use of the term. He states:

> Postsecular civil society on my account is paradoxically consistent with the view that the state would regulate manifestations of religion and impose civil values, where need be, on forms of religious education and practice. ... On my account postsecular civil society can only realistically allow a greater role for the sacral if it is committed to state-based regulation and reform of religion.[53]

On accounts such as Habermas and Hudson's the term denotes neither an increase in religiosity, after an era of decrease, nor does it call into question the terms and conditions of a secular public life. Rather, it seeks to account for and positively demand a change in mindset among those who previously felt justified in considering religions to be irrelevant or moribund. In such a reading, as Hent de Vries and Lawrence Sullivan put it:

> What undergoes transformation is less the nature of the secular state, let alone its constitutional arrangements guaranteeing, say, a separation between church and state, but rather the state's "secularist self understanding." Needless to say, it is far from clear what kind of "self-understanding" might come to substitute for the secularism (or "secular fundamentalism") of old, not least because the phenomenon on which the postsecular condition reflects – namely, religion's persistent role – is increasingly difficult to grasp conceptually and to situate empirically.[54]

Note, however, that the term postsecular as used by de Vries, Sullivan, and Habermas is one deployed by dominant power holders – whether political or intellectual – to describe a situation that religious groups themselves may describe in very different terms. This is certainly the case within Christian theology as the example of Radical Orthodoxy illustrates.

Most uses of the term "postsecular" remain committed to a notion of the secular as a neutral, autonomous, and rationally governed sphere of social and political relations.[55] By contrast, Radical Orthodoxy uses the term to call into question the very possibility of a secular space understood as neutral and uncommitted. On this account there are only pagan/religious or apostate spaces and one cannot divorce politics (or reason itself) from either relationship with God or some form of determinate confession.[56] For example, John Milbank argues that much modern social theory is itself deeply religious and constitutes a form of anti-theology. He states: "The most important governing assumptions of such theory are bound up with the modification or the rejection of orthodox Christian positions."[57] For Milbank, supposedly secular social theory is supported not by a neutral, universal rationality free from determinate commitments, but by an alternative confession. As understood by Radical Orthodoxy, a postsecular politics – whether of Christian or some other origin – recognizes the inescapability of worship and belief in public life and how "secular" politics is parasitic upon and a parody of religious forms.

As the contrast between Habermas and Milbank illustrates, uses of the term "postsecular" are various and contested and it is questionable how helpful the term is in describing the contemporary relationship between religion and politics. Habermas asserts that: "A 'post-secular' society must at some point have been in a 'secular' state." Yet it is arguable that in terms of religious adherence and the public significance of religion we never lived in a "secular age" even if, as Charles Taylor argues, we do now live in an age when religious belief has become a self-reflexive act. Taylor gives three meanings to the term "secular": The first denotes a decline in the public role of religion and the second posits a "falling off" in religious adherence. The third refers to the conditions of belief whereby belief in God moves from being a given to becoming "one option among others."[58] For Taylor, this third development was itself a partially religious development rather than an inevitable outcome of processes of modernization. This third meaning of the term does have traction. For Taylor, our "secular age" is characterized neither by a necessary decline in religious belief nor by an incompatibility between religion and modernity, but by a plurality of forms of belief and unbelief which are themselves constantly interacting and changing. On this account, secularism and the secularity of both particular institutions, such as a university, and of a society are as much the result of dynamics and discourses within Christianity as the fruit of external pressures. In the light of Taylor's thesis, use of the term "postsecular" in the ways Habermas uses it can be seen as illustrative of the condition of belief and unbelief within the contemporary context wherein everyone, including the ardent "secularist," has to be self-reflexive and critical about their commitments.[59] No one, from the confessional Darwinist to the so-called fundamentalist, can assume that their view is "normal" or simply the way things will be.[60]

Against the assumptions of the secularization thesis, religion has always played a prominent role in public and political life – even in Europe. At the macro level, with the exception of France and the USA, churches have been incorporated into the state through a variety of forms of establishment. And throughout Europe and the USA, not only have churches been involved in the delivery of welfare services, but the very formation of the different welfare systems and policies regarding poverty has been directly shaped by differences in belief and practice between the Catholic, Lutheran, and Reformed traditions.[61] At the micro level, for example, within supposedly secular institutions such as prisons, the military, and hospitals, chaplains have continued to have an established and often prominent role. However, even if religion never really went away, what is clear is that we are currently going through a period of deconstruction and reconstruction in which perennial questions about the relationship between religious and political authority are being asked again and previous settlements renegotiated.

There are specific material changes that can be identified that have led to this process of renegotiation. Many of these changes are set out in more detail in Chapter 1 through a case study of the UK context. However, the three most prominent ones are the following: new patterns of immigration are changing the religious demography of Western liberal democracies such that there is greater and deeper religious diversity (albeit in limited, mostly urban pockets); the events of September 11, 2001, the "war on terror," and the wars in Iraq and Afghanistan have led to an increased consciousness of Islam as a world religion and political force and raised questions about whether tolerance is an adequate response to religious diversity; and the state is increasingly situating itself as a partner, not a provider of social welfare services, which in turn is creating new opportunities for and new forms of engagement between religious groups, the state, and the market.

Material changes such as changes in religious demography have led to new moments emerging within existing patterns of relationship within the contemporary context. These moments are ones in which the relationship between religious groups, the state, and the market is undetermined and ambiguous while at the same time those from many different religious traditions and non-religious actors are encountering each other in new and deeper ways within shared territory. The contemporary context may be described as a postsecular*ist* space as far as the state and certain elite groups are concerned, but it is better understood overall *as a period in which, for the first time, multiple modernities, each with their respective relationship to religious belief and practice, are overlapping and interacting within the same shared, predominantly urban spaces.* Within such interactions, existing binary oppositions, such as secular and religious, tolerant and intolerant, public and private, conservative and radical, and left and right, that tend to frame political relationships break down. Yet incommensurable otherness remains to be negotiated within a shared territory in pursuit of goods in common.

What I am describing is best articulated through a concrete example. In Brixton, an area of South London characterized by multifaceted religious and ethnic diversity and a high rate of youth delinquency, which was a recruiting ground for those involved in the July 7, 2005 terrorist events in London, there are a number of pilot projects developing a new partnership between statutory bodies and Islamic groups in assessing and intervening with young people considered "at risk" of involvement in crime, gangs, and social disorder. One such project, run by a group which can be broadly characterized as "Salafi," receives referrals from the probation service to work with at-risk youths while simultaneously being monitored by the security services as a source of Islamic "radicalization" and violent opposition to the liberal democratic state.[62] Thus, the same group is perceived by the state both as contributing to law and order and as a source of violent opposition to its regime of law and order. The non-religious or secular statutory bodies are being forced to move beyond mere tolerance and ignorance of the religious "other" to make fine-grained distinctions between different groups within the same tradition as they seek to work with some and monitor others, or do both at the same time. This more intensive engagement is leading to a felt need to engage directly with what are understood as theological questions by government agencies. A measure of this shift to engage with (or some might say intrude upon) the "theological" is given by the creation of two posts in the UK's Department of Communities and Local Government, as of November 2008, entitled "Theology and Institutions" and "Theology" and by the advocacy of direct engagement with "theological" debate.[63] From the perspective of the youth project, the state is a threat, in that it is making its religiously framed dissent a security issue rather than a religious or political one and is seeking to intrude upon the formulation of its belief and practice. But it is also a source of opportunity to the group for it to achieve goals commensurate with their religious commitments: the formation of faithful young men. Both the religious group and the statutory bodies involved have an undetermined, constantly shifting and deepening relationship with each other as they negotiate a common life within the same territory in pursuit of a shared good – namely, stopping young men becoming involved in crime. Religious belief and practice, in particular the place of the authority of revelation as against the status of political authority, is central to the negotiation of this relationship in a context where, at the micro level, no single religious or non-religious hegemony is dominant. The example given here is a particularly acute one, but it illustrates experiences common to many religious groups where even though there is not the direct securitization of religion, there is a deep suspicion of religious groups. The example represents a particular spatial-temporal *moment* within a much wider, more variegated array of relationships.

Theologically understood, these moments are neither new nor, as de Vries and Sullivan suggest, "difficult to grasp conceptually." Rather, through drawing on Augustine's conception of the *saeculum* as that time after Christ's resurrection and before Christ's return, the *saeculum* can be understood as an ambiguous time, a field of wheat and tares, neither wholly profane nor sacred. What we might call postsecularist moments can be viewed as part of the normative condition of the church as it seeks to bear faithful witness within the ambiguous, undetermined time of the *saeculum*, wherein both "Christians" and "non-Christians" are constituted in their personhood by the earthly city and the city of God, where both the church and those various others with whom it must negotiate an earthly peace are capable of good and evil, pride and love, and where there is often a hazy boundary between church and non-church. This theologically defined understanding of the secular/*saeculum* is discussed in greater detail in Chapter 2 where a contrast is drawn between my own approach and that of John Milbank.

Theological Politics and the Ecclesial-Turn

As well as situating the book within some of the dominant ways of conceptualizing the conditions and possibilities of contemporary political life and the relationship between religion and politics, it is necessary to locate it in a specific theological conversation about the relationship between Christianity and politics. It is this conversation that lies at the heart of the book. A key problem in contemporary Christian political thought is whether the church has a distinctive politics and is itself a particular polity or whether it is best understood as a constituency within civil society whose politics takes the form of democratization and a commitment to a liberal state. In the mid-twentieth century, Jacques Maritain, Reinhold Niebuhr, and others argued, first, for the compatibility of Christianity and liberal democracy, and second, against both totalitarianism and an ideologically secular liberalism.[64] In recent years a growing number of theologians have emphasized that the first task of the church is to be a church. For them, it is not the business of the church to invest itself in one particular form of temporal political order – namely liberal democracy. In the view of one of the most prominent exponents of this critique, Stanley Hauerwas, the church has its own politics and should refrain from turning to the state as the first or only way of addressing social and political problems.[65] As will be set out in Chapter 1, the move toward a "theological politics" can also characterize the work of John Milbank, William Cavanaugh, and Oliver and Joan Lockwood O'Donovan. Figures such as Milbank, Cavanaugh, and the O'Donovans rightly contend that the church cannot simply derive an understanding of its political vision from outside of Christian belief and practice. In turn, they each conceptualize a particular relationship between the church, the state, and the market, and in one way or another, they envisage different aspects of Christian worship as a counter-performance of social and political relationships to those conditioned by the modern state and the capitalist economy.

I am broadly in sympathy with the shift to a theological politics. However, the central question of this book is not what does it mean to be the church in relation to the state and the market, but what does it mean for the church qua church to negotiate a common life with various non-Christian others in relation to the state and the market. A further distinction to work representative of what I call the "ecclesial-turn" is that this book conceptualizes the relationship between church, state, and market in response to already existing practices that have developed within the conditions of contemporary political life. The focus on how Christians are already acting politically makes no inherent claim for a first-order theory of practice. Rather, it is simply an attempt to conceptualize the relationship between church, state, and market through attention to the givenness of what is already going on; that is, to the reality of existent political relationships. In attending to such practices we may discover that the already existing forms of action are suggestive of alternative ways of framing faithful witness than are currently available in contemporary Christian political thought. More significantly though, through paying attention to existent forms of political action a theological account of what faithful political action involves can be developed. It is at this point that the contrast between this book and many of the key figures in contemporary political theology can be seen. O'Donovan, Milbank, and Hauerwas, each in their own way, set out the terms and conditions of political life and of how the church qua church is to act politically. Like the lawmaker or the builder of the city wall, they establish normative boundaries within which the church's social and political life takes place. As Hannah Arendt comments on Greek conceptions of political life:

> Before men began to act, a definite space had to be secured and a structure built where all subsequent actions could take place, the space being the public realm of the *polis* and its structure the law. ... But these tangible entities themselves were not the content of politics.[66]

Rather, politics is what takes place subsequent upon these boundaries being established. Contemporary advocates of theological politics, like the architect and legislator, establish the parameters of political life within the earthly city and build theological foundations for Christian political witness. But this should not be confused with or used as a substitute for an account of Christian political action.[67] Yet some such account is necessary in order to say what kind of political action is warranted within the cut and thrust of negotiating faithfully the contemporary Western political context. It is just such an account of political action that this book attempts to develop. Thus a central concern of this book is the theological articulation and practical description of what it means, in the contemporary context, to maintain the specificity and particularity of Christian witness, and at the same time, cooperate with religious and non-religious others in pursuit of goods in common.[68] By goods in common I do not mean the aggregation of different vested interests, but substantive goods in which the flourishing of all is invested. Such substantive goods, for example, health or education, are goods in which the good of each is conditional upon the good of all.[69] However, these substantive goods take determinate form within different contexts and so what the pursuit of health or education involves will necessarily vary according to context. Determining what is appropriate in order to fulfill such goods within the conditions and possibilities of a particular context requires political judgment. The book delineates various ways in which the church contributes to judgment about such goods in common at a local, national, and global level. To do this, I map the interrelationship between different theological responses to liberal democracy – ranging from Niebuhr and Maritain to Milbank and Hauerwas – and concrete forms of political action within the contemporary context. Out of attention to this interaction an account is developed of what the faithful pursuit of Babylon's peace may involve.

Summary of Aims and Methodology

The book has a number of interrelated aims. The first is to develop a particular theological vision of the relationship between Christianity and politics. Such a vision, I contend, is best glimpsed through attention to how the church fosters just or right judgments and neighbor love within the temporal, fallen order.[70] An account of neighbor love forms a central theme of the book, while an account of political judgment is given in the conclusion.[71] Following the first aim, a second aim of the book is to assesses various attempts to foster just judgments and neighbor love within Western, religiously plural, liberal nation-states in order to delineate the conditions and possibilities of faithful witness within the contemporary context. Conversely, the third aim is to discern how the "principalities and powers" are manifested in the contemporary life of the church and identify forms of action that school the church in resisting temptation.

A fourth aim of the book is to extend and develop earlier work that argued that hospitality is the normative pattern of faithful relations between Christians and those who are strangers to them. This book extends the theologic of the arguments developed in my earlier work in order to draw out the implications of my account of hospitality for faithful witness in contemporary politics. Developing my account of hospitality as a way of structuring relations between Christians and non-Christians leads, of necessity, to a theological form of political analysis. This analysis maps the conditions under which hospitable relations operate and identifies what form Christian hospitality takes within such conditions. It is necessarily a political analysis because, as defined here, politics is *the ongoing process through which to maintain commonality and recognize and conciliate conflict (including the use of coercive force) in pursuit of shared, temporal goods.*[72] And following Aristotle, politics properly relates to what pertains to the general, comprehensive, or public order of a polity. Christian hospitality, as a way of framing relations between Christians and non-Christians, pertains to politics because it is a way of conceptualizing how to forge a common life – that is, a public life – with others with whom we disagree or who are, at some level, strangers to us.

Lastly, the book aims to develop a theological form of political analysis in critical dialogue with a range of other disciplines and in response to a generic context, namely, Western liberal democracies. The approach taken is born out of an attempt to avoid an essentialized conception or abstract blueprint of church–state relations and, building on previous work, to pay attention to the ad hoc commensurability between Christian and non-Christian conceptions of the good, especially as these come to be manifested in common action. Where the book extends my earlier work is in developing a form of analysis that accords with what Nicholas Healy calls an "ecclesiological ethnography"; that is, it seeks to give a theological account of the church in relation to the world that draws on historical and social scientific accounts while being mindful of and not capitulating to the methodological atheism that often undergirds such research.[73] The aim of this kind of approach is neatly summarized by Healy who states that such analysis "must be critical, carefully assessing our ecclesial culture and the cultural patterns of other traditions of inquiry in an effort to render the church's witness and discipleship more truthful."[74] Without rehearsing the debate about the relationship between "Reason" (including the social sciences) and "Revelation" from Karl Barth and Paul Tillich onward, it suffices to say that this form of theological political analysis is developed out of a trialogue between the Christian tradition of belief and practice, various non-theological studies, and contextually situated critical reflection in which a theological methodology sets the parameters of the conversation. The fruit of such conversation is an ecclesially forged and theologically conditioned discernment of what constitutes faithful witness within the contingent flux of prevailing political conditions.[75] This conversation is an academic form of what the first two chapters argue: that is, that a constitutive moment in the fermentation of Christian practical reason involves listening simultaneously to the Word of God and to strangers. Through such listening encounters our conceptions of ourselves in relation to God and others undergo a deepening moral conversion that enables our reasoning to be healed and purified in order that we may make increasingly just, wise, and faithful judgments.

Theological deliberation is crucial for discerning what might be the appropriate response to a particular issue and judging what form that response might take in a particular context. At the same time, there can be no direct correlation between a particular theological conception of the relationship between Christianity and politics and a particular mode of political action. Different theologies can warrant the same kinds of action. In response to the need for theological deliberation and the plausibility of multiple theological evaluations of any one action, the case studies in this book are meant to constitute thick, theological descriptions of how political witness has been developed in relation to particular issues or in particular settings. These case studies are, to use John Milbank's phrase, "judicious narratives of ecclesial happenings" meant to indicate what it might mean to be a church in the contemporary context.[76] Yet the chapters also analyze different strands of theological reflection in relation to the same political issue in order to assess how different theologies frame what faithful witness requires in relation to that issue. In conversation with these different theological conceptions and existing forms of practice the book as a whole develops a constructive account of the conditions and possibilities of faithful witness within contemporary politics.

There is scope for normative or prescriptive accounts of the relationship between Christianity and politics. However, these can never be definitive and must be related to theological reflection on the processes, arenas, and conditions of political life in any given context. As Bernd Wannenwetsch argues, building on the work of Oliver O'Donovan, theories of church–state relations are a necessity, yet they are also necessarily contingent because the "relevant and appropriate theological theories" can only emerge from a "sensitive awareness of the given missionary situation."[77] Any attempt to arrive at a definitive classification not only ignores changes in historical context but also the dynamic relationship between the prior actions of Christ and different dimensions of society whereby Christ's Lordship comes to be exercised in different degrees over different aspects of society at different times. Accordingly, Christians need to develop the ability to improvise faithfully in response to Christ within a variety of different political environments. Part of learning how to improvise faithfully is done by attending to assessments of pivotal political issues, to theological critiques of these issues, and to how Christians have responded, both negatively and positively, to these issues in practice. At the same time, a completely fragmentary approach that forgoes any pattern or consistent shape to Christian political witness is theologically and practically unsustainable. What is needed is a more ad hoc yet consistent approach to conceptualizing Christian political witness, one that involves close attention both to the particularities of the contemporary context and the ongoing tradition of Christian political thought as it has sought to respond to the Lordship of Christ within different historical contexts.

In order to navigate these methodological issues, the book assesses the relationship between Christianity and contemporary politics through an analysis of various "telling" or paradigmatic case studies. These case studies are taken to have what Hannah Arendt called an "exemplary validity"; that is, while retaining their particularity, and without reducing or subsuming them to expressions of a prior universal (whether it be a Platonic ideal or a Kantian schema), the cases provide insight into the generality that otherwise could not be discerned by us as those who are participants in the very context under scrutiny.[78] Through the theological analysis of these case studies the book develops a constructive account of how Christians can engage in forms of hospitable witness in a multi-faith, morally plural liberal democratic polity. The case studies analyzed in the book address issues central to political debates in the USA and Europe (but also relate to developments in Australia and New Zealand). Given the necessary attention to detail there is a certain specificity to the focus of each chapter, although parallels and analogous developments in other contexts are constantly referred to: the assessment of the funding of faith-based organizations in Chapter 1 is focused primarily on the UK; the evaluation of broad-based community organizing and the Sanctuary movement in Chapters 2 and 3 are predominantly focused on the North American context; and the examination of Fair Trade mainly discusses the situation in the UK and continental Europe. However, as already suggested, analysis of these case studies illuminates wider and more generic issues in contemporary political, social, and economic life. The studies are thus invitations to further deliberation on related or analogous issues.

Notes

1 Graham Ward, "Questioning God," in *Questioning God*, eds. John D. Caputo, Michael Scanlon, and Mark Dooley (Bloomington, IN: Indiana University Press, 2001), p. 277.

2 Augustine, *City of God* XX, 17. All references refer to Augustine, *The City of God Against the Pagans*, trans. R. W. Dyson (Cambridge: Cambridge University Press, 1998).

3 Augustine, *City of God*, XIX, 7.

4 *City of God*, XIX, 15.

5 *City of God*, XIX, 5.

6 Jeremiah 29.4–7. Daniel Smith describes verses 5–7 "as the essence of the letter from Jeremiah." Daniel Smith, "Jeremiah as Prophet of Nonviolence," *Journal for the Study of the Old Testament* (1989) 13.43, p. 97.

7 *City of God* XIX, 26.

8 Richard Bauckham, *The Theology of the Book of Revelation* (Cambridge: Cambridge University Press, 1993), pp. 101, 161.

9 See also I Timothy 2.1–6.

10 This particular emphasis is drawn from Calvin's reading of Jeremiah 29. See John Calvin, *Calvin's Commentary – Volume 10 – Jeremiah 20–47* (Grand Rapids, MI: Baker, 1999).

11 In common with much Old Testament scholarship, Andrew Mein holds that the exiled Israelites were not slaves or prisoners and were allowed a degree of personal freedom and communal self-organization. In addition, they were able to gather both to hear a letter and to debate the issues that affected them as a community. However, at the same time, Mein points out that the exiles' very identity and existence as a people were under threat and the experience of domination and oppression a constant reality. Andrew Mein, *Ezekiel and the Ethics of Exile* (Oxford: Oxford University Press, 2001), pp. 66–71. Daniel Smith-Christopher goes further, contesting readings of the exilic experience as relatively benign, noting that to say that the Israelites were not "slaves" is too imprecise. While agreeing that a degree of self-organization was possible, Smith-Christopher argues that the Israelites did suffer forced labor and that the process of exile entailed severe trauma. Daniel Smith-Christopher, *A Biblical Theology of Exile* (Minneapolis, MN: Augsberg Fortress, 2002), pp. 65–73. For Smith-Christopher,

the advice given in Jeremiah to "build, plant and marry" should not be read as an indication of the favorable conditions of life in Babylonia. Rather, he reads it as an echo of Deuteronomy 20 and its list of those who were exempted from fighting in war. Smith-Christopher argues that these exemptions are to ensure that no one misses out on enjoying the good things of life bestowed on the covenant nation by the Lord. In his reading, Jeremiah is declaring that although the exiles are in a situation of war with their oppressors, the condition of the exiles themselves is not one of active military service: in other words, despite their perilous circumstances, they are not to resort to violence to address their situation. Instead, Jeremiah's advice to the exiles represents an emergent Jewish ethic of "nonviolent social resistance" that Smith-Christopher sees evidence of in Daniel, later Pharisaic practice, and early Christianity. He states: "It is a militant non-violence that has very little in common with an appeasing liberal pacifism because it is an engaged, strategic position towards authority and power that is certainly aware of the requirements for success and survival." Daniel Smith, "Jeremiah as Prophet of Nonviolence," p. 104.

12   As Christopher Seitz comments: "There can be no life in the land after 597 which is not under false illusions, and which does not stand under God's ultimate judgment. God spoke this word through his prophet Jeremiah early and often. ... Only those already exiled could be sure that judgement had fallen. As such, they alone could properly hear a divine word regarding restoration." Christopher Seitz, *Theology in Conflict: Reactions to the Exile in the Book of Jeremiah* (Berlin: Walter de Gruyter, 1989), p. 5.

13   Walter Brueggemann, *A Commentary of Jeremiah: Exile and Homecoming* (Grand Rapids, MI: Eerdmans, 1998), p. 256.

14   John Howard Yoder, *The Jewish–Christian Schism Revisited*, eds. Michael Cartwright and Peter Ochs (Grand Rapids, MI: Eerdmans, 2003), pp. 161–2. For Yoder, Babylon becomes a stand-in for Jerusalem because it more faithfully represents what Jerusalem was meant to be. Jerusalem became the site for the Tabernacle and thence the Temple because historically it had belonged to no tribe. It was foreign ground possessed by none. Following the logic of the Tabernacle's former itinerant ministry, God could be present to the People in Jerusalem without being possessed or controlled by any particular tribe. On Yoder's reading Babylon functions in the same way, both in Jeremiah and historically. As Yoder puts it: "The transcendence of the Most High is acted out in the fact that the place of his manifestation is not our own turf. God's choosing to pitch his tent in our midst is his mercy, not our merit or our property" (ibid., p. 161). Peter Ochs points to the danger of Yoder's understanding of *galut* (diaspora or exile) as the normative condition of Israel and in particular of Yoder's reading of Jeremiah 29 as an attempt to avoid the "embarrassment, burden, and unreasonable complexity of Israel's landedness" (ibid., p. 203). Och's critique of Yoder from a Jewish perspective points to a problem with Yoder's prescription of a diasporic identity for the church; that is, it has little room for a deep valuation of place and the way we come to be persons through

particular histories in a given place. Chapter 3 in this book can be read as an attempt to reconcile a Yoderian vision of *galut* as vocation with a theology of place within an account of what I call Christian cosmopolitanism.

15 Ibid., pp. 170–1; 190–2. Reference to Yoder should not be read as signaling a complete convergence between Yoder's political theology and my own. As will become apparent in subsequent chapters, there are significant points of divergence.

16 Ibid., p. 202, n. 60. Cartwright holds that Yoder's translation collapses into what he calls "monologic" (ibid., p. 29, n. 68). Yet such a criticism ignores the connection between dialogue and mission in Yoder's work and more broadly the normatively dialogic nature of Christian mission. Lamin Sanneh argues that Christianity, from its very origins, has demonstrated an enormous appetite for engaging with and learning from materials from other religious traditions and cultures (Lamin Sanneh, *Translating the Message: The Missionary Impact on Culture* (Maryknoll, NY: Orbis Books, 1989), p. 43). Yet it never simply absorbs or merges with other cultures. Rather, there is always a process of translation and inculturation that involves simultaneous affirmation, critique, and transformation that results in a point of new departure for *both* Christianity *and* the culture or religious system it is interpenetrating (ibid., p. 37). On this see also Andrew Walls, *The Missionary Movement in Christian History* (Edinburgh: T&T Clark, 1996). The dynamic of translation and inculturation is arguably a dynamic specific to Christianity and its missiological stance, leading to a perhaps different implication of Jeremiah 29 for Christians than for Jews.

17 This logic is constantly repeated through the Gospels' depiction of Jesus' ministry. A particularly forceful example is given in Mark 5.1–20 and Luke 8.26–39 (with a variation in Matthew 8.28–34), when Jesus heals a demoniac. Jesus goes out to Gerasene/Gadarene (a pagan country), and lands in a graveyard (a place of death) and thus is located in a place of utter pollution. There he meets a demoniac (one completely cut off from human community and self-destructively subject to the principalities and powers), and in this barren, derelict place brings healing, new life, and the restoration of social relationships.

18 Alasdair MacIntyre, *After Virtue: A Study in Moral Theory*, 2nd edn (London: Duckworth, 1994); Alasdair MacIntyre, *Dependent Rational Animals: Why Human Beings Need the Virtues* (London: Duckworth, 1999); Sheldon Wolin, *Politics and Vision: Continuity and Innovation in Western Political Thought*, expanded edn (Princeton, NJ: Princeton University Press, 2004).

19 For an overview of MacIntyre's critique of modern politics and a summary of his account of local politics as a constructive response see Luke Bretherton, *Hospitality as Holiness: Christian Witness Amid Moral Diversity* (Aldershot: Ashgate, 2006), chs. 1 and 4.

20 Robert Putnam, *Bowling Alone: The Collapse and Revival of American Community* (New York: Simon & Schuster, 2000), pp. 15–47. Some dispute Putnam's findings for America. Likewise, the situation across Europe is ambiguous: there is much evidence to suggest that while some forms of voluntary and

civic associations may decline, other forms have hugely increased. In many parts of Europe volunteering, civic association, and political engagement are relatively buoyant. For a summary of this debate see John Field, *Social Capital* (London: Routledge, 2003), pp. 94–8.

21 Dietland Stolle and Marc Hooghe, "Consumers as Political Participants? Shifts in Political Action Repertoires in Western Societies," in *Politics, Products, Markets: Exploring Political Consumerism Past and Present*, eds. Michele Micheletti, Andreas Follesdal, and Dietlind Stolle (New Brunswick, NJ: Transaction Publishers, 2004), p. 268.

22 Ibid., pp. 268–9.

23 Putnam, *Bowling Alone*, pp. 287–90.

24 Theda Skocpol, *Diminished Democracy: From Membership to Management in American Civic Life* (Norman, OK: University of Oklahoma Press, 2004).

25 Putnam, *Bowling Alone*, pp. 153–60.

26 Manuel Castells, *The Rise of the Network Society* (Oxford: Blackwell, 1997); Anthony Giddens, *Self and Society in the Late Modern Age* (Cambridge: Polity Press, 1991); and Anthony Giddens, *Beyond Left and Right – the Future of Radical Politics* (Cambridge: Polity Press, 1994).

27 Ulrich Beck, *Risk Society: Towards a New Modernity*, trans. Mark Ritter (London: Sage, 1992), pp. 87–138.

28 Ibid., p. 90.

29 Ibid., pp. 90, 100.

30 Ibid., p. 23; Beck, *Risk Society*, pp. 193–9, 223–35.

31 Ulrich Beck, "World Risk Society as Cosmopolitan Society? Ecological Questions in a Framework of Manufactured Uncertainties," *World Risk Society* (Cambridge: Polity Press, 1999), p. 39. In direct contrast to Putnam, Beck cites the example of the mass consumer boycotts organized by Greenpeace against Shell in 1995 as an example of this new kind of direct political action (ibid., pp. 40–3).

32 Ulrich Beck, "The Reinvention of Politics: Towards a Theory of Reflexive Modernization" in Ulrich Beck, Anthony Giddens, and Scott Lash, *Reflexive Modernization: Politics, Tradition and Aesthetics in the Modern Social Order* (Cambridge: Polity Press, 1994), p. 23.

33 Ibid., p. 40.

34 Pippa Norris, *Democratic Phoenix: Reinventing Political Activism* (Cambridge: Cambridge University Press, 2002), p. 4.

35 See Ronald Inglehart, *Modernization and Postmodernization* (Princeton, NJ: Princeton University Press, 1997); and Ronald Inglehart, "Postmodernization Erodes Respect for Authority, but Increases Support for Democracy," in Pippa Norris, ed., *Critical Citizens: Global Support for Democratic Government* (Oxford: Oxford University Press, 1999), pp. 236–56.

36 Use of the term "post-Marxist" denotes thinkers who are indebted to Marxism while at the same time seeking to move beyond its limitations.

37 Michael Hardt and Antonio Negri, *Multitude: War and Democracy in the Age of Empire* (London: Hamish Hamilton, 2005), p. 87–8.

38   Ibid., p. 350.

39   Ibid., p. 336.

40   Luc Boltanski and Eve Chiapello, trans. Gregory Elliot, *The New Spirit of Capitalism* (London: Verso, 2005), pp. 352–3. Following Weber, Boltanski and Chiapello use the term "spirit" to denote the legitimating moral framework and plausibility structure that motivates and generates commitment to capitalism. As they point out, capitalism cannot sustain itself by force alone. Since the nineteenth century, they argue, there have been a number of different "spirits" of capitalism, each of which incorporates elements of its own critique. Ibid., pp. 8–12.

41   Ibid., pp. 201, 426–9.

42   A rider to this statement is that the characterization of the four accounts set out above is inevitably truncated and there are more nuances at work in any one voice within each of the positions. However, even given this, the typology developed here provides a helpful, heuristic rubric for reflecting on Christian practice in relation to contemporary politics.

43   For example, Michelle Micheletti demonstrates in relation to a case study of the "Good Environmental Choice" forestry labeling scheme in Sweden that political consumerism both builds on and extends existing patterns of political and social life. In summary, Miceletti notes: "The case study reports how successful use of political consumerism builds upon the already accumulated and institutionalized social capital found in established civil society associations." Michele Micheletti, *Political Virtue and Shopping: Individuals, Consumerism, and Collective Action* (New York: Palgrave MacMillan, 2003), p. 155.

44   Jürgen Habermas, "Notes on a Post-Secular Society," www.signandsight.com/features/1714.html (accessed: September 5, 2007).

45   Bryan Wilson, *Religion in Sociological Perspective* (Oxford: Oxford University Press, 1982), p. 49. For a summary of debate over the secularization thesis see Linda Woodhead, ed., *Peter Berger and the Study of Religion* (London: Routledge, 2001). See also Steve Bruce, *Religion and Modernization: Sociologists and Historians Debate the Secularization Thesis* (Oxford: Clarendon Press, 1992); Steve Bruce, *God Is Dead: Secularization in the West* (Oxford: Blackwell, 2002); and David Herbert, *Religion and Civil Society: Rethinking Public Religion in the Contemporary World* (Aldershot: Ashgate, 2003).

46   Peter Berger, *The Desecularization of the World* (Washington, DC: Ethics and Public Policy Centre, 1999), p. 2.

47   Rodney Stark, "Secularization, R.I.P.," *Sociology of Religion* 60.3 (1999), 249–73.

48   S. N. Eisenstadt, "The Reconstruction of Religious Arenas in the Framework of 'Multiple Modernities,'" *Millennium: Journal of International Studies* 29.3 (2000), p. 593.

49   David Lyon, *Jesus in Disneyland: Religion in Postmodern Times* (Oxford: Polity Press, 2000); Herbert, *Religion and Civil Society*.

50   Grace Davie, *Religion in Modern Europe: A Memory Mutates* (Oxford University Press, 2000).

51 José Casanova, "Immigration and the New Religious Pluralism: A European Union/United States Comparison," in Thomas Banchoff, ed., *Democracy and the New Religious Pluralism* (Oxford: Oxford University Press, 2007), p. 63.

52 Jürgen Habermas, "Religion in the Public Sphere," *European Journal of Philosophy* 14.1 (2006), 1–25.

53 Wayne Hudson, "Postsecular Civil Society," in *Civil Society, Religion and Global Governance: Paradigms of Power and Persuasion*, ed. Helen James (London: Routledge, 2007), pp. 153–4.

54 Hent de Vries and Lawrence E. Sullivan, *Political Theologies: Public Religions in a Post-Secular World* (New York: Fordham University Press, 2006), p. 3.

55 Other, parallel deployments of the term include John D. Caputo, who uses it to denote a postmodern religious position – a "religion without religion." He envisages the secular as a necessary stage that religions must pass through before they can become postsecular. John D. Caputo, *On Religion* (London: Routledge, 2001), pp. 60–1. Similarly, Romand Coles seeks a "post-secular caritas" by which he means a post-Christian and post-metaphysically grounded conception of receptive generosity or love that is alive to its own historical contingency and relevant to a context of radical pluralism. Romand Coles, *Rethinking Generosity: Critical Theory and the Politics of Caritas* (Ithaca, NY: Cornell University Press, 1997). In a different key, Patrick Curry uses the term to position "deep green ethics" as spiritual rather than religious, drawing as it does on a wide variety of influences to restore a sense of the sacred and the spiritual to an ecocentric appreciation of the environment. Patrick Curry, *Ecological Ethics: An Introduction* (London: Polity Press, 2005), pp. 103–7. With a more sociological focus, Kim Knott uses the term descriptively to account for emergent "postsecular confessions" which are the fruit of a dialectical relation between religious and secular beliefs and commitments and constitute a critical engagement drawing on both. Kim Knott, *The Location of Religion: A Spatial Analysis* (London: Equinox, 2005), pp. 71–2. By contrast, Ananda Abeysekara uses the term as a way of framing a critique of modernist or secularist ideologies. Ananda Abeysekara, *The Politics of Postsecular Religion: Mourning Secular Futures* (New York: Columbia University Press, 2008).

56 Philip Blond, "Introduction," *Post-secular Philosophy: Between Philosophy and Theology*, ed. Philip Blond (London: Routledge, 1998), pp. 1–65; James K. A. Smith, *Introducing Radical Orthodoxy: Mapping a Post-secular Theology* (Grand Rapids, MI: Baker Academic, 2004); Graham Ward, *True Religion* (Oxford: Blackwell, 2003).

57 John Milbank, *Theology and Social Theory: Beyond Secular Reason* (Oxford: Blackwell, 1993), p. 1.

58 Charles Taylor, *A Secular Age* (Cambridge, MA: Harvard University Press, 2007), pp. 2–3.

59 Habermas himself seems to be calling for such a position of mutual self-reflexivity between secular and religious citizens. Habermas, "Religion in the Public Sphere," p. 20.

60 The increasing vehemence and vigor of certain anti-religious exponents of Darwinism can be understood as a growing self-awareness and felt need to argue their corner as against the previous assumption that their view would inevitably prevail.

61 Sigrun Kahl, "The Religious Roots of Modern Poverty Policy: Catholic, Lutheran, and Reformed Protestant Traditions Compared," *European Journal of Sociology* 46.1 (2005), 91–126. While it does not undermine the central tenets of her argument, Kahl's article is marred by a Weberian caricature of Calvin and Calvinism that fails to engage with either Calvin's own work or the historical literature on Calvin's response to poverty in Geneva. For a corrective account see Fred Graham, *The Constructive Revolutionary: John Calvin and His Socio-Economic Impact* (East Lansing, MI: Michigan State University Press, 1987).

62 Robert Lambert, "Empowering Salafis and Islamists against Al-Qaeda: A London Counter-terrorism Case Study," *Political Science (PS) Online* January 2008, pp. 31–5. I am very grateful to Robert Lambert and Gwen Griffith-Dickson for further details on the work of the project described here with which they have both worked closely. In the interests of confidentiality I have not included the name of the project.

63 *Preventing Violent Extremism: Winning Hearts and Minds* (London: Department of Communities and Local Government, 2007).

64 Jacques Maritain, *Christianity and Democracy*, trans. Doris C. Anson (London: Geoffrey Bles, 1945); Jacques Maritain, *Man and the State* (Chicago, IL: University of Chicago, 1951); Reinhold Niebuhr, *The Children of Light and the Children of Darkness* (London: Nisbet & Co., 1945).

65 See, for example, Stanley Hauerwas, *After Christendom? How the Church Is to Behave if Freedom, Justice, and a Christian Nation Are Bad Ideas* (Nashville, TN: Abingdon Press, 1991).

66 Hannah Arendt, *The Human Condition*, 2nd edn (Chicago, IL: University of Chicago Press, 1958), pp. 194–5.

67 It remains to be seen whether John Milbank's "blue socialism" constitutes the basis for an account of political action. Philip Blond's development of the "Red Tory" thesis could claim to be such an account, yet it is not clear quite how his arguments are derived from or related to theological precepts and what the role of the church qua church is within his emerging account.

68 The conception of the church as a *res publica* in itself draws on Augustine, *City of God*, II, 21, XIX, 21 wherein, building on Cicero's definition of a people as a multitude "united in fellowship by a agreement as to what is right and by a community of interest," Augustine defines a people as "an assembled multitude of rational creatures bound together by a common agreement as to the objects of their love." *City of God*, XIX, 24.

69 I have tended not to use the term "common good" for the reason that within the Augustinian account of the nature of politics within the *saeculum* developed in Chapter 2, talk of "the" common good is problematic. An all-encompassing

common good seems only an ever-deferred horizon of possibility rather than a plausible political reality under conditions of a fallen and finite political life, although, arguably, its deferred status does not render conceptualizing the common good irrelevant as it may still operate as a regulative ideal or guiding point of reference. In this latter sense it is quite proper to talk about "the" common good of a particular society. However, a second issue is that it is not clear at what level the common good is to be pursued – local, regional, national, or global. (For an account of the necessarily non-national and local location of the common good see Alisdair MacIntyre, "Politics, Philosophy and the Common Good," in *The Macintyre Reader*, ed. Kelvin Knight (London: Polity Press, 1998), pp. 235–66). Given the focus of this book on political action, I use the plural and talk of goods in common or common goods. It is the discernment and formation of these goods through politics, primarily at a local or regional level, that constitutes the process of glimpsing the common good.

70 The terms "just" and "right" are taken as synonyms for each other in relation to the proper exercise of judgment and denote what is the fitting or most appropriate moral discrimination and decision to be made given the circumstances.

71 By way of preface to the account of judgment, judgment is understood as having the double, simultaneous aspect of discrimination and decision. Following O'Donovan's analysis of judgment, such just or right judgment has a retrospective element (as an act of discrimination it pronounces upon an existent state of affairs) and as a decision it has a prospective aspect (it is effective in establishing or clearing a space for a common field of action in which moral relations are possible). Oliver O'Donovan, *The Ways of Judgement* (Grand Rapids, MI: Eerdmans, 2005), pp. 7–12. I draw on O'Donovan's account of judgment because it is the fullest account available of political judgment that takes seriously what it means to make judgments in a sinful world after the exaltation of Jesus Christ. Thus, while it is alive to the concerns and developments of the accounts of judgment given by Kant and Arendt (although both of their accounts of political judgment are at best fragmentary), it is a fully theological account of political judgment.

72 I use the term conciliate to denote both mediation and coming to a position of friendliness with those with whom one disagrees. The definition of politics given here can be broadly characterized as Aristotelian. For contemporary restatements of this conception of politics see Sheldon Wolin's *Politics and Vision* and the parallel account of politics in Bernard Crick, *In Defence of Politics*, 5th edn (London: Continuum, 2005).

73 Nicholas Healy, *Church, World and the Christian Life: Practical-Prophetic Ecclesiology* (Cambridge: Cambridge University Press, 2000), pp. 154–85. In contrast to Healy, whose primary focus is systematic theology, the focus of this work is the field of theological ethics, although, following Karl Barth's location of ethics within dogmatics, this is not meant to imply any disjuncture between the two, simply a focus of attention. In addition to Healy's work, Reinhard Hütter's conception of theology as a catechetical church practice involving a

creative, theologically determined form of "thick description" illuminates and resonates with the methodological approach taken in this book. See Reinhard Hütter, *Suffering Divine Things: Theology as Church Practice*, trans. Doug Scott (Grand Rapids, MI: Eerdmans, 2000). As such it differs considerably in its appropriation and conceptualization of social scientific accounts of what is the case from those developed within either liberation theology or practical theology as exemplified in the work of Don Browning (Don Browning, *A Fundamental Practical Theology* (Minneapolis, MN: Fortress Press, 1996)). A key point of difference from these approaches is the attention given to the possibility of God's agency, and thus the need for theology, in the *description* of what is the case rather than confining it to the *analysis* of data generated by supposedly neutral social scientific methods.

74   Healy, *Church, World and the Christian Life*, p. 174.

75   One could insert the term "*phronesis*" or practical wisdom in place of "discernment." However, use of the term "discernment" better emphasizes how faithful political judgments are responses to the prior and ongoing creative action of God in the midst of the world.

76   John Milbank, "Enclaves, or Where is the Church?" *New Blackfriars* 73.861 (1992), p. 344.

77   Bernd Wannenwetsch, *Political Worship: Ethics for Christian Citizens* (Oxford: Oxford University Press, 2004), p. 260.

78   Hannah Arendt, *Lectures on Kant's Political Philosophy*, ed. Ronald Beiner (Chicago, IL: Chicago University Press, 1982), pp. 76–7.

1

Faith-Based Organizations and the Emerging Shape of Church–State Relations

Introduction

The most common way Christians seek the welfare of their neighbors is through their various pastoral ministries. There are myriad ministries, from soup runs to international aid agencies, from visiting the elderly to prison chaplaincy, that embody the pastoral or diaconal ministry of the church. These pastoral ministries have no explicit political agenda but are more often than not simply a response to an immediate human need. They can be viewed as more a form of humanitarian than political action. Nevertheless, the pastoral ministries of the church have a political discussion because, by seeking to heal, care for, and enable the flourishing of others, the church contributes to the earthly peace of society as a whole. In the modern period there are a variety of ways in which church and state have cooperated so as to address issues of social welfare and individual human needs. As part of this cooperation, state funding of Christian pastoral care is nothing new, even in the USA. However, since the 1990s, both in the USA and the UK, this relationship has changed and cooperation between church and state and state funding of what are now called faith-based organizations are both increasing in some areas and more contested in others.

This chapter examines the terms and conditions of the relationship between church and state through a case study of the emerging pattern of this relationship as it affects the funding of faith-based organizations. While a particular focus is given to the situation in the UK, parallel developments and issues in the USA are also addressed. The first section charts the developments that have shaped this emerging relationship since the early 1990s, most notably, the strengthening of the public voice of minority faith communities. The second section analyses the debates about the role of religious communities in generating social cohesion and social capital in the context of debates about the importance of civil society to liberal democracy. The third section assesses whether the emergent shape of relations between the state and faith communities conforms to or contradicts a liberal account of the role of religious discourse in the public square. In contrast, the last two sections focus on the place of the church in this emergent relationship and analyze the opportunities and pitfalls confronting the church in the light of contemporary developments in Christian political thought. The overall line of argument is that the church, in light of what is actually being offered to it by the state, should be extremely wary about partnership given the current terms and conditions of cooperation on offer. The purpose of this chapter is to set the scene for subsequent analysis of the relationship between church, state, and market at work in various forms of Christian political witness where the terms of cooperation are not set by the state.

"Working Together": The Shaping of Relations between the State and Religious Groups in a Multi-Faith Society

A number of developments contribute to the emergent shape of relations between the state and religious groups in the West. First, there is the advent of deep religious diversity owing to large-scale immigration since the 1950s. For example, in the UK, a number of religious minorities refuse to be categorized as an "ethnic" group and demand recognition and access to state resources on the basis of their religious identity. Political advocacy on the basis of religious identity forms part of a wider shift away from ideologically driven politics to the "politics of recognition."[1] From the controversy surrounding the publication of Salman Rushdie's *Satanic Verses* in 1988 to protests by the Sikh community over the play *Behzti* in 2004 there has been a steady increase in the political mobilization and strengthening of the public voice of minority faith communities in Britain.[2] Throughout Europe it is the political mobilization of Islam that is most prominent. However, it is not only reactive protest that determines the public political presence of minority faith communities. As will be seen, there is an increasingly constructive engagement between the state and minority religious groups.

Second, across the political spectrum, from the end of the Cold War onward there was a more communitarian direction in British politics, coupled, perhaps paradoxically, with an embrace by all parties of a more libertarian economic vision.[3] The communitarian turn in British politics since the early 1990s emphasizes the need to balance rights with responsibilities; strengthen participation in civil society and the formation of mediating structures between the state and the individual; devolve power; encourage widespread consultation and participation in decision making; and foster social inclusion. This shift echoes parallel developments in both the USA and continental Europe. However, the renewed emphasis on civil society inevitably led to greater scrutiny of what was really going on. As noted in the Introduction, some hold that civil society is not flourishing.[4] Faith communities, in one way or another, both fit the communitarian vision and are seen to be a resilient part of civil society and so vital to its renewal. Thus, particularly in the UK and the USA, religious groups can both present themselves, and be perceived as, a constructive part of the post-Cold War political landscape.[5]

Third, the communitarian turn, and the emphasis on the free market, legitimized the retreat of the state from welfare provision. A key factor in this retreat was the spiraling cost of the welfare state. However, the solution, proposed in one way or another by all political parties in the UK, was to recast the state as a "partner" rather than sole provider of welfare services.[6] The result is that the state is angling for groups to partner with. Faith communities are seen as an obvious partner and are increasingly being used as conduits for the provision of welfare services and education. Examples range from contracting a local church to provide a program for young people at risk to the Prison Service giving a Christian charity, the Kainos Community, responsibility for running whole prison wings.[7] Parallel developments can be seen both in the USA with, for example, the outsourcing of welfare-to-work programs to faith-based organizations,[8] and in the arena of international development aid.[9]

Fourth, a factor more evident in the USA but latent in the UK was the return of moral questions in the distribution of welfare. The structural conditions of poverty and inequality began to inform government policy from the beginning of the twentieth century onward. However, structural issues only came to the fore with Roosevelt's New Deal politics after the Great Depression in the USA and the creation of the welfare state in the UK after 1945. With these shifts the relationship between welfare provision and virtue began to be uncoupled. In the process moral concerns about fecklessness became delegitimized.[10] By contrast, questions about the relationship between lifestyle and indigence were a central part of nineteenth-century discourses of poverty. For example, Samuel Smiles in his book *Self Help* (1859) wrote: "No laws, however stringent, can make the idle industrious, the thriftless provident, or the drunken sober. Such reforms can only be effected by means of individual actions, economy, and self-denial, by better habits, rather than by greater rights."[11] Frank Prochaska charts the shift away from such a view and how from the early twentieth century onward both secular intellectuals like Sidney and Beatrice Webb and churchmen such as the Christian socialist Canon Samuel Barnett developed an impersonal, "scientific," and professional approach to welfare, belief in the efficacy of legislation, and advocacy of state intervention paid for by taxation.[12] After World War II this became the dominant approach both in Europe and America. However, from the 1980s onward, with the return to laissez-faire economics, such an approach has increasingly been called into question. A key element of the discourses informing welfare reform from Thatcher and Reagan onward, on both left and right, has been the return of questions of personal accountability and character and the need to balance rights and responsibilities.[13] Religious groups have positioned themselves and been perceived as able to incorporate advocacy of individual responsibility with personalized care and compassion in their provision of welfare services. Even with a shift away from more doctrinaire forms of laissez-faire economics or neoliberalism in the wake of the crises of capitalism from 2008 onward, the linkage between personal responsibility and welfare provision looks set to remain.

Fifth, in a shift that is directly related to the recoupling of welfare provision and personal responsibility there has been a move toward what is called participative or co-governance. Western governments are realizing that good governance cannot be the state's responsibility alone and that many social issues need non-state actors in order to be addressed effectively. Governments seek and are expected to address issues like anti-social behavior, obesity, parenting, and the "radicalization" of religious groups. Yet such issues are not amenable to the kinds of policy and regulatory instruments available to central government. They require cultural and personal changes that governments are not able to tackle alone. The distinctive character of the move to co-governance lies in the development of a broad repertoire of delivery mechanisms that seek to combine the diverse knowledge and resources of stakeholders in the business, public, and charity or "third" sectors in order to address a specific issue.[14] Faith groups are a key constituency that governments are seeking to enlist in addressing these issues as they are seen as repositories of the kinds of cultural, moral, and social resources vital for effecting change.[15] The move toward co-governance not only relates to a national level but also to an international one, especially in relation to development work and humanitarian aid.[16] However, as John Ackerman argues, if co-governance is to avoid being a synonym for co-option then it must combine shared responsibility for addressing issues of social concern with decentralized decision-making powers, a clear regulatory framework, and an increase in measures to hold government to account. Ackerman cites the examples of participatory budgeting in Porto Alegre in Brazil and Mexico's Federal Electoral Institute as concrete examples of "co-governance for accountability" that enhanced democratic participation, strengthened the rule of law, and addressed a systemic problem of corruption.[17] The UK government is beginning to address this need for co-governance for accountability as evidenced in talk of "active citizenship" and a focus on "empowering communities."[18] Broad-based community organizing, analyzed in Chapter 2, can be seen as a particularly robust example of such co-governance for accountability.

Lastly, the most recent dynamic affecting the emerging shape of relations between the state and religious groups is the "securitization" of religion in response to the real and perceived links between ongoing terrorist activities and some Islamic groups. Barry Bulzan et al. define securitization as meaning an "issue is presented as an existential threat, requiring emergency measures and justifying actions outside the normal bounds of political procedure."[19] The securitization of religion entails rhetorically constructing religion as a direct security threat to the state and presenting it as an issue of supreme priority that needs to be dealt with outside the normal legal and political processes within which religion is dealt with. In turn, this legitimates the exceptional treatment of some religious groups and extra resources and greater attention being directed toward them. It is Muslims who are most directly affected by this process, but it is impacting the relationship between the state and religion more generally as well. As the example of the Brixton group outlined in the Introduction indicates, these resources can take the form of monitoring and intervening in certain religious groups ("hard" policing) as well as "community-based approaches" that entail funding and intentionally building relationships between religious groups and state agencies ("soft" policing). In the UK, responses to Muslim groups highlight a lack of consensus on what constitutes best practice, both in approaches to intervention and in policies on "Muslim engagement" by government departments. Some agencies view "radical" dissenting religious-political behavior (whether Christian or Muslim) as necessarily a security problem, whereas others seek partnership with law-abiding groups. In this fast-changing and controversial area, what is clear is that there are many operational differences between government departments, police, and the security services.[20] A crucial question in all such strategies is whether they allow religious groups scope for critique and dissent of wider government policies. The danger is that through a combination of co-option and securitization government agencies render dissenting but public and law-abiding groups inoperative as mediums for expressing religiously framed grievances and political critiques, delegitimizing any form of political activism and thereby inadvertently directing this dissent toward secrecy and violence.[21] An overall impact of processes of securitization, in the UK at least, is a deeper level of engagement between state agencies and many religious groups as the government seeks to understand and address internal dynamics within religious groups, Islamic groups in particular, that might exacerbate or diminish resort to violence.

The result of these six factors is a new openness and intensity in the level of engagement between the state and religious groups in the UK. Indeed, the multi-faith nature of contemporary Britain, while often used as an argument for strict separation of church and state, seems, in effect, to be producing a new form of "establishment." A measure of this emergent "multi-faith" establishment was the formation of a Home Office Faith Communities Unit in 2003; the appointment of a "faith envoy" for the Prime Minister; and the inclusion of religious leaders in the formation of social policy through such bodies as the Faith Communities Consultative Council formed in 2006.[22] A significant move in this direction was the establishment of the Inner Cities Religious Council (ICRC) in 1992.[23] Such developments are not limited to national government. They are mirrored at a regional and local level: most local authorities now have an officer responsible for liaison with faith communities;[24] and Local Strategic Partnerships (LSPs), established by local authorities to contribute to planning delivery of services to local people, often have a place reserved on them for a faith representative and are required to make specific efforts to involve and consult faith groups.[25] The cementing of this constructive relationship was marked by the report *Working Together: Cooperation between Government and Faith Communities* produced by the Home Office Communities Unit in 2004.[26] The report calls for greater "religious literacy" on the part of government at all levels and sets out guidelines for consulting faith communities in the formulation of public policy and guidance for faith communities on working with government. A parallel process of increased openness to active cooperation between the state and faith-based groups can be seen in the USA, a process that culminated in the inclusion of the Charitable Choice provision in the Personal Responsibility and Work Opportunity Reconciliation Act in 1996 and the formation of the White House Office of Faith-Based and Community Initiatives in 2001.[27] This is an initiative that President Barack Obama is continuing and developing in the form of the Office for Faith-Based and Neighborhood Partnerships.

It may be premature to talk of a new multi-faith establishment. What is clear is that in the UK a far more variegated pattern of relationships now exists. There is the continuing bilateral relationship between the state and the Church of England; for example, in relation to the provision of chaplains in the military and some prisons, hospitals, and universities. Within this bilateral arrangement the Church of England effectively acts as a broker and gatekeeper, enabling other faith groups, as well as other Christian denominations, to access state resources. The *primus inter pares* role of the Anglican

Church coexists with new, formal, multilateral patterns of cooperation such as existed in the former Inner Cities Religious Council wherein the Anglican Church was just one among many religious participants, all of whom had an equal relationship with the state.[28] These bilateral and multilateral forms of direct cooperation operate alongside and in the midst of intended – because hostile or militantly secularist – and unintended – because ignorant – prejudice by state authorities against religious groups seeking state support or cooperation.[29] All this suggests that although the political influence of the Christian church may be less, the influence of other religions is not declining, but beginning, while that of the churches, and of the Established Church in particular, is having to be renegotiated.

Social Cohesion, Social Capital, and the "Salvation" of Civil Society

From the perspective of the state, the justification for, and hostility against, closer cooperation between faith communities and the state, both in the USA and the UK, revolve around the same question: Can faith communities generate social cohesion or are they agents of division? Sociological research suggests that the answer is ambivalent.[30] However, the evidence for or against faith communities generating social cohesion is perhaps less significant than the motivations of government to work with faith groups and the impact of government policy on the practice of these groups.

Before proceeding further it is important to define some terms and deconstruct the analytical biases apparent in much of the commonly used terminology. As noted in the Introduction, this book seeks to give a theological account of the church in relation to the world that draws on historical and social scientific accounts while being alert to where such accounts conflict with or contradict theological modes of description and analysis. The need for such reflexivity is especially pressing when drawing on current social scientific literature related to debates about the relationship between religion and politics. My aim is not to rule out their use altogether but simply to draw attention to some of the more problematic aspects of widely used terms in order to articulate their limited currency for a theological analysis. Where such terms are retained they function as a form of pidgin English that bears enough meaning to allow for common conversation with the wide variety of social theorists who have adopted them.

In policy-related discussion of the relationship between religion and politics, the current vogue is to use the term "faith community" and assess whether faith communities generate "social capital." However, the term faith community is highly problematic. First, use of the term "faith" denotes a certain "Christianization," or even a "Protestantization," of other religious groups. Faith is a central frame of reference within Christianity and a key theological emphasis in Protestant churches.[31] Second, use of the term faith, like its equivalent, the term "religion," indicates a modernist, essentializing metaphysics at work that seeks to homogenize disparate and arguably incommensurable phenomena.[32] The refusal to take the particularity of different religious traditions seriously is problematic because it fails to evaluate these traditions in terms of their own frames of reference and thereby repeatedly misinterprets and misunderstands what is going on within them. Such misinterpretation leads to ill-judged action on the part of "outsiders": for example, regeneration professionals often fail to make appropriate distinctions between groups so that Sikhs are confused with Muslims or Reformed Jews are not distinguished from Ultra-Orthodox ones.[33] Farnell et al., mindful of this problem, call for secular agencies to resist assuming a homogenous "faith sector" and be prepared to engage with different faiths in terms of their own heterogeneous frames of reference.[34] Third, use of the term "faith" suggests a focus on what is personal and by implication private as opposed to the term "religion" that connotes a public, institutionally mediated power.

Any use of the term "faith communities" and its correlate "faith-based organization" must be alert to the power relations intrinsic within the use of this term. These are labels ascribed to certain groups by others rather than one intrinsic to the internal discourses of any faith group labeled as such. I will use instead the term *faith designated group* (FDG) in order to render explicit how the label "faith" carries an essentializing and latently stigmatizing bias. The term faith designated group indicates both the work of religious or "faith-based" nongovernmental organizations and the work undertaken by Christian congregations, Mosques, Gurdwaras, etc., in themselves. Use of the term "group" as opposed to "community" circumvents the problematic association with the term community that implies a homogenous and cohesive small-scale society. Religious traditions are highly contested and fractious entities with diverse and at times global social and institutional forms (for example, the Roman Catholic Church).

In reality, lines of demarcation between "faith" and "secular" organizations are very hard to determine. As will be argued later, the phenomenon of institutional isomorphism whereby FDGs take on the norms and structures of state bureaucracies and nongovernmental organizations (NGOs) means that "faith" organizations increasingly mimic "secular" organizations. Even without this process of convergence there is still the basic question of what makes a social service or welfare organization (as distinct from a congregation, denomination, or individual) religious or "faith based." This is a growing area of debate and one of the most influential accounts is given by Thomas Jeavons who identifies seven key areas where religious characteristic manifest themselves.[35] These are: i) the self-identity of the organization; ii) the religious convictions of participants; iii) the extent to which religion helps or hinders the acquisition of resources; iv) the extent to which religion shapes the goals, products, and services of the organization; v) the impact of religion on decision making; vi) the remit of religious authority and leadership within the organization; and vii) the extent to which religion determines inter-organizational relationships. Jeavons argues that instead of there being a strict separation between faith and secular organizations the above variables determine the *degree* of organizational "religiosity." These range from the explicitly religious to the completely secular such that in their identity, internal cultures, organizational structure, and service delivery "faith" and "secular" NGOs exist on a continuum and overlap a great deal. Thus, rather than envisioning "faith" and "secular" groups as distinct or separate from each other, it is better to identify the particular and historically contingent ways in which FDGs partially differentiate themselves from "secular" groups within common organizational fields and shared spheres of activity.[36]

The term "social capital" is equally problematic. Robert Putnam provides what he calls a "lean and mean" definition, stating that the term denotes: "social networks and the associated norms of reciprocity and trustworthiness."[37] He goes on to say: "The core insight of this approach is extremely simple: like tools (physical capital) and training (human capital), social networks have value."[38] For Putnam, social capital is a glue that bridges and bonds society in a way that enables the smooth running of social interactions both at an interpersonal level and between groups and organizations. However, there are two key problems with the term and both relate to the metaphor of capital applied to social relations. Use of the term "social capital," as opposed to political, institutional, or more organic metaphors, conceives of economics as the most basic or fundamental way of thinking about how to organize human society. This was an explicit assumption in the early development of the term in the work of Pierre Bourdieu but is mostly implicit in its more recent usage. Sheldon Wolin develops a genealogy of how economics came to provide the most basic way of thinking about human relations and outlines how this development undermines the plausibility of the existence of a common good. Wolin gives an account of the centralization of sovereignty in the nation-state and the subsequent attempt to overcome political conflict within liberal nation-states through a combination of rational administration, use of technology, and the demarcation of the economy as the sphere of free, uncoerced relations.[39] On Wolin's account, liberalism identifies freedom with private interest rather than the pursuit of common action and shared advantage. The corollary of this is to grant the economy – envisaged as the sphere of private interest and uncoerced relations – maximal scope and priority over the requirements of good government or the goods of any institution, whether it is a family, a farm, or a football club. Economics becomes the sovereign knowledge "pertaining to the welfare of the community as a whole."[40] Social harmony ceases to issue from a prior set of institutional and political arrangements, but is construed as flowing from the spontaneous equilibrium of economic forces. Within such a vision the status of the citizen becomes absorbed into that of the producer or consumer.[41] For Wolin, liberalism follows both Marx and the classical economists such as Adam Smith in seeing social and political relations as secondary to and dependent on economic relations, and economic relations as the means to move beyond politics. Capitalism rather than politics is the means to order the world and the basis of society. Wolin's account is illustrated in Alan Finlayson's analysis of Tony Blair and New Labour's policies. Finlayson notes:

> New Labour does not like politics very much and certainly doesn't like it to happen outside its purview. It would prefer to imagine a permanent consensus under its permanent management. It sometimes seems to be dreaming of a world of pure individuals, permanently innovating new products and managing social relations through the terms and practices of trade. Economic rather than political exchange become understood as the basis of community and its freest expression is the private market not the public meeting.[42]

The move away from politics is reflected in the use of the term "social capital" as a way of talking about social relations wherein economic relations rather than political ones are the basic paradigm.

The fruit of economics becoming the sovereign knowledge pertaining to the welfare of the community as a whole is that it becomes plausible to envisage social relations as equivalent to capital flows and monetary exchange. Re-rendering social relations as analogous to capital flows has a similar effect to the reduction of heterogeneous religious beliefs and practices to a single, homogeneous category of "faith community": that is, use of the term "social capital" abstracts diverse patterns of relationship from the historical, geographic, and political contexts and traditions that give them meaning, reinterpreting and reducing them to bonding and bridging relationships that serve some other goal such as social cohesion.[43] A particularly egregious example of exactly this is the definition of the term "church" given by Robert Putnam who states: "For simplicity's sake I use the term church here to refer to all religious institutions of whatever faith, including mosques, temples, and synagogues."[44] Yet social relations are only ever embodied in particular institutions, traditions, and contexts that give them meaning and shape. So it is questionable whether reducing and essentializing them to social capital, as if all social relations were equivalent and fungible (marriage being equivalent to and exchangeable with participation in a bowling league), tells us much about them at all.[45] However, while recognizing that use of the term is to perpetuate a distorting mirror that ontologizes capitalism as a natural or necessary reality rather than a contingent one, I retain it for pragmatic reasons in certain places through the book.[46]

I turn now to the motivations of the state to seek partnership with FDGs. Many of the justifications given for a partnership between the state and FDGs envisage FDGs as vital partners in generating social cohesion.[47] In addition to this somewhat functionalist aim, working with FDGs denotes a desire to be inclusive and tolerate diversity.[48] Thus, FDGs can be seen as representing the resolution of a seeming antinomy at the heart of contemporary Western society: that is, how to simultaneously foster social cohesion and respect diversity. Underlying the desire to work with FDGs in order to generate social cohesion and respect diversity is a vision of partnership between FDGs and the state as contributing to the renewal of civil society.[49] Civil society is a key topic in both political theory and policy debates, the dominant assumption being what Michael Walzer calls the "civil society argument" that "the strength and stability of liberal democracy depends on a vibrant and healthy sphere of associational participation."[50] Walzer argues that for civil society to flourish, it depends on the nurture of both solidarity and pluralism in order that both human freedom and sociality might be fulfilled.[51] On this account, something like the modern liberal state is the polity best suited to enabling and framing a flourishing civil society in which humans can live the good life.[52] Religious groups, as long as they stay within civil society, can be accommodated because they are seen as contributing to civil society both in their diversity and in their patterns of association.

A review of relevant UK government reports and speeches by British politicians reveals other more prosaic, instrumental reasons given for partnering with FDGs. FDGs are seen as: 1) effective means of achieving social policy goals in areas where government has had little success (for example, in inner city schooling and urban regeneration); 2) good entry points for reaching socially excluded groups in culturally sensitive ways;[53] 3) having concrete resources that can be utilized (for example, buildings and local staff);[54] 4) having a long-term commitment to, and past experience within, particular localities in contrast to welfare professionals who commute in and out and who tend to operate with a very different worldview than those they serve;[55] and 5) being cost effective and able to provide best value for money.[56] However, these motivations fail to reckon with two things: first, the difficulties FDGs have in accessing government resources; and second, the transformative impact government has on FDGs when they become conduits for state resources. These two factors undermine the hoped-for outcomes of government policy in this area.[57]

The aspiration to work with FDGs is plagued by practical difficulties. Richard Farnell et al. set out a wide range of obstacles that block partnership between FDGs and the state.[58] They note that from the perspective of FDGs the "bureaucratic demands, the resources needed to ensure a successful bid and the compromises that need to be made to meet secular objectives" means that "some faith groups decide to focus on their worship and small-scale self-funded activities rather than get involved in formal regeneration programmes."[59] On the government side cooperation is hampered by numerous factors. In their study of faith-based volunteering Priya Lukka and Michael Locke point out that despite government rhetoric about engagement, "there is still only a limited understanding of the mechanisms that exist to achieve this, or of the nature and capacity of existing social action by different faith communities."[60] They go on to say that "it is not clear if the groups themselves know what is being asked of them, how they can get involved and what the terms of a regeneration partnership involving them would be."[61] Even if these practical difficulties could be resolved, it is far from clear whether partnership between the state and the FDGs can foster social cohesion and renew the kind of vibrant associational life understood as vital for the health of liberal democracy.

The partnership between government and FDGs is an unequal one and one that can both distort the FDGs themselves and foster conflict between different religious traditions. Much of the anxiety about drawing FDGs into partnership with the state centers on the fear that religion is a socially divisive force.[62] However, it is not necessarily FDGs that cause the conflict. Rather, the cause is often the way in which the state structures its relationships with them. The dominance of the market model in the provision of welfare services, and the demand of competitive tendering for government contracts, frames relations between FDGs in terms of rivalry rather than cooperation. Based on his fieldwork in Southall, West London, Gerd Baumann states:

> In Southall ... the fact that public resources are, as the word goes, targeted at cultural communities leads to a political scene in which the common good is seen as a competition of any one community with [every] other community ... In the process, every minority has to struggle against all others and each of them becomes a community of disappointment and suspicion that complains that some other community is getting a better deal while the common good gets nowhere.[63]

As David Herbert comments: "This competition rewards groups for identifying communally on a religious or ethnic basis, potentially aggravating and even creating divisions."[64] This analysis is borne out by the Ouseley and Cantle reports that came out in the aftermath of riots in the towns of Bradford, Oldham, and Burnley in 2001. Both these reports note that self-separation between different ethnic and religious communities is exacerbated by government policy which encourages competition between communities for urban renewal funds.[65] Thus the state establishes an agonistic or competitive field of encounter for FDGs to meet each other and the processes by which the state recognizes groups has a divisive effect. In short, government policy, far from contributing to social cohesion, can undermine its stated aim through the way it structures its relations with FDGs. However, the deleterious impact of its policy is masked because any conflict that arises is subsequently interpreted through the Enlightenment critique of religion as a source of division – religion is the chaos monster – and no attention is given to how such division is itself a result of state-induced competition.[66] Left to themselves, many religious groups are just as liable to establish convivial relations of reciprocity and trust in pursuit of goods in common. One form of such convivial relations will be explored in Chapter 2 in the analysis of broad-based community organizing.

In addition to setting up competitive relations between different religious groups, relationships between FDGs and the state can create distance between the targeted client group and the religious organization acting as a conduit for state resources. This difficulty arises through a process of what is called "institutional isomorphism." This is a process where religious organizations reshape themselves to fit government policy and thereby lose their unique characteristics, while taking on the same institutional shape and processes as state agencies. Paul DiMaggio and Walter Powell identify three interrelated dynamics at work in institutional isomorphism – the coercive, the mimetic, and the normative – each of which leads to a convergence within a particular organizational field.[67]

First, *coercive* isomorphism involves the adaptation by FDGs to state norms and procedures due to formal or informal pressures or generalized expectations.[68] For example, abstaining from religious activities such as proselytization in order to comply with conditions set for receiving government grants. A further example is the demand for, or the adoption of, bureaucratic organizational forms and values by FDGs in order to qualify for state funding or to cope with accountability procedures. The FDG is thereby recast in the image of the state and the very elements that make it distinctive are diminished: that is, the engagement with the whole person and the "spiritual" dimensions of the problems being addressed are squeezed out by bureaucratic procedures. At the level of state funding of work undertaken by local churches, mosques, etc., there is the question of how the integrity of the worshiping community can be maintained at the same time as energy is channeled into maintaining government-sponsored projects which grow larger and are better resourced than the "core business" of the church being the church or the mosque being the mosque. This can affect congregations in numerous ways: for example, burnout of key personnel as they are caught up in paperwork to account for grants, or action being increasingly directed toward tangible outcomes and away from "spiritual" goals such as praying with and pastoring people.

Second, *mimetic* isomorphism means the adaptation of technologies or organizational procedures so as to copy or conform to prevailing or hegemonic organizational structures and procedures. The pressure here is not external but comes from a desire within an organization to be like everyone else or follow a model that is perceived as successful or effective. Lastly, *normative* isomorphism signifies adaptation mediated by processes of professionalization. An example of this process is set out by Alexander Kenneth Nagel who states: "Although FBOs [faith-based organizations] may apply religious criteria when they recruit new staff, just like secular nonprofits they choose their managerial staff according to formal qualifications, thus exposing themselves to normative isomorphism."[69] Noting how partnership with the state encourages a process of professionalization among FDGs, Charles Glenn argues: "Professionalization, while it may raise the standards of service or teaching in significant respects, may also distance nonprofit organizations or schools from those they serve and from their communities."[70] This is because, as Glenn puts it: "Imposition of professional norms upon a faith-based school or agency by government requirements or, more subtly, by acceptance of professional norms, may lead to a fundamental shift in its way of understanding and living its mission."[71] The professionalization of the "program" distances the work and employees from the congregation out of which it came. The result is that many faith-based organizations and projects are not that different from their non-religiously affiliated counterparts.[72] Drawing on the results of extensive research in the USA, Robert Wuthnow suggests that: "The 'secular' influences of government regulations, bureaucratic structure, and professional norms appeared to outweigh the influences of being associated with religious traditions and practices."[73] Thus, like the claim to be seeking partnership with FDGs in the name of social cohesion, the justification of working with FDGs in order to respect diversity is somewhat hollow.

Analysis of the interaction between faith groups and the state suggests that the state: one, affects religious practice in ways that generate social conflict rather than civic association for the common good; two, its terms and conditions for partnership are often at odds with the aims and objectives of faith groups themselves; and three, partnership with the state can have a secularizing impact upon FDGs, alienating them from their own communities. The incorporation of faith groups into state policy, on conditions set by the state, and justified in instrumental terms, risks closing down the free, non-instrumental space that religious belief and practice holds open and which, as David Herbert argues, is central for the formation of civil society as a space of free deliberation.[74]

The wider question of whether civil society can be conceived of as a sphere of free deliberation and non-instrumental relations will be addressed in the next chapter. What can be said is that the co-option by the state of religious actors in a bid for efficiency and effectiveness of social policy does tend toward forming a new establishment. However, unlike the establishment of the Church of England wherein there is, *de jure*, a joint jurisdiction between church and state and a built-in dialectic between the two, this new, Erastian establishment is one in which the state monopolizes jurisdiction over the ordering of society and the religious institutions and initiatives are rendered wholly subordinate to the state. In accepting the current terms and conditions of cooperation as structured by the state, the church distorts its ministry and mission and remolds its witness around the instrumental requirements of the state. What will be explored in subsequent chapters is whether the church can structure its cooperation with the state in ways that avoid these outcomes.

Liberalism and the Continuing Requirements of Public Reason

Within debates about the place of the religions in Western democracies the primary discourse framing this relationship is liberalism. What then are we to make of the emergent relationship between the state and FDGs within the context of liberal political thought? For liberalism, ecclesiastical and religious sources of authority are ruled inadmissible as justifications for public policy. Within the liberal settlement "religion" is confined to the private sphere and public policy must be justified in terms of "public" reasons. However, this does not mean that all liberals are inherently hostile to "religion." John Rawls explicitly distances himself from what he calls anti-Christian "Enlightenment Liberalism" and advocates a political form of toleration and autonomy that is not *necessarily* committed to a conception of the individual agent as a skeptical self-reflexive subject who stands at one remove from any particular tradition.[75] In Rawls's later work his concern is not the exclusion of religious discourse from public debate, but that no comprehensive doctrine of whatever kind, including religious, can form the basis for political decisions regarding the use of coercive public power. Rawls's approach is what Paul Weitham characterizes as the "liberalism of reasoned respect," or as it is more widely referred to, "political liberalism."[76] The liberalism of reasoned respect has direct parallels with both the work of Jürgen Habermas, whose discursive or communicative ethics is similar in trajectory to Rawls's "deliberative democracy,"[77] and John Gray's *modus vivendi* model of liberalism.[78] Rawls gives what is termed a proceduralist theory of equality and justice: that is, his account seeks to secure justice by emphasizing procedures rather than a normative or substantive account of what justice consists of. In theory at least, such an approach allows for a range of different "comprehensive" doctrines to accept its terms and conditions without having to agree with one another.[79] Rawls's central concern is how those with differing conceptions of the good life can live together in a polity and provide justification for the use of coercive political force in terms acceptable to one another.

Within political liberalism religion is problematic because it is seen to threaten the basis of *political* cooperation – which is distinct from the wider social cooperation in civil society that religion may indeed foster. Reason – or specifically "public reason" – becomes the basis of political cooperation and just judgment between competing claims.[80] For the state, or another citizen, to base cooperation and the exercise of coercive power on terms that any citizen could not reasonably endorse as a free and equal person is to show a form of disrespect.[81] As already noted, a primary value at work in the liberalism of reasoned respect is the generation of consensus. The desire for consensus is born out of a vision of the political ordering of society as a cooperative as opposed to a competitive enterprise.[82] In order to participate in public deliberation about the common good, religiously motivated actors must "translate" their reasons for advocating a particular policy that may involve the coercive use of force into "public reasons"; that is, reasons that all may accept because they accord with a liberal political conception of justice.[83] For Rawls, although one may have religious reasons for acting, ultimately these must be justified by public reasons and can never in and of themselves constitute a public justification. The result is that the church qua church must give public reasons (as Rawls defines them) for the positions it holds in relation to decisions about public policy. As already indicated, the demand to translate Christian reasons into public reasons does not mean that Christianity is reduced to the realm of private opinion. Churches and Christian belief and practices can have an important role to play in civil society and contribute to informing deliberation on a wide variety of moral and political issues.[84] Yet while the "acceptable" face of Christianity may contribute to the background political culture, the church is, in effect, depoliticized. One could argue that the church, via its participation in civil society, is not depoliticized. However, its public political role is restricted to participation in civil society, which is, within Rawls's scheme, a form of depoliticization.[85]

It seems, at first glance, that in Britain at least, liberal arguments that demand that churches conform their speech to public reason have been directly reversed. For example, government officials are now being encouraged to be "religiously literate" and priests and imams contribute directly to the formation of public policy. However, as already stated, the call for greater partnership between the state and FDGs is justified in largely pragmatic terms. Where they are not, justifications in terms of the contribution of FDGs to generating social cohesion, social capital, and renewing civil society are, in effect, public reasons: that is, these kinds of justifications do not appeal to religious sources of authority. Conversely, most FDGs, including those with strong religious affiliations, justify their own patterns of service delivery in terms of what Smith and Sosin call a "dignity-and-rights philosophy" that neither makes distinctions between recipients of services on the basis of creed or culture nor demands conformity to a particular religious worldview.[86] Such an approach directly conforms to a Rawlsian conception of the overlapping consensus wherein a religious group gives public reasons for acting that are themselves grounded or located within ultimately religious reasons. Those agencies more directly oriented to proselytism or other overtly religious goals tend neither to receive funding nor seek state resources and so are self-excluding.[87] Any remaining anxieties or concerns a political liberal might have about partnership between the state and FDGs can be allayed by attention to the terms and conditions of entry that are set for religious groups to receive public money.[88] Moreover, as argued above, while the language is of partnership the reality is that the state controls the relationship.

In North America and Britain, many Christian groups have embraced the offer of partnership as both an opportunity to reengage the churches with the political process and to overcome what they see as a false divide between church and state.[89] At the local level, many congregations are involved in partnerships with local government to provide a variety of different services. These partnerships operate as if the church is but one piece of the jigsaw that makes up civil society and constitutes part of what Rawls calls the "background culture" of liberal democracy. Pragmatically, working within the constraints of the liberal settlement is not necessarily problematic: the church can contribute to public policy but only on grounds of public reason and as long as it restricts itself to being just another voluntary agency within civil society rather than a corporate actor with its own political authority. Some go beyond simply a pragmatic consideration, accepting the Rawlsian-type liberal settlement as a positive construction of the relationship between church and state. This is particularly the case with those who see liberal democracy and human rights as intrinsically congruent with Christianity and unproblematic for the church to adopt as its primary language of political engagement. However, questions arise as to what impact the liberal settlement has on the church and whether it is one that is congruent with Christian belief and practice. In order to clear the ground for a range of theological responses to these questions and establish the need to move beyond political liberalism to a post-liberal, postsecularist politics, I will outline three problems with Rawls's conception of political life.

Before doing so it is important to say that the advocacy of a post-liberal, theological politics presumes a liberal constitutional order, the rule of law and a self-limiting state. This may seem a self-contradictory statement; however, as suggested in the Introduction to the book, politics is the process through which to maintain commonality and recognize and conciliate conflict with others in pursuit of shared goods. As Hannah Arendt argues, politics is distinct from and subsequent to the constitutional-legal order.[90] A liberal constitutional-legal order guarantees certain positive and negative liberties, equality before the law, and sets out various procedures and institutions, for example a legal system and judiciary, for buttressing these liberties. These freedoms – which against most current thinking do not, of necessity, have to be conceptualized in terms of human rights – include positive freedoms such as freedom of worship, freedom of assembly, and freedom of speech; and negative freedoms, such as freedom from torture, inhuman or degrading treatment, or punishment, freedom from slavery, and freedom from arbitrary arrest, detention, or exile. In short, the liberal legal-constitutional order sets the boundaries within which politics takes place. For Arendt these rights or freedoms are not natural or self-evident. Rather, they are conventions or forms of human agreement forged through common action. As Jeffrey Isaacs summarizes it, for Arendt:

> It is only in concert, on the basis of claims that are mutually recognized and agreed to, that human dignity can be secured and continually resecured in a recalcitrant world. If we fail to act, we will simply be acted upon. Given the forces at work in the modern world, such a course is unlikely to afford either security or freedom.[91]

Building on Arendt, I contend that while the liberal constitutional order seeks to guarantee a basic set of freedoms these cannot exist without the politics to forge and actualize them and such a politics can only occur within particular kinds of place-based and time-intensive relationships.

There are a number of ways to give an account of the foundations of this liberal polity. For example, Oliver O'Donovan gives a theological-historical justification of this order as a fruit of the Christ-event.[92] Alasdair MacIntyre develops a Thomist-Aristotelian account that draws on natural law and pursuit of the common good.[93] Historic examples include the 1628 "Petition of Rights" pressed on Charles I by Parliament and the 1641 *Body of Liberties* formulated by the Massachusetts Bay colonists, both of which drew on chartered rights and liberties (in particular the Magna Carta), custom, and common law in order to establish constitutional bills of rights.[94] As the historic examples suggest, a liberal constitutional order does not necessarily entail a democracy but is compatible with a variety of forms of rule, including a constitutional monarchy. Following Aristotle, what this order defines is the space of politics, and it is politics that necessitates self-restraint and the conciliation of different interests within a territorial unit under a common rule. Rawls stands in the modern tradition of justifications of a liberal constitutional order based on some account of a social contract that goes back to Kant, Rousseau, and Hobbes. While I dispute Rawls's contractarian account of the foundation of the liberal constitutional-legal order, his emphasis on the importance of such an order is exactly right. Theologically, a central claim of Scripture, paradigmatically articulated in the Decalogue, is that human social and political order is one determined not by the personal fiat of a single ruler or an oligarchy but by law and covenant (that is, committed, faithful, mutually responsible social relationships). Where Rawls's understanding of the place of law, along with that of many liberals, becomes unworkable and self-destructive is in the attempt to expand the liberal constitutional-legal order, primarily through an emphasis on human rights, so that it functions as a substitute for and overrides concrete social and political relationships in particular places. This kind of substitution falls prey to the following charge by Arendt:

> Escape from the frailty of human affairs into the solidity of quiet and order has in fact so much to recommend it that the greater part of political philosophy since Plato could easily be interpreted as various attempts to find theoretical foundations and practical ways for an escape from politics altogether.[95]

Liberalism as a form of politics, rather than as a commitment to a particular form of legal-constitutional order, represents the attempt to eliminate frailty, historical contingency, and creatureliness from political life. As already set out, Sheldon Wolin argues that libera*lism*, along with Communism, represents a modern attempt to replace politics with procedure. For Wolin, an "adequate political logic must be framed to cope with contraries and dissymetries arising out of a mobile and conflict-laden situation. Its tutelary deity is Proteus, not Procrustus."[96] To use Wolin's terms, the liberal legal-constitutional order is not a contract but a birthright or inheritance that can be either squandered or tended and handed on. Whether or not they are grounded in some account of natural rights or creation order, the freedoms this constitutional order guarantees are in practice civil and political freedoms that have to be reappropriated and fulfilled through shared political action.

What I argue for in Chapter 2 is the need for a post-liberal *politics* within the boundaries of a liberal constitutional-legal order that at the same time brews and dialectically lives out the promise of this order. The rest of this book presumes such an order and Chapter 3 gives a theological account of its importance while at the same time pointing to a crisis within its current forms. This is not to say that a commitment to a liberal constitutional order is a *sine qua non* of faithful witness: as an earthly political order it is fallen, imperfect, and by no means immutable. However, as will be argued more extensively in Chapters 2 and 3 it is an existing realm of earthly peace and is to be valued as such.

The first problem with Rawls's political liberalism as an account of politics and its exclusion of religious discourse from political life relates directly to the issue of conflict. Rawls seeks to avoid particular kinds of conflict in politics, specifically over questions of ultimate meaning. However, conflict is inevitable and political decisions are necessarily contested. Good government does not spring fully formed like Athene from Zeus's brow out of the actions of bureaucrats and the writing of laws. It is the result of cumulative judgments that are come to through a time-intensive and often conflict-ridden process of deliberation. Moreover, questions of ultimate meaning cannot be forever avoided and addressing them necessarily involves highly contested debates over the vision of the good – the debate over abortion being a case in point. Conflict is not in and of itself bad. It can be creative and disagreement can clarify what is important and enable better judgments to be made. The issue is how we handle conflict – violently or nonviolently, with respect for the rule of law or flouting it. Religiously motivated actors are no better – but certainly no worse – than others at handling conflict constructively. What we need is a politics that can live with deep plurality over questions of ultimate meaning and can encompass the fact that many communities and traditions contribute to the common good – each in their own way.

Rawls's analysis and his quest for rationally derived consensus are based on a false specter. Political liberalism is a response to an imagined threat:

that religion is the primary or most dangerous source of chaos and violence in the political sphere.[97] This threat has plausibility because of the *mythos* of liberalism – its own *Enuma Elish* – wherein liberal modernity plays the hero who slays the chaos monster of religion, thus returning peace and civility to the social order after the "wars of religion" in the seventeenth century.[98] To maintain the social order religion cannot be allowed to enter the public domain, lest chaos and violent disorder once again hold sway.[99] Events since September 11, 2001 would seem to confirm this view. Yet this *mythos* masks the fact that the modern chaos monster has been played by anti-religious or agnostic political regimes, whether colonialist, nationalist, fascist, or communist. Moreover, liberalism itself, married as it has been to capitalism and a technocratic, instrumental rationality, is party to untold ecological, economic, and social misery and violent chaos around the world.[100] As Nicholas Wolterstorff points out: "It would be dangerously myopic to focus one's attention on the danger that religion poses to the polity while ignoring the equal or greater danger posed by secular causes."[101] All of this is simply to underline the point that, as stated before, religiously motivated actors are no better, but certainly no worse, at handling conflict and power constructively. Theologically this should not be surprising. One of the fundamental insights of Augustine was that every participant in the earthly city – which includes the church as well as political authorities – is subject to the *libido dominandi*.

A second problem revolves around how Rawls's account of the proper relationship between religion and liberal democracy occludes people's most basic reasons for acting. His approach inhibits the formation of a genuinely common life with others because we are never able to respond to and engage with their primary concerns and self-understanding. As already noted, Rawls's political liberalism demands that, at certain points, all comprehensive doctrines translate their "thick" patterns of thought and speech into the "thin" or common discourse of public reason. For Rawls, religiously motivated political actors are required to reframe their theological reasons into public reasons before advocating policy positions. By contrast, Jeffrey Stout, in his critique of Rawls's conception of public reason, highlights why religious speech should be able to contribute directly to public deliberation about common action. For Stout it is vital that "religiously committed citizens" articulate their reasons for acting politically "in as much depth and detail as they see fit," otherwise, as Stout puts it: "[i]f they are discouraged from speaking up in this way, we will remain ignorant of the real reasons that many of our fellow citizens have of reaching some of the ethical and political conclusions they do."[102] Jeremy Waldron, in explicit contrast to Rawls's notion of public reason, argues that the first responsibility in contested arguments about the common good is to "make whatever effort we can to converse with others on their own terms, as they attempt to converse with us on ours, to see what we can understand of their reasons, and to present our reasons as well as we can to them."[103] Rawls's account prevents real dialogue and encounter and thus precludes the formation of a genuinely common good; that is, a common good in which both differences and commonalities together constitute an arena of mutual ground.[104] Or as Clarke Cochran puts it: "Public civil discourse is genuine to the extent that participants learn to speak with one another in their differences as well as their shared languages."[105]

A third problem with Rawls's approach is that it overly narrows the range of what constitutes public deliberation and excludes nonverbal and non-rational forms of contribution. This is a point drawn out by Iris Marion Young who argues for the need to move beyond "deliberative democracy" to what she calls "communicative democracy."[106] For Young, "when political dialogue aims at solving collective problems, it justly requires a plurality of perspectives, speaking styles and ways of expressing the particularity of social situations as well as the general applicability of principles."[107] She points out that what counts as deliberation that can contribute to public reason excludes other, more tradition-specific forms of communication, notably, greeting, rhetoric, and storytelling.[108] For Young, these modes of communication supplement rational argument by providing "ways of speaking across difference in the absence of significant shared understanding."[109] As such, keeping diverse and thick forms of communication in play in public deliberation ensures that on the one hand, difference is respected, and on the other, that there is "both the expression and the extension of shared understandings, where they exist, and the offering and acknowledgement of unshared meanings."[110] One aspect of the fuller range of legitimate contributions to public deliberation that Young does not pick up on is that comprising embodied witness and symbolic action or gesture. Action – whether a hunger strike, a march, or an act of charity – is often a powerful contribution to public deliberation. In action, as well as in forms of speech such as greetings, we reach the limit of rational argument, yet the surplus of meaning made available by action and tradition-specific forms of communication to political life and the negotiation of goods in common can open up new political possibilities. Actions explored in later chapters, such as sanctuary and fair trade, are examples of exactly this process of opening up new possibilities. The implication of this more pluralist, variegated, and "agonistic" conception of public deliberation is that, as William Connolly puts it: "You transfigure the drive to reach a consensus on justice above contending faiths into the effort to negotiate a positive ethos of engagement between multiple constituencies who bring chunks and pieces of their faiths with them into the public realm."[111]

These three critiques suggest there is no good political reason to accept a Rawlsian liberal settlement in relation to the role of the church in politics. What remains to be addressed is the theological rationale for refusing such a settlement.

Theological Politics and the Question of What Constitutes Faithful Witness

Liberal political thought may be able to rest easy at the emergent relationship between FDGs and the state; however, should the church? A growing number of theologians are highly critical of the liberal settlement and the restriction of the church to the background culture. Echoing Karl Barth, they argue that the first task of the church is to be the church and it is not the business of the church to legitimize one particular form of political order – namely liberal democracy. These approaches argue that liberal democracy itself, like any political regime, can be tyrannous, inhumane, and idolatrous, serving what John Paul II called the "culture of death."[112] What follows is a brief consideration of three prominent theological critics of contemporary liberal democracy whose work represents a shift to a post-liberal, theological politics. These approaches can be characterized in the following terms: one, the priority given to enabling the church to be an alternative *polis* as set out in the work of Stanley Hauerwas; two, the politics of moral suasion and upholding the common good as delineated within contemporary Catholic social teaching (with a particular focus on John Paul II as the most significant figure in its recent development); and three, a vision of the political dimension of mission as ensuring the obedience of rulers to Christ as articulated by Joan Lockwood and Oliver O'Donovan. Attention to the work of Hauerwas, John Paul II, and the O'Donovans is not meant to be exhaustive. Rather, it sets the scene for the theological analysis of particular issues in subsequent chapters, locating the engagement with a diverse range of theological voices within the broad contours and concerns of post-liberal, Christian political thought.

Ecclesiology and the Political Mission of the Church

Hauerwas, John Paul II, and the O'Donovans are engaged with the late-modern context in which the seeds of the Enlightenment have come to fruition. For all these figures, the political dimensions of the church qua church are central. For Hauerwas, John Paul II, the O'Donovans, and, we might add, Radical Orthodox theologians such as John Milbank, William Cavanaugh, and Catherine Pickstock, the first question we need to ask is not what is practical or relevant but what does it mean to be the church?[113] In effect, theological politics constitutes a renewed emphasis on the political dimensions of ecclesiology.[114] Consequent upon the emphasis on the church being the church is the refusal to allow the state to set the terms and conditions of entry into the public square: if the church, to be authentically itself, is a public political body which speaks in its own specific language, then so be it. The state oversteps its proper limits when it seeks to determine when, where, and in what voice the church may speak. Conversely, the church falsely limits itself when it only acts and speaks within conditions set for it externally.

None of these theologians would fully endorse the emergent shape of church–state relations in contemporary Britain and the USA. For Hauerwas, involvement with the state is permissible, but only on an ad hoc basis. A fuller examination of Hauerwas's approach is set out in Chapter 4; however, his position can be summarized as follows. Hauerwas calls for discriminating engagement rather than either complete withdrawal or general involvement.[115] Hauerwas opposes foundationalist attempts to find a common language or a form of "public reason" on which church and state can systematically cooperate and understand each other. For Hauerwas, the church contributes to civil society but at the same time is an alternative civil society. Its purposes are never simply to help the nation-state and liberal democracy to function. Hauerwas writes that "while I am not opposed to trying to harness the resources of state power to alleviate the needs of people, I think it is unfortunate when we think only in those terms."[116] For Hauerwas, the call to work together with the state risks compromising the true gift of the church to the state: that is, its ability to open new horizons, provide new languages of description, and embody alternative practices. This contribution is sustained by the worship life of the church, which constitutes the church as a distinct society or body within the body politic.

Unlike Hauerwas, contemporary Roman Catholic social teaching holds open the possibility of systematic cooperation between the state and the church on the basis of a shared pursuit of the common good.[117] However, what this means is very different than the demands of Rawls's conception of political liberalism. For John Paul II the church can never simply be confined to civil society, and where partnership with the state undermines the autonomous and free witness of the church, the church must resist co-option.[118] John Paul II argued that civil society in particular and culture more generally has priority over politics and economics as that which drives historical change and is the true sphere of human freedom.[119] For it is in our cultural life and forms of association that constitute civil society that humans become persons through the pursuit of transcendent, nonmaterial goods. And at the heart of culture is a cult or religion.[120] The contrast here is with political realists on the left and right who wish to define politics solely in terms of the exercise of power and reduce what it means to be human to material concerns alone.[121] His anthropology, which has as its centerpiece the dignity of every human person and the interdependence and mutual responsibility of all humans, forms the basis of the polarity that John Paul II sets up in *Evangelium Vitae* between a "culture of death" – which undermines and opposes human dignity and solidarity – and a "culture of life" – which contributes to and promotes these goods.[122] John Paul II's anthropology underlies his emphasis on evangelization as the primary political task of the church: the conversion of hearts and minds will usher in a culture of life that gives rise to positive political change.[123] For John Paul II, as *Centesimus Annus* puts it, "there can be no genuine solution of the 'social question' apart from the Gospel."[124] Thus John Paul II locates the primary political responsibility of the church in its faithful witness. This is put most forcefully in the following statement from *Centesimus Annus* given in support of the approach that John Paul II identifies as first articulated in *Rerum Novarum*:

> In effect, to teach and to spread her social doctrine pertains to the Church's evangelizing mission and is an essential part of the Christian message, since this doctrine points out the direct consequences of that message in the life of society and situates daily work and struggles for justice in the context of bearing witness to Christ the Saviour.[125]

However, faithful witness includes pursuing the common good through partnership with people of good will, who may or may not be found in the apparatus of state.[126] For example, the task of the laity is defined as "infusing the temporal order with Christian values, all the while respecting the nature and rightful autonomy of that order, and cooperating with other citizens according to their particular competence and responsibility."[127]

Perhaps the most pertinent critique of the emergent establishment can be derived from the work of the O'Donovans, who are directly engaged with the question of the church's establishment. Like Hauerwas and John Paul II, the O'Donovans see the church as the paradigmatic social body or good society. For the O'Donovans, the generic shape of the church is modeled on the Christ-event which they conceive as the structuring principle for all ecclesiology. Oliver O'Donovan states that the church "recapitulates the Christ-event in itself, and so proclaims the Christ-event to the world."[128] Faithful Christian witness necessarily reframes every aspect of human life, including its political ordering, through the prism of church order which is an icon of the Christ-event. That other, non-ecclesial social orders – such as nations – should, over time and in *response* to successful mission, begin to bear the imprint of this ecclesial order is, for the O'Donovans, right and proper.[129] A key feature of this imprint is the chastening of political authority. For the O'Donovans: "The reign of Christ in heaven has left *judgment* as the single remaining political need. ... The secular princes of this earth, shorn of pretensions to our loyalty and worship, are left with the sole function of judging between innocent and guilty."[130] Yet political authority is not alone in this task. For the O'Donovans and, they would argue, the main thrust of Christian political thought, ecclesial and political authority share a joint responsibility for ordering society and offering judgment. The judgment of the church takes the form of proclamation of the Gospel – that is, the promulgation of God's judgment in Christ – while the judgment of political authority is the limited arena of coercive human legal and political judgment. The interrelationship of these two forms of judgment are drawn out by Joan Lockwood O'Donovan who states: "The whole of human jurisdiction has the purpose of sustaining a social and moral space for the church's ministry of proclamation."[131] Establishment, understood as the constitutional priority for Christianity so as to ensure that the state formally recognizes the lordship of Christ, enables ecclesiastical and civil institutions to form a public juridical totality that maintains the dual character of judgment after Christ.[132] The O'Donovans do not see Establishment as the only theologically acceptable form of church–state relationship; however, Establishment can positively and practically maintain the dialectical relationship between jurisdiction and proclamation that together form and maintain a just social order.

For the O'Donovans the political responsibility of the church in a post-Christendom context is mission. Mission is understood not simply as an urge to increase the influence and size of the church, but as the church being "at the disposal of the Holy Spirit in making Christ's victory known. It requires, therefore, a discernment of the working of the Spirit and of the Antichrist."[133] This dual approach of discerning the work of the Spirit in history and of the Antichrist – understood as any attempt to form a unified or total political and sacral authority opposed to or apart from Christ – drives their theology of church–state relations. Unlike Hauerwas, the O'Donovans do not see the relationship between church and state as antagonistic but, under the right conditions, as complementary. However, in contrast to John Paul II, the O'Donovans do not think that there can be a shared rationality on which the church and a state that denies the lordship of Christ can base their cooperation. Rather, Christian mission involves promoting and upholding the practice of a distinctive Christian liberalism; that is, a social order based on freedom, mercy, natural rights (as distinct from human rights), and openness to free speech.[134] However, in a society that simultaneously bears the marks of Christian mission and subverts Christian teaching, a central feature of the church's mission is to serve as a watchman: it must discern and give a critique of the marks of the Antichrist on the prevailing social and political order.[135] The O'Donovans identify late-modern liberalism, and its technocratic basis, as one such "parodic and corrupt development of the Christian social order" that should be resisted.[136] If the above analysis of what is meant by FDGs and the state "working together" is correct, then it seems that the O'Donovans would counsel the church to avoid the lure of partnership.

Summary

The changing pattern of the relationship between religious communities and the state in liberal polities presents the church with a difficult task of discernment. After experiencing many years of being marginalized by the state when it came to the formulation of public policy and the distribution of public funds, a new openness on the part of the state to work with churches can appear a welcome development. However, close analysis of the impact of partnership with the state, under present conditions, suggests that the church should be cautious about receiving money from the state. Involvement with the state often exacerbates social division and forces the church to mimic the state in its form and practices. Assessment of whether the emergent shape of relations between the state and faith communities conforms to or contradicts a liberal account of the role of religious discourse in the public square suggests that the new opportunities for partnership can be seen as simply another chapter, albeit a postsecularist one, in the modern subversion of the church by the state. The work of Hauerwas, John Paul II, and the O'Donovans furnishes the church with some theological frameworks for discerning the way ahead. While each of these theologians has a different emphasis, the common conclusion they point to is that the church, in order to fulfill its mission to the state, should be discriminating about when and how it enters into partnership. It is not that cooperation is always and in every circumstance ruled out; it is rather that wise discernment is needed about when and how to cooperate in order to avoid co-option and the instrumentalization of the church by the state. Hauerwas would allow exceptions on an ad hoc, minimal level. John Paul II, and Catholic Social Teaching in general, maintains that closer cooperation is possible where pursuit of the common good can be upheld and partnership contributes to the formation of a "culture of life." The O'Donovans' work suggests that real partnership is possible only in situations where a genuine dialectic between political authority and ecclesial proclama-tion of the Gospel can be either maintained or created. These writers consti-tute different theological lenses through which to assess the emergent relationship between church and state at a local and national level. What they all suggest, however, is that while present legal and political arrangements create a fruitful space for Christian mission and ministry that will overlap and intersect with the state at a variety of levels, direct partnership with the state, as it is currently envisaged, is more of a Trojan than a gift horse. What will be explored in the following chapter is a way of situating the church in relation to the liberal state that is consciously alert to the problems of co-option and contests the confinement of the church to generating social cohesion and delivering social welfare by exploring how community organizing enables a critical but constructive relationship between church, state, and market.

Notes

1   Charles Taylor, "Multiculturalism and the 'Politics of Recognition,'" in *Multiculturalism and the "Politics of Recognition": An Essay by Charles Taylor*, ed. Amy Gutmann (Princeton, NJ: Princeton University Press, 1992), pp. 25–73.

2   For an in-depth analysis of the controversy surrounding the *Satanic Verses*, the mutual misinterpretations at work between secular and Islamic "publics," and the subsequent politicization of Muslims in the UK see Herbert, *Religion and Civil Society: Rethinking Public Religion in the Contemporary World* (Aldershot: Ashgate, 2003), pp. 157–96.

3   There is, in theory at least, a division between what might be called the civic republican communitarianism of New Labour and the neoliberal communitari-anism of the Conservative Party, influenced as it is by the "compassionate con-servativism" of George W. Bush and Marvin Olasky. However, in practice, New Labour seems to elide the two. See John Annette, "Faith Communities, Social Capital and Education for Citizenship" (Political Studies Association, Conference Proceedings, Leicester, 2003).

4   Robert Putnam's work on America suggests a downward trend in civic participa-tion and social capital. See Putnam, *Bowling Alone*. The evidence from the UK is less clear-cut. Warde et al. argue that in Britain social capital is not necessarily in decline. However, there is a growing division, with professionals and managerial workers participating most in society and other classes decreasing in participa-tion. Meanwhile, membership of civic associations itself is becoming more vola-tile. See A. Warde, G. Tampubolon, M. Tomlinson, K. Ray, B. Longhurst, and M. Savage, "Trends in Social Capital: Membership of Associations in Great Britain, 1991–98," *British Journal of Political Science* 33.3 (2003), 515–25.

5   On this see Richard Farnell et al., *"Faith" in Urban Regeneration: Engaging Faith Communities in Urban Regeneration* (Bristol: Policy Press, 2003), pp. 7–8.

For an assessment of the perception and contribution of congregations to civil society in the USA see Jerome Baggett, "Congregations and Civil Society: A Double-edged Connection," *Journal of Church and State* 44 (2002), 425–54.

6 This is central to Labour's "Third Way" vision. See Tony Blair, *The Third Way: New Politics for a New Society*, Fabian Pamphlet 588 (London: The Fabian Society, 1998), p. 4. For an equivalent statement by the Conservative Party see the speech by the then Shadow Home Secretary, Oliver Letwin, to the Adam Smith Institute, "Sustainability and Society," July 2002.

7 Kainos currently runs programs in the following prisons: The Verne in Portland, Dorset and Swaleside on the Isle of Sheppey. There has been some debate over whether it should continue to do so.

8 For studies of such programs see Stephen Monsma and J. Christopher Soper, *Faith, Hope and Jobs: Welfare-to Work in Los Angeles* (Washington, DC: Georgetown University Press, 2007); and Sheila Suess Kennedy and Wolfgang Bielefeld, *Charitable Choice at Work* (Washington, DC: Georgetown University Press, 2006).

9 For an account of the shift to a greater openness of state funders to faith-based development agencies see Gerard Clarke, "Faith Matters: Faith-Based Organizations, Civil Society and International Development," *Journal of International Development* 18 (2006), 835–48.

10 Stanley Carlson-Thies, "Charitable Choice: Bringing Religion Back into American Welfare," *Journal of Policy History* 13 (2001), p. 112.

11 Quoted from Frank Prochaska, *Christianity and Social Service in Modern Britain: The Disinherited Spirit* (Oxford: Oxford University Press, 2006), pp. 10–11.

12 Ibid., pp. 76–9. However, we should be wary of positing an absolute disjuncture. As Kahl argues, the formation of modern welfare systems in Europe and the USA owe much to the prior systems of poor relief and theological conceptualizations of poverty in the dominant Christian tradition in each country. Kahl, "The Religious Roots of Modern Poverty Policy: Catholic, Lutheran, and Reformed Protestant Traditions Compared," *European Journal of Sociology* 46.1 (2005), 91–126.

13 On the political right the advocacy of "compassionate conservatism" as articulated in the work of Marvin Olasky is a striking example of a call for the need for reintroducing moral considerations into the distribution of welfare. See in particular Marvin Olasky, *The Tragedy of American Compassion* (Washington, DC: Regnery Publishing, 1992). Omri Elisha notes that what set Olasky's work apart from other conservative critiques of reform was "his ability to present a moral and historical (some would say revisionist) narrative that encompasses notions of Christian faith, meritocratic individualism, communitarian ethics and nationalist pride all at once." She goes on to argue that Olasky directly contributed to an ideological movement that detached issues related to poverty relief from wider questions about social justice. Omri Elisha, "Moral Ambitions of Grace: The Paradox of Compassion and Accountability in Evangelical Faith-Based Activism," *Cultural Anthropology* 23.1 (2008), p. 174.

14   Gerry Stoker, *Transforming Local Governance: from Thatcherism to New Labour* (London, Palgrave Macmillan 2004), p. 11. Stoker refers to co-governance as "networked community governance."

15   Vivien Lowndes and Adam Dinham, "Religion, Resources and Representation: Three Narratives of Faith Engagement in British Urban Governance," *Urban Affairs Review* 43.6 (2008), 817–45.

16   One significant example of this shift in the arena of international development is the World Faiths Development Dialogue (WFDD). WFDD was set up in 1998 as an initiative of James D. Wolfensohn, then President of the World Bank, and Lord Carey, then Archbishop of Canterbury. Its aim was to facilitate a dialogue on poverty and development among people from different religions and between them and the international development institutions in order to develop more effective policy and action among all those involved (www.wfdd.org.uk. Accessed October 12, 2007). It is significant because the World Bank, which up to then had little or no engagement with religious groups, led it. See also Katherine Marshall and Marisa Van Saanen, *Development and Faith: Where Mind, Heart and Soul Work Together* (Washington, DC: World Bank, 2007).

Parallel problems of co-option attend the relationship between government funding and faith-based development agencies. For a somewhat polemical account of the process of co-option from the 1990s onward in relation human-itarian work in general see David Rieff, *A Bed for the Night: Humanitarianism in Crises* (London: Vintage, 2002).

17   John Ackerman, "Co-governance for accountability: Beyond 'exit' and 'voice,' " *World Development* 32.3 (2004), pp. 447–63. Participatory budgeting is now being piloted in the UK context as a way of empowering poor communities to have more control over the quality of services delivered in their communities and neighborhoods. See www.participatorybudgeting.org.uk (accessed October 12, 2008).

18   The fullest expression of this recognition is given in the White Paper: *Communities in Control: Real People, Real Power* (London: Department for Communities and Local Government, 2008).

19   Barry Buzan, Ole Waever, and Jaap de Wilde, *Security: A New Framework for Analysis* (Boulder, CO: Lynne Rienner, 1997), pp. 23–4. The term "securitiza-tion" draws on the "Copenhagen school" of international relations established by Buzan, Waever, and de Wilde. Drawing on Austin's speech-act theory, their notion of "securitization" outlines how particular issues are framed through various speech-acts as a security rather than a political problem and thereby these issues are at once intensively politicized and rendered above politics.

20   This can be seen in the differences between two key documents that set out the current approaches to addressing terrorism: *Preventing Violent Extremism – Winning Hearts and Minds* (London: Department of Communities and Local Government, 2007) and *Pursue Prevent Protect Prepare: The United Kingdom's Strategy for Countering International Terrorism* (London: Home Office, 2009).

21 Recent research suggests that this is exactly what is going on. Basia Spalek, Salwa El Awa, and Laura McDonald, *Police–Muslim Engagement and Partnerships for the Purpose of Counter-Terrorism: An Examination, Summary Report* (Arts and Humanities Research Council/University of Birmingham, 2008).

22 Located under the auspices of the Department of Communities and Local Government, the Faith Communities Consultative Council (FCCC) is a non-statutory body that aims to provide a national forum focused primarily on issues related to social cohesion, social inclusion, and neighborhood and urban regeneration. It also acts as an important primary structural reference point and means of liaison between central government and faith communities.

23 For an account of the formation of the ICRC and a critique of the new discourse around the role of religion in politics see Jenny Taylor, "There's Life in Establishment – But Not as We Know It," *Political Theology* 5.3 (2004), 329–49. The ICRC was initially replaced by the Faiths Consultative Council in 2005. The Faith Communities Unit (FCU) was established within the Home Office with responsibility for leading government engagement with faith communities. The FCU was subsequently replaced by the Race, Equality, Cohesion and Faith Directorate within the Department of Communities and Local Government. Its latest incarnation is the Faith Communities Consultative Council mentioned above. However, all such units are liable to change and be relocated in what is a fast-changing policy area as government struggles to conceptualize and formalize its evolving engagement with religious groups.

24 Home Office, *Working Together: Cooperation between Government and Faith Communities* (2004), p. 20.

25 A report for the Church Urban Fund argued that LSPs are "the only form of local public partnership that has really endorsed the concept of 'faith representatives' being there to represent the constituency of local faith communities." A contrast is drawn with experience in the National Health Service, where some non-executive directors on primary care trusts are identified as faith representatives, but tend to see themselves as "people of faith" rather than spokespeople for a specific constituency (Church Urban Fund, *Faithful Representation: Faith Representatives on Local Public Partnerships* (London: Church Urban Fund, 2006), p. 3).

26 This has been developed subsequently in the report: *Face to Face and Side by Side: A Framework for Partnership in Our Multi Faith Society* (London: Department of Communities and Local Government, 2008).

27 Amy E. Black, Douglas L. Koopman, and David K. Ryden, *Of Little Faith: The Politics of George W. Bush's Faith-Based Initiatives* (Washington, DC: Georgetown University Press, 2004); Lewis D. Solomon, *In God We Trust? Faith-based Organizations and the Quest to Solve America's Social Ills* (Lanham, MD: Lexington Books, 2003).

28 The pattern for these bilateral and multilateral arrangements with central government is given in *Working Together*, pp. 71–5.

29   See Greg Smith, "Faith in Community and Communities of Faith? Government Rhetoric and Religious Identity in Urban Britain," *Journal of Contemporary Religion* 19.2 (2004), p. 200.

30   See Robert Wuthnow, *Saving America? Faith-based Services and the Future of Civil Society* (Princeton, NJ: Princeton University Press, 2004); and Putnam, *Bowling Alone*, pp. 65–115. Derek Bacon in an assessment of faith-based organizations in Northern Ireland gives a more directly positive assessment. Derek Bacon, "Revitalizing Civil Society through Social Capital Formation in Faith-Based Organizations: Reflections from Northern Ireland," *Social Development Issues* 26.1 (2004), pp. 14–24.

31   Wuthnow, *Saving America?*, p. 20.

32   On this see Christoph Schwöbel, "Particularity, Universality, and the Religions: Towards a Christian Theology of Religions," in *Christian Uniqueness Reconsidered: The Myth of a Pluralistic Theology of Religions*, ed. Gavin D'Costa (New York: Orbis Books, 1996), pp. 30–46.

33   Farnell et al., *"Faith" in Urban Regeneration*, p. 31.

34   Ibid., p. 9.

35   Thomas Jeavons, "Identifying Characteristics of 'Religious' Organizations: An Exploratory Proposal," in *Sacred Companies: Organizational Aspects of Religion and Religious Aspects of Organizations*, eds. N. J. Demerath, Peter Hall, Terry Schmitt, and Rhys Williams (Oxford: Oxford University Press, 1998), pp. 79–95. For a further development and empirical testing of Jeavons' framework see also, Helen Rose Ebaugh, Janet Chafetz, and Paula Pipes, "Where's the Faith in Faith-Based Organizations? Measures and Correlates of Religiosity in Faith-based Social Service Coalitions," *Social Forces* 84.4 (2006), 2259–72. For an alternative typology to Jeavons see Ronald Sider, "Typology of Religious Characteristics of Social Service and Educational Organizations and Programs," *Nonprofit and Voluntary Sector Quarterly* 33.1 (2004), 109–34.

36   Use of the term "differentiation" is borrowed from the work of David Martin. In contrast to other theories of secularization that interpret the convergence of religious and secular organizational forms as signifying the decline in the authority of religious belief and practice, his use of the term differentiation allows for the continuing authority of religious belief and practice even as organizational forms converge. See David Martin, *A General Theory of Secularization* (New York: Harper & Row, 1979).

37   Robert Putnam, "*E Pluribus Unum*: Diversity and Community in the Twenty-first Century. The 2006 Johan Skytte Prize Lecture," *Scandinavian Political Studies* 30.2 (2007), p. 137. For an extended definition and genealogy of the term "social capital" see Putnam, *Bowling Alone*, pp. 18–26. For an overview of the debate surrounding the definition of the term social capital, the different forms of social capital and how the term is applied to faith-based organizations, see Christine Hepworth and Sean Stitt, "Social Capital and Faith-Based Organizations," *Heythrop Journal* XLVIII (2007), 895–910.

38   Putnam, "*E Pluribus Unum*," p. 137.

39 Sheldon Wolin, *Politics and Vision: Continuity and Innovation in Western Political Thought*, exp. edn (Princeton, NJ: Princeton University Press, 2004), p. 261.

40 Ibid., p. 271.

41 Ibid., p. 273.

42 Alan Finlayson, *Making Sense of New Labour* (London: Lawrence and Wishart, 2003), p. 11.

43 J. K. Gibson-Graham, *Postcapitalist Politics* (Minneapolis, MN: University of Minnesota Press, 2006), pp. 58–9.

44 Putnam, *Bowling Alone*, p. 65.

45 Mark R. Warren, *Dry Bones Rattling: Community Building to Revitalize American Democracy* (Princeton, NJ: Princeton University Press, 2001), p. 20.

46 For an altogether more positive assessment of the term "social capital" and its extension in the term "faith capital" see John Atherton, *Transfiguring Capitalism: An Enquiry into Religion and Global Change* (London: SCM-Canterbury, 2008), pp. 87–102. Atherton perceives the term as a way of restating the importance of social relationship within economic discourses (ibid., p. 91) and his use of the term "faithful capital" seems more polemical than substantive (ibid., p. 102).

47 Farnell et al., *"Faith" in Urban Regeneration*, p. 7.

48 Ibid.

49 For example, see Local Government Association, *Faith and Community: A Good Practice Guide for Local Authorities* (London: Local Government Association, 2002), p. 3.

50 Simone Chambers and Will Kymlicka, *Alternative Conceptions of Civil Society* (Princeton, NJ: Princeton University Press, 2002), p. 2. For a critique and overview of accounts of civil society see Charles Taylor, "Invoking Civil Society," in *Contemporary Political Philosophy: An Anthology* (Oxford: Blackwell, 1997), pp. 66–77.

51 Michael Walzer, "The Civil Society Argument," in *Theorizing Citizenship*, ed. R. Beiner (New York: SUNY Press, 1995), p. 162. Walzer envisages his account as a "corrective" to the other major arguments for the importance of civil society.

52 Ibid., p. 167–71.

53 For example, see Local Government Association, *Guidance on Community Cohesion* (London: Local Government Association, 2002), p. 21.

54 For example, see Tony Blair, Speech to the Christian Socialist Movement, Westminster Central Hall, March 29, 2001.

55 For example, see Local Government Association, *Faith and Community*, p. 1.

56 For example, see ibid., p. 3.

57 For a case study in how the relationship between the state and FDGs works out at the grassroots and the difficulties FDGs have in accessing resources see Greg Smith, "Religion as a Source of Social Capital in the Regeneration of East London," *Rising East* 4.3 (2001), 128–57.

58 Farnell et al., *"Faith" in Urban Regeneration*, pp. 21–9.

59 Ibid., p. 26.

60 Priya Lukka and Michael Locke, *Faith and Voluntary Action: Community, Values and Resources* (London: Institute for Volunteering Research and University of East London, 2003), p. 16.

61 Ibid.

62 See Farnell et al., *"Faith" in Urban Regeneration*, p. 2. It is a fear that pervades the Cantle Report: see Community Cohesion Unit, *Community Cohesion: A Report of the Independent Review Team Chaired by Ted Cantle* (London: Home Office, 2003).

63 Gerd Baumann, *The Multicultural Riddle: Rethinking National, Ethnic, and Religious Identities* (London: Routledge, 1999), p. 124. Citation from David Herbert, *Religion and Civil Society*, p. 83. For an account of how this works out in practice see Gerd Baumann, *Contesting Culture: Discourse of Identity in Multicultural London* (Cambridge: Cambridge University Press, 1996).

64 Ibid., p. 83.

65 Bradford Race Review, *Community Pride Not Prejudice: Making Diversity Work in Bradford, Presented to Bradford Vision by Sir Herman Ouseley* (2001), p. 11; Community Cohesion Unit, *Community Cohesion*, p. 17 and p. 57.

66 For a critique of the "myth of the state as savior" see William Cavanaugh, *Theopolitical Imagination: Discovering the Liturgy as a Political Act in an Age of Global Consumerism* (Edinburgh: T&T Clark, 2002), pp. 9–52.

67 Paul J. DiMaggio and Walter W. Powell, "The Iron Cage Revisited: Institutional Isomorphism and Collective Rationality in Organizational Fields," *American Sociological Review* 48.2 (1983), 147–60. In contrast to Weber, who viewed processes of bureaucratization as being driven largely by capitalism and market competition, DiMaggio and Powell contend that the main factors driving processes of rationalization and bureaucratization are the state and professionalization. Evidence would suggest that this is case in the relationship between FDGs and the state.

It should be noted that many of the problems identified here in relation to institutional isomorphism in the relationship between FDGs and the state correlate with dynamics at work more broadly in the relationship between the "third" or voluntary sector and the state.

68 Alexander-Kenneth Nagel, "Charitable Choice: The Religious Component of the US Welfare Reform – Theoretical and Methodological Reflections On 'Faith-Based-Organizations' as Social Service Agencies," *Numen* 53 (2006), p. 97.

69 Ibid.

70 Charles Glenn, *The Ambiguous Embrace: Government and Faith-Based Schools and Social Agencies* (Princeton, NJ: Princeton University Press, 2000), p. 192.

71 Ibid.

72 As D. Scott Cormode argues, the problems associated with institutional isomorphism can be seen as simply a reversal of the same process in the nineteenth century in the USA and Britain whereby secular organizations took on ecclesial

forms. He notes how such groups as fraternal lodges, women's associations, labor unions, and ethnic societies borrowed symbols, patterns of meeting, organization, and structures from the churches, gaining credibility and authority through doing so. D. Scott Cormode, "Does Institutional Isomorphism Imply Secularization? Churches and Secular Voluntary Associations in the Turn-of-the-Century City," in N. J. Demerath et al., *Sacred Companies*, pp. 116–31.

73   Wuthnow, *Saving America?*, p. 148. See also Steven Smith and Michael Sosin, "The Varieties of Faith-Related Agencies," *Public Administration Review* 61.6 (2001), 651–70.

74   For examples of how the church upholds the space for free speech in the formation of modern states see Herbert, *Religion and Civil Society*, pp. 96–8.

75   John Rawls, "The Idea of Public Reason Revisited," in *The Law of Peoples* (Cambridge, MA: Harvard University Press, 2001), pp. 176, 146, 152.

76   See Paul Weitham, "Introduction: Religion and the Liberalism of Reasoned Respect," in *Religion and Contemporary Liberalism*, ed. Paul Weitham (Notre Dame, IN: University of Notre Dame Press, 1997), pp. 1–37. Rawls is the key proponent of this approach. Other advocates include Robert Audi, Ronald Dworkin, and Thomas Nagel and can be said to include the Roman Catholic theologian, John Courtney Murray. It is to be distinguished from the "value pluralism" of Isaiah Berlin and William Galston which, on Rawlsian terms, is a comprehensive doctrine. See Isaiah Berlin, *Liberty*, ed. Henry Hardy (Oxford: Oxford University Press, 2002) and William Galston, *Liberal Pluralism: The Implications of Value Pluralism for Political Theory and Practice* (Cambridge: Cambridge University Press, 2002).

77   See Jürgen Habermas, *Between Facts and Norms: Contributions to a Discourse Theory of Law and Democracy*, trans. William Rehg (Cambridge, MA: MIT Press, 1996).

78   See John Gray, *Post-liberalism: Studies in Political Thought* (London: Routledge, 1996).

79   John Rawls, "The Idea of Public Reason Revisited," pp. 172–3.

80   John Rawls, *Political Liberalism* (New York: Columbia University Press, 1996), p. 213.

81   As Nicholas Wolterstorff points out, Rawls simply assumes that the "morality of respect" is a constituent feature of liberal democracy, which its participants should inherently recognize. Robert Audi and Nicholas Wolterstorff, *Religion in the Public Square: The Place of Religious Convictions in Political Debate* (Lanham, MD: Rowman & Littlefield, 1997), p. 110.

82   Wolterstorff (ibid., p. 109) notes that Rawls's account of political liberalism is in many ways "communitarian" in outlook, refusing as it does to live with a politics of "multiple communities." Instead, Rawls seeks to delineate the politics of a "community with a shared perspective."

83   John Rawls, "The Idea of Public Reason Revisited," p. 141; *Political Liberalism*, pp. 214–15. Although the need to translate a comprehensive doctrine into public reasons applies only to decisions that involve the coercive use of force to

achieve public ends, it is difficult to see how this does not affect most areas of public policy, resting as it ultimately does on appeal to law and the threat of coercion.

84   However, only certain kinds of Christianity can play this constructive role: so-called "fundamentalist" forms are rendered "political heretics" on Rawls's account. John Rawls, "The Idea of Public Reason Revisited," p. 178; Nicholas Wolterstorff, *Religion in the Public Square*, p. 149.

85   In contrast to the account given here, Christopher Insole (*The Politics of Human Frailty: A Theological Defense of Political Liberalism* (London: SCM Press, 2004)) argues that Rawls's position is consonant with an Augustinian political theology. However, Insole does not give sufficient attention to how the church, in terms of its own theological self-description, is itself a *polis*, *res publica*, or political society. This relates to the somewhat under-realized eschatology at work in his account. For him, the impact of sin is such that the only political response of the church is humility in the face of the claims of others to say what the good life consists of; and all actions of the Spirit in manifesting the kingdom of God are so fragmentary and hidden that we should have little, if any, confidence in being able to identify them. However, to assume that the kingdom of God is hidden by the manifold sins and oppressive practices of the church is to be guilty of false humility because it is to overvalue the church. The church is in constant need of divine authorization: Christian witness is not an expression of its own perfection but points to the prior and independent actions of God. The proper response to the sins of the church is not the denial of knowledge of the kingdom to come, but repentance and penitence which themselves constitute forms of witness to the future that God is bringing into being.

86   Smith and Sosin, "The Varieties of Faith-Related Agencies," p. 664. This is not to say there are not contradictions at work within the internal discourses of FDGs. The same organization may take a "no strings attached" approach to its service delivery, basing this on a theologically grounded view of compassion or of all people being made in the image of God, but at the same time have an expectation of moral change or conversion based on a particular sotierology. For a case study of this kind of contradiction in the work of conservative evangelical social activism in the USA see Omri Elisha, "Moral Ambitions of Grace," pp. 154–89.

87   Evidence for this in the USA is given in the following empirical study: Ebaugh, Chafetz, and Pipes, "Where's the Faith in Faith-Based Organizations?" p. 2269.

88   See, for example, *Working Together*, p. 36.

89   In Britain, Steve Chalke's Faithworks Campaign, launched in 2001, is an example of this. Another example is the partnership between the government and Christian groups in establishing a number of new city academies in areas of urban deprivation.

90   Hannah Arendt, *The Human Condition*, 2nd edn (Chicago, IL: University of Chicago Press, 1958), pp. 194–5. For an account of how Arendt's conception

of democracy relates to and upholds a liberal constitutional order see Jeffrey Isaac, *Democracy in Dark Times* (Ithaca, NY: Cornell University Press, 1998), pp. 100–22.

91 Isaac, *Democracy in Dark Times*, p. 83.

92 Oliver O'Donovan goes so far as to say: "The liberal tradition ... has right of possession. There is no other model available to us of a political order derived from a millennium of close engagement between state and church. It ought, therefore, to have the first word in any discussion of what Christians can approve, even if it ought not to have the last word. ... We cannot simply go behind it; it has the status of a church tradition, and demands to be treated with respect." Oliver O'Donovan, *The Desire of the Nations: Rediscovering the Roots of Political Theory* (Cambridge: Cambridge University Press, 1996), pp. 228–9.

93 See Alasdair MacIntyre, "Community, Law and the Idiom and Rhetoric of Rights," *Listening* 26 (1991), 96–110; "Politics, Philosophy and the Common Good," in *The Macintyre Reader*, ed. Kelvin Knight (London: Polity Press, 1998), pp. 235–66; and *Dependent Rational Animals: Why Human Beings Need the Virtues (The Paul Carus Lectures)* (London: Duckworth, 1999).

94 John Witte, *The Reformation of Rights: Law, Religion and Human Rights in Early Modern Calvinism* (Cambridge: Cambridge University Press, 2008), p. 214, 279–88. See also Harold Berman, *Law and Revolution II: The Impact of the Protestant Reformation on the Western Legal Tradition* (Cambridge, MA: Belknap Press, 2003), pp. 225–6.

95 Arendt, *The Human Condition*, p. 222.

96 Sheldon Wolin, "Contract and Birthright," *Political Theory* 14.2 (1986), p. 60.

97 On this see William Cavanaugh, "The Myth of the State as Savior," *Theopolitical Imagination*, pp. 9–52; William Connolly, *Why I Am Not a Secularist* (Minneapolis, MN: University of Minnesota Press, 1999), pp. 20–1.

98 John Rawls, *Political Liberalism*, pp. xxv–xxvi.

99 Anxiety about the threat that religion poses to the social and political stability of liberal democracy is a central assumption of liberal political philosophy. For example, Richard Rorty sees the disenchantment of public life as a central achievement of the Enlightenment and the way in which liberal democracies have achieved civil peace. Richard Rorty, "Religion as a Conversation-Stopper," *Common Knowledge* 3.1 (1994), 1–6.

100 For an extensive critique of this mythos see William Cavanaugh, "Killing for the Telephone Company: Why the Nation-State is Not the Keeper of the Common Good," in *In Search of the Common Good*, eds. Patrick D. Miller and Dennis McCann (New York: T&T Clark International, 2005), pp. 310–32.

101 Nicholas Wolterstorff, "The Role of Religion in Decision and Discussion of Political Issues," in Robert Audi and Nicholas Wolterstorff, *Religion in the Public Square: The Place of Religious Convictions in Political Debate* (Lanham, MD: Rowman & Littlefield, 1997), p. 80.

102 Jeffrey Stout, *Democracy and Tradition* (Princeton, NJ: Princeton University Press, 2004), p. 64. For Stout's critique of Rawls's conception of public reason see ibid., pp. 68–77.

103 Jeremy Waldron, "Cultural Identity and Civic Responsibility," in *Citizenship in Diverse Societies*, eds. Will Kymlicka and Wayne Norman (Oxford: Oxford University Press, 2000), p. 163. For Waldron's critique of Rawls's *Political Liberalism* see his *Law and Disagreement* (Oxford: Clarendon Press, 1999), pp. 149–63.

104 For an extensive critique of Rawls in relation to this point see Kristen Deede Johnson, *Theology, Political Theory, and Pluralism: Beyond Tolerance and Difference* (Cambridge: Cambridge University Press, 2007), pp. 35–67.

105 Clarke Cochran, *Religion in Public and Private Life* (London: Routledge, 1990), p. 94.

106 For her critique of the notion of impartiality and public reason, see Iris Marion Young, *Justice and the Politics of Difference* (Princeton, NJ: Princeton University Press, 1990).

107 Iris Marion Young, "Communication and the Other: Beyond Deliberative Democracy," in *Democracy and Difference*, ed. Seyla Benhabib (Princeton, NJ: Princeton University Press, 1996), p. 132.

108 Similarly, Connolly argues that the requirement that rational arguments alone are sufficient in public deliberation "suppresses complex registers of persuasion, judgment, and discourse operative in public life." Connolly, *Why I Am Not a Secularist*, p. 20.

109 Young, "Communication and the Other: Beyond Deliberative Democracy," p. 129.

110 Ibid., p. 133.

111 William Connolly, *Pluralism* (Durham: Duke University Press, 2005), p. 60.

112 "As history demonstrates, a democracy without values easily turns into open or thinly disguised totalitarianism," *Centesimus Annus*, #46.

113 John Paul II may seem the odd one out in this list. However, as Charles Curran notes, post-Vatican II social teaching has shifted away from an emphasis on natural law towards a more Scriptural, theological, and Christological approach to grounding Roman Catholic social teaching, with John Paul II making the greatest contribution to this development. Charles Curran, *The Moral Theology of Pope John Paul II* (Washington, DC: Georgetown University Press, 2005), pp. 205–6. For example, this can be seen clearly in *Gaudium et Spes* in which arguments for the dignity of all persons are located primarily within a theological anthropology rather than a natural law account (*Gaudium et Spes*, #11–19). With the publication of *Deus Caritas Est*, Pope Benedict XVI continued and deepened this shift. What is more, a central concern of the theological politics at work in contemporary Roman Catholic social teaching is the question of what does it mean for the church qua church to act faithfully in relation to its political responsibilities.

114 A renewed emphasis on the political dimensions of ecclesiology is not without its own risks. The danger is that the church presents itself as the answer to all modern problems, from individualism, consumerism, and reliance on technical rationality to family and moral breakdown. As Nicholas Healey puts it, Christianity is presented as "the way of life or the way of being that saves us from the evident evils of the modern world. Ecclesiology thereby takes on a new kind of apologetic function, that of ameliorating the starkness of the Gospel claims by situating them within a communal solution to contemporary social problems that appeals to well meaning moderns and post-moderns." Nicholas Healy, "Ecclesiology and Communion," *Perspectives in Religious Studies* 31.3 (2004), p. 289. The problem with this is that the Gospel becomes a salve rather than good news of salvation.

115 Arne Rasmusson, *The Church as Polis: From Political Theology to Theological Politics as Exemplified by Jürgen Moltmann and Stanley Hauerwas* (Notre Dame, IN: University of Notre Dame Press, 1995), p. 227.

116 Stanley Hauerwas, "Will the Real Sectarian Please Stand Up," *Theology Today* 44.1 (1987), p. 90.

117 *Gaudium et Spes*, #76; Pontifical Council for Justice and Peace, *Compendium of the Social Doctrine of the Church* (London: Continuum, 2004), p. 214 (#425); and *Deus Caritas Est*, #26–30. Benedict XVI frames the relationship in terms of "mutual coordination" between state and church in the delivery of social welfare and pursuit of the common good (*Deus Caritas Est*, #30.b).

118 *Compendium of the Social Doctrine of the Church*, pp. 213–14 (#424–7).

119 *Centesimus Annus*, #24; *Compendium of the Social Doctrine of the Church*, pp. 210–11 (#417–18). In arguing this he is consistent with and following a line of argument set out in Vatican II (see *Gaudium et Spes*, #53).

120 On this see George Weigel, "John Paul II and the Priority of Culture," *First Things* 80 (1998), 19–25.

121 Charles Curran notes that for John Paul II both capitalism and Marxism share the same root problem – materialism. He states: "Wojtyla's philosophical personalism opposes the materialism of both Marxism and capitalism. *Laborem exercens*, the first social encyclical of the Wojtyla papacy continues the same approach by showing that capitalism and Marxism are based on what the pope calls 'materialistic economism,' a form of materialism that gives priority to the objective rather than the subjective aspects of work." Curran, *The Moral Theology of Pope John Paul II*, p. 219.

122 John Paul II, *Evangelium Vitae* (London: Catholic Truth Society, 1995), pp. 37, 142.

123 On this see Derek Jeffreys, *Defending Human Dignity: John Paul II and Political Realism* (Grand Rapids, MI: Brazos Press, 2004).

124 *Centesimus Annus*, #5. The interrelationship between truth and freedom and how these are grounded in the Gospel has been a central theme in many of John Paul II's encyclicals, see especially: *Redemptor Hominis* (1979), *Veritatis Splendor* (1993) and *Evangelium Vitae* (1995). Likewise, Benedict XVI's *Deus*

Caritas Est with its emphasis on the centrality of the love of God and neighbor to authentic charitable service can be read as a profound reaffirmation of John Paul II's link between the Gospel and the "social question" (see in particular *Deus Caritas Est*, #33–8). This is developed further in Benedict XVI's recent encyclical *Caritas in Veritate* (2009). Unfortunately, this rich statement, highly relevant to this book, appeared just after the main manuscript was submitted and so precluded any systematic analysis of its content.

125   *Centesimus Annus*, #5.

126   For example, *Sollicitudo Rei Socialis* (#47) and *Centesimus Annus* (#60) end with pleas for all people of good will to work together to overcome injustice and pursue the common good. There is, however, a clear tension that arises between John Paul II's attempt to uphold an authoritative religious and moral tradition that embodies and proclaims a set of public truths which all "people of good will" can grasp and his recognition that public moral discourse is incoherent and the foundations of morality on the Gospel require explicitly restating.

127   *The Participation of Catholics in Political Life* (Vatican Congregation for the Doctrine of the Faith, 2002), #1.

128   O'Donovan, *The Desire of the Nations*, p. 174.

129   Oliver O'Donovan is often misunderstood as advocating that some form of Christendom is a necessary political project of the church. This is not the case. Rather, for O'Donovan, the church engages in mission, eschewing any imperialistic or totalizing political project, yet in response to this mission something Christendom-like may emerge at the point where rulers seek to bow the knee to the Lordship of Christ. Against the likes of Hauerwas, O'Donovan is content with such an eventuality as right and proper and as not something to be ashamed of where it has occurred in the history of the church.

130   O'Donovan, "Government as Judgment," in Oliver and Joan Lockwood O'Donovan, *Bonds of Imperfection: Christian Politics, Past and Present*, (Grand Rapids, MI: Eerdmans, 2004), p. 208. For Oliver O'Donovan, it is from the founding act of judgment depicted in Revelation that all other judgments flow and derive their authority. Political authority in this secular age do not create law but keep and maintain law through acts of judgment rather than the formulation of justice. See also Oliver O'Donovan, *The Ways of Judgment* (Grand Rapids, MI: Eerdmans, 2005), pp. 52–66.

131   Joan Lockwood O'Donovan, "The Church of England and the Anglican Communion: A Timely Engagement with the National Church Tradition?" *Scottish Journal of Theology* 57.3 (2004), pp. 336–7.

132   Joan Lockwood O'Donovan envisages a new kind of Establishment, one that is "predominantly Christian" yet includes the "public accommodation of non-Christian minorities within the public affirmation of an historical Christian tradition." Ibid., p. 333.

133   *Desire of the Nations*, p. 214.

134   Ibid, pp. 262–8.

135   Ibid, p. 273.

136   Ibid., p. 275.

2

Local
Augustine, Alinsky, and the Politics of the Common Good

Introduction

The previous chapter analyzed the emerging pattern of church–state relations in the contemporary context and set out some of the problems at work in this relationship. This chapter represents a constructive response to these problems. It examines the participation of churches in broad-based community organizing to assess whether it demonstrates in practice that there are more ways to pursue the peace of Babylon than accepting either the liberal settlement or an unspecified form of ad hoc or dialectical cooperation. A further aim of the chapter is to assess whether broad-based community organizing constitutes an example of the kind of place-based, time-intensive political action that sustains and actualizes human dignity in the face of the intensive pressures acting against it in the contemporary context.

Examining the involvement of churches in community organizing necessitates a close interrogation of the work and legacy of Saul Alinsky. This of course begs the question: Who was Alinsky? From the 1940s onward Saul Alinsky (d. 1972) initiated and developed a particular form of local, pre-dominantly urban, democratic politics, often referred to as broad-based community organizing. Alinsky's methods, as distinct from his political theory, have been very influential on a wide variety of social movements and political initiatives around the world. There are a number of community organizing networks and groups that draw explicitly on Alinsky's approach. These include, among others, COPS (Community Organized for Public Service), ACORN (Association of Community Organizations for Reform Now), PICO (People Improving Communities through Organizing), DART (Direct Action Research and Training), and the Gamalial Foundation. His direct legacy is the Industrial Areas Foundation (IAF), which he founded in 1940. This has 57 affiliate groups operating throughout the USA, and in Canada, Britain, Australia, and Germany.[1] A distinctive feature of Alinsky's work and legacy is its close relationship with churches.

What I set out here is an explicitly theological reading of Alinsky. Such a reading is warranted for a number of reasons. The first is biographical. Alinsky was an agnostic Jew, yet his own life and work calls forth a theological reading. There were a number of key influences on his development, notably: his work with the Chicago sociologist Clifford Shaw; his relationship with the trade union organizer John L. Lewis; his observations of organized crime when working with Shaw; and his own experience of the *shtetl* tradition and Jewish community self-organization when growing up in Chicago.[2] However, throughout his life, the majority of Alinsky's primary interlocutors were either clergy (for example, Bishop Shiels), theologically trained (for example, Ed Chambers), or, in the case of his friendship with Jacques Maritain, they were theologians of major standing.[3] The second reason is historical. It is churches of all denominations that have most intensively and fruitfully engaged with his work, both during his life and subsequently, and this relationship alone warrants theological excavation.[4] The third reason is theological and follows on directly from the second. As noted in the Introduction, a key problem confronting the church is whether the church can uphold the specificity of the church's political witness and at the same time cooperate with religious and non-religious others. A theological reading of Alinsky is a necessary precursor to discerning whether church involvement in Alinsky-style political initiatives points to a resolution of this problem. The final reason for an intensive, theological reading of Alinsky is that he is a very fruitful conversation partner for opening out and examining further the theological debates about the relationship between Christianity and politics in modern liberal states that were touched on in Chapter 1.

The first section summarizes Alinsky's approach and the dynamics of what broad-based community organizing involves. The second sets out the terms and conditions of faithful citizenship through an account of Augustine's conception of the *saeculum* as the mutual ground in which the non-eschatological and relative goods that sustain and form the basis of the limited earthly peace may be pursued. In the third a distinction is drawn with Niebuhr's Augustinian political realism in order to argue that Alinsky's work keeps a central place for the church qua church as a political actor without instrumentalizing it or subsuming the church to some superordinate project such as democratic renewal. The fourth part argues that Alinsky's approach is better understood in the light of Jacques Maritain's Thomistic account of Christian democracy. An underlying implication of the chapter as a whole is that Alinsky's approach represents a generative and faithful form of political witness in a religiously plural liberal polity. In contrast to the note of caution struck in the previous chapter, this chapter develops a more positive appraisal of the conditions and possibilities of faithful witness in the contemporary context and, in particular, of how such witness relates to democracy.

The Alinsky Approach: The Work of Broad-Based Community Organizing

The central thrust of community organizing for Alinsky is the fostering of a common life amid the fractured anomie and injustice of the modern city through ensuring that those excluded from the decision-making process that affects them have power through being organized to act together in the defense and pursuit of common goods. For Alinsky democracy provides the opportunity and means by which to achieve this while, at the same time, democracy encapsulates a vision of a common life in which the dignity and worth of every person is intrinsically valued. For Alinsky: "The complete man is one who is making a definite contribution to the general social welfare and who is a vital part of that community of interests, values, and purposes that makes life and people meaningful."[5] By contrast: "The denial of the opportunity for participation *is* the denial of human dignity and democracy."[6]

Alinsky summarizes the point of community organization in the following terms:

> This, then, is our real job – the opportunity to work directly with our people. It is the breaking down of the feeling on the part of our people that they are social automatons with no stake in the future, rather than human beings in possession of all the responsibility, strength, and human dignity which constitute the heritage of free citizens of a democracy. This can be done only through the democratic organization of our people for democracy. It is the job of building People's Organizations.[7]

The program for such a "People's Organization" was to emerge from the "principles, purposes, and practices which have been commonly agreed upon by the people."[8] These were to be discerned through a process of listening and relationship building orchestrated by an external organizer. Then, "[o]ut of all this social interplay emerges a common agreement, and that I call the people's program. Then the other function of organization becomes important: the use of power in order to fulfill the program."[9] For Alinsky the development of the program is simultaneously the process of organizing the people. An example of this in practice was how Alinsky established the Back of the Yards Neighborhood Council in Chicago through recruiting parishes and businesses to join the organization via a job referral agency that was simultaneously a way of addressing the issue of youth delinquency.[10]

Crucially for Alinsky, the process of organization was not a top-down exercise imposing an alien structure and the organizer was not envisaged in terms of an intellectual *avant garde* working to an abstract ideology. The organizer was a kind of agitator or *agent provocateur*, working to develop "native leadership" and enlisting and collaborating with the existing institutions and traditions already present.[11] As Alinsky puts it: "The foundation of a People's Organization is in the communal life of the local people. Therefore the first stage in the building of a People's Organization is the understanding of the life of a community."[12] The program and organizational form grows out of what is latent within the locality itself or, in the words of an IAF maxim, "the people is the program." However, none of this should imply an idealization or reification of the "people." Alinsky was acutely aware of the demoralized and disorganized condition and self-destructive anomy that often goes hand in hand with poverty. This was why there was a need for organization. Alinsky was also a "realist" about the context and process of organizing, stating:

> A People's Organization lives … in the midst of smashing forces, clashing struggles, sweeping cross-currents, ripping passions, conflict, confusion, seeming chaos, the hot and the cold, the squalor and the drama, which people prosaically refer to as life and students describe as "society."[13]

For Alinsky, organizing was built on a non-ideological, prudential politics that worked from the experience and possibilities of the world as it is. Alinsky envisaged the organizer as a "pragmatic social changer" for whom compromise was a beautiful word.[14] Yet, for Alinsky, the commitment to the inclusion of the poor and the dignity of each person meant that within a context of injustice, community organizing warranted the label radical. Alinsky's pragmatism was subject to much criticism from many different quarters. Protestant critics such as Walter Kloetzli, writing in the *Christian Century*, saw Alinsky's approach as amoral. Meanwhile, the American New Left in the 1960s accused Alinsky of lacking an ideology and a transcendent vision.[15] But Alinsky's pragmatism was neither amoral nor lacking in vision; rather it grew out of the insight that people can only act together within traditions that bind them and motivate them to act and require institutions within which they can learn to trust and cooperate within particular contexts.[16] Only by working with the grain of the institutions and traditions already in place can real change be effected. This necessitated both avoiding top-down, ideologically or theoretically driven political programs and inductively deriving specific policy proposals from the lived experience of the people those policies would affect.[17] At the same time, his commitment to the dignity of all enabled him to denounce the idolatry of any tradition or practice that threatened this dignity. Within American history, Alinsky frames this approach to politics as being both Revolutionary and Tory.[18] It is akin to the kind of conservative radicalism advocated by Sheldon Wolin who argues for the intrinsic connection between "archaic" and diverse historic institutions, traditions and patterns of local participation, and the ability to "tend" democracy and resist centralizing and technocratic forms of modern power.[19] Wolin's account of democracy helps articulate the interrelationship between Alinsky's conception of democratic politics and establishing a contradiction to totalizing forms of dominatory power. He states:

> The power of a democratic politics lies in the multiplicity of modest sites dispersed among local governments and institutions under local control (schools, community health services, police and fire protection, recreation, cultural institutions, property taxes) and the ingenuity of ordinary people in inventing temporary forms to meet their needs. Multiplicity is anti-totality politics: small politics, small projects, small business, much improvisation, and hence anathema to centralization, whether of the centralized state or of the huge corporation.[20]

While for Wolin moments of democratic politics are episodic, circumstantial, and primarily local, they draw on longstanding, local patterns of association and what he calls "archaic" traditions such as Christianity. These provide the means for the re-creation of political experience and extending to a wider circle the benefits of social cooperation and achievements made possible by previous generations. Wolin states, in almost a direct echo of Alinsky, that the aim of democracy should be neither equality nor nostalgic preservation but restoring

> some measure of control over the conditions and decisions intimately affecting the everyday lives of ordinary citizens, to relieve serious and remediable distress and to extend inclusion beyond the enjoyment of equal civil rights by making access to educational and cultural experiences and healthy living conditions a normal expectation.[21]

Alinsky's response to race relations illustrates the relationship between his pragmatism and his passionate commitment to the dignity of every person and the need for solidarity between all people. He was concerned with racial inequality from the 1940s onward and the emergence of segregation in Chicago with the migration of African-Americans from the South to the North. However, rather than advocate integration or expound a rhetoric of equality he tried to identify the concrete factors that exacerbated race relations and the quality of life of the new immigrants and organize around these: the most pressing issue was housing and the destructive impact of "block busting" and white flight. The fruit of his engagement was the establishment of the Organization for the Southwest Community (OSC) in 1959, which drew together white and black neighbors, via their churches, in a single organization focused on issues of law and order and maintaining property prices. Subsequently, in 1960, he helped establish The Woodlawn Organization (TWO), which along with the civil rights movement was the most significant black-led political organization in Chicago at that time (and arguably beyond it as well). TWO's focus was community development, greater accountability of social service agencies, and the construction of low-income housing.[22]

Alinsky's vision of organizing meant that he was very critical of state welfare programs, the "apostles of planning," and nongovernmental charity.[23] He saw such endeavors as paternalism that failed to address the real needs of people, served to reinforce existing structures of injustice, and undermined people's dignity. He states:

> It is living in dignity to achieve things through your own intelligence and efforts. It is living as a human being. To live otherwise and not to share in the securing of your own objectives but simply to receive them as gifts or as the benevolent expression of either a government which does not consult with you or as the hand-out of a private philanthropist, places you in the position of a pauper.[24]

His approach to social, economic, and political injustice aimed to empower those excluded so that they could take responsibility and act for themselves and thereby forge a common world with (rather than against) the existing power holders. This is summarized in a central maxim of community organizing: "Never do for others what they can do for themselves."[25] Alinsky's analysis was not, strictly speaking, class based as the interests of the poor were not intrinsically opposed to those of the rich. His concern was the identification and pursuit of a genuinely common good, premised on justice, understood as the right judgment to be made for the benefit for all. Hence he was equally critical of the sectarian interest group politics pursued by organized labor and business, and the identity group politics pursued by religious groups and the Black Power movement, all of which denied the possibility of such a good.[26] Ed Chambers summarizes Alinsky's and IAF's approach as working with people from all backgrounds

> to build broad organizations that don't rely on liberal belief in the welfare state or conservative faith in the invisible hand of the market. Instead, IAF has invested in the power of organized families and congregations acting together to refound democratic public life.[27]

For Alinsky, community organization involves a form of political *ascesis* or disciplined formation: it educates and apprentices people into the practices necessary for sustaining public or civic friendships and, through these friendships, forging a common world with those who are different or with whom they disagree.[28] Alinsky envisaged community organizing as a process by which people are awakened or called out from a private world to participate in a public or common life.[29] He states:

> Through the People's Organization these groups discover that what they considered primarily their individual problem is also the problem of the others, and that furthermore the only hope for solving an issue of such titanic proportions is by pooling all their efforts and strengths. That appreciation and conclusion is an educational process.[30]

Central to elucidating what this education in public friendship involves are Alinsky's parables. Many of these are conversion narratives where someone who is an enemy becomes a friend. These tales, some true, some fictional, are often humorous stories involving trickery and a transformation against the odds which lead to reconciliation and a new order being established out of chaos and injustice.[31] However, while public friendship was the goal, it could not bypass judgment against and confrontation with the structures, institutions, and people who opposed a just and common life. This is best encapsulated by Alinsky's juxtaposition of the following two quotes to express the "hopes, aspirations and dreams" of those committed to community organizing. He quotes St Francis of Assisi's prayer: " 'Lord, make me an instrument of Thy peace; where there is hatred, let me sow love; where there is doubt, faith; where there is despair, hope; where there is darkness, light; and where there is sadness, joy.' " He then goes on to say that the prayer is undergirded by the words of Jehovah: " 'When I whet my glittering sword, and my hand taketh hold on Judgement: I will render vengeance unto my enemies and those that hate me will I requite. I will make my arrow drunken with blood, and my sword devour flesh; from the blood of the slain and of the captives, from the crushed head of the enemy.' "[32] Thus for Alinsky, building real relationships must encompass judging your enemy as an enemy and identifying the nature of the conflict or injured right that stands between you before there can be any possibility of reconciliation and friendship.

In his second book, written a few years before he died, Alinsky set out a series of "rules" through which he summarizes the tactics of organizing. A central focus of these rules is how to provoke conflict, such conflict being the precursor to building mutual civic friendships.[33] These tactics, while highly conflictual, are nonviolent and Alinsky was always concerned about remaining within the bounds of the law. Alinsky sees imagination, humor, and irony as central and there is a strong trickster element to his whole approach.[34] For example, rule six states: "A good tactic is one that your people enjoy,"[35] rule five advocates ridicule as a potent weapon, rule four deploys the ironic gesture of forcing the enemy to live up to their reputed value system, and rule one advocates deceiving one's opponent into thinking that you have more power than you have. Crucial to all this is working within the experience of your people (rule two) but at the same time, wrong-footing your opponent by going outside their experience (rule three).

One example illustrates both how these rules operate in practice and their inherent tricksterism. In 1965 Alinsky began working with the African-American community in Rochester. The main focus of this work was achieving equal employment conditions between blacks and whites at the Eastman Kodak Company. One of his suggestions (never actually carried through) was to buy one hundred tickets to the opening performance of the Rochester Symphony Orchestra, the nexus of the elite cultural life of that city. The tickets would be given to blacks who would then eat huge amounts of baked beans before the concert and would proceed to fart their way through the event. While highly disturbing of polite society, it is within the law and any attempt to act against the group would make a mockery of the authorities. It would be very funny, ridiculing the establishment, while at the same time highlighting the racism of the status quo by physically placing poor blacks in an exclusive environment frequented only by whites. It was completely outside the experience of the establishment while within the experience and abilities of the people. As Alinsky puts it: "The one thing that all oppressed people want to do to their oppressors is shit on them."[36] Yet at the same time, it recognizes that the alien and formal surroundings of the concert hall would intimidate the blacks, so the measure involves involuntary physical action that overcomes any reticence on the part of the participants. The merit of the action would be in the reaction of the racist ladies-who-lunch berating their executive husbands who worked at Eastman Kodak to do something to stop the fouling up of "their" concert hall.[37]

All his tactics involve articulating and dramatizing the conflict between the people and their "enemies" or targets. This is notoriously summarized in rule thirteen, which states: "Pick the target, freeze it, personalize it, and polarize it."[38] Each tactic constitutes a form of conscientization, articulating the conflicts of interest at work in a situation and unveiling the existing dramaturgy of power relations.[39] The making of explicit and self-conscious engagement with inherent conflicts of interest also serves to foster the solidarity, cohesiveness, and identity of the organization and thereby builds the power of the organization by increasing the capacity of its members to act together. Each of these rules assumes the stance of those who do not possess sovereign power and so, akin to Michel de Certeau's explicitly trickster conception of *bricolage*, the rules constitute a means by which to make creative use of the prevailing power relations in order to divert and adapt them to different ends.[40] Or as Alinsky put it, "The basic tactic in warfare against the Haves is a mass political jujitsu: the Have-Nots do not rigidly oppose the Haves, but yield in such planned and skilled ways that the superior strength of the Haves becomes their own undoing."[41] However, the point of these tactics is not conflict per se, but the opening up of a space for new ways of relating or addressing an issue, ways that reconfigure the unjust status quo.[42] As Alinsky puts it in rule twelve: "The price of a successful attack is a constructive alternative."[43]

This brings us to a crucial difference between Alinsky's approach to politics and other forms of protest. Alinsky's approach is neither oppositional nor does it simply aim to become a protest movement nor can it be reduced to a means of social critique.[44] Neither is its aim to establish some kind of contrast or dissident society. Rather it is best understood as a means by which to formulate and embody a *contradiction* to any given instance of injustice. By contradiction I mean that his approach represents a way to show forth a contrary logic of relationship to that existing in a particular hegemony.[45] Political actions for Alinsky are simultaneously to declare the unjust way to be untrue and to present a possible alternative through which all may flourish. Alinsky's insistence on having a constructive alternative means that the declaration of a "No" to something is always premised on the prior celebration and upholding of a "Yes" to another way, a way in which both oppressor and oppressed are invited to participate. Examples of this dynamic are seen in numerous recent IAF campaigns; for example, the Living Wage initiatives in Baltimore, London, and elsewhere are not against poor pay, but for a living wage that brings benefits to both employer and employee as well as the wider community. As in this example, the contradiction itself emerges out of an act of listening rather than the application of a prior principle, theory, or ideology. The contradiction is neither an act of assertion over and against what exists nor does it set itself up as in competition with what exists, nor is it a straightforward contrast, but through first listening, then deliberating on what could be the common good in this case, it unveils a way of reformulating what exists so that all may benefit. As will become apparent in the discussion of the analogue between Alinsky and Augustine, it is in his advocacy and display of a politics of contradiction that Alinsky finds his closest point of connection with a theological politics. The Christian conceptualization of contradiction is of course "martyrdom": the witnessing to an order in which all may flourish in communion with God and each other. As O'Donovan notes:

> No honour is paid to martyrs if they are presented as mere dissidents, whose sole glory was to refuse the cultural order that was on offer to them. Martyrdom is, as the word itself indicates, witness, pointing to an alternative offer. The witness is vindicated when it is carried through in a positive mode, saying yes as well as saying no, encouraging the act of repentance and change by which the powers offer homage to Christ.[46]

Mark Warren, in his sociological study of contemporary IAF community organizing, identifies five key component parts to it.[47] There is a direct continuity and consistency between these five elements and the summary of Alinsky's approach already outlined.[48] First, membership of an organization is not as an individual but as institutions, whether it is a parish, a school, or a union branch. It is these local institutions that mainly fund the full-time organizer and it is from these institutions that leaders are drawn. Second, organizing is not issues based but is done via building relationships based on common values and the desire to meets the needs of the wider community. As Ernesto Cortes, one of the most influential organizers since Alinsky, puts it: "The issues fade and they lose interest. But what they really care about remains – family, dignity, justice and hope."[49] The identification of issues around which participants are prepared to act together is accomplished through conversation and relationship building via what are called "one on ones."[50] Third, organizing is not focused on particular groups or sectional interests but works primarily with congregations and other local institutions, building links between these different institutions. It is thus broad based, so for example, London Citizens (the UK affiliate of the IAF) involves over one hundred different faith and secular organizations, including Anglicans, Catholics, Methodists, Pentecostals, Buddhists, Muslims, trade union branches, schools, and university departments. Fourth, IAF organizations work to maintain an independent, nonpartisan political strategy, remaining unaligned with any political party (for example, they will never endorse a candidate) or government agency (for example, they will not accept money from state agencies). It thereby avoids a clientelistic politics and co-option by the state. Independence is ritually dramatized in what are called "accountability sessions" which are staged dialogues/arguments with elected or business officials. However, they are also willing to compromise and work with anyone willing to work with them, using both tension and conflict to open up dialogue, plus negotiation to sustain dialogue and achieve results.[51] Fifth, there is a clear authority structure, with professional organizers and leaders drawn from affiliated institutions making decisions. This is combined with high levels of participation. My own research suggests that there are two further key components to organizing in addition to those identified by Warren. As already noted, it has a strong trickster element to it. And lastly, organizing is best understood as a craft with "rules" – rather akin to a monastic rule – that one is apprenticed into. These rules shape the practice and approach of organizing and give its specific character. They act as guidelines for a creative engagement that must be fresh in each instance and particular to each context.

Given Alinsky's approach it is not surprising that he was a controversial figure. Alinsky himself actively promoted his own notoriety. It is somewhat surprising then to find such a close historic relationship between his work and a large number of churches. What is more surprising still is that there might be a deep affinity between Alinsky's work and Christian theology. To outline this affinity, I begin with Augustine, whose conception of the relationship between eschatology and politics helps establish the terms and conditions of faithful citizenship and of the relationship between Alinsky's approach and Christian political witness. Without the Augustinian "ground rules" for what a faithful citizenship may involve it is easy to either overinflate or underestimate what Alinsky offers. It is my contention that Alinsky's approach opens up a way of identifying and tilling the kind of common objects of love that Augustine identifies as the basis of any stable social and political order. At the same time, Alinsky's approach both enables the contingency of the political order to be kept to the fore and enables a tolerable earthly peace to exist through upholding a plurality of institutional and associational forms.

Eschatology, Politics, and the Mutual Ground of the *Saeculum*

There is a growing scholarly consensus that, for Augustine, while political authority is not neutral (it is either directed toward or away from God), the *saeculum* (the time between Christ's ascension and his return) is open, ambivalent, and undetermined.[52] Augustine's eschatology constitutes a response to both Constantinian triumphalism (marked by an expectation of progress until the church would overcome the world and universally display heaven's glory in history) and Donatist separatism from the world (wherein history is oriented toward regress or a movement away from God).[53] In place of both these polarities, Augustine reestablishes a Pauline eschatological perspective through his conception of the two cities.[54] For Augustine the city of God is an alternative, yet co-terminus society to the earthly city. These two cities are two political entities coexistent in time and space and thus part of this non-eternal age or *saeculum*. Within this framework human history is "secular" (rather than neutral): that is, it neither promises nor sets at risk the kingdom of God. The kingdom of God is established, if not fully manifest, and the "end" of history is already achieved and fulfilled in Christ. Thus the church can reside in this age, regarding its structures and patterns of life as relativized by what is to come and therefore see them as contingent and provisional. Charles Mathewes draws out the implications of this as follows: "Christians' attitude to history should not be one of anxious grasping after control, but of a relaxed playfulness."[55]

R. A. Markus argues that Augustine's eschatology warrants positing an autonomous secular sphere which is neither wholly demonic, sinful, or profane nor wholly sacred, either for the pagan or the Christian.[56] However, this seems an overstatement that does not keep in play the dynamic relationship between the earthly city and the city of God within the *saeculum*.[57] Markus is right in so far as the *saeculum* is an ambiguous time, a field of wheat and tares, neither wholly profane nor sacred. However, it is not autonomous; Christ's sovereignty holds sway over all that happens in this age.[58] The *saeculum* constitutes a single reality or realm, ruled by Christ, and this reality is the mutual ground on which the city of God and the earthly city coexist. Eric Gregory helpfully summarizes this conception of the secular as follows:

> The drama of the secular lies precisely in the human capacity for good or evil, rather than in some autonomous *tertium quid* that is delivered from moral or religious significance. The "secular" refers simply to that mixed time when no single religious vision can presume to command comprehensive, confessional, and visible authority. Secularity ... is interdefined by its relation to eschatology. This definition does not deny the Christian claim that the state remains under the Lordship of Christ, providentially secured in its identity "in Christ." But it does claim that the secular is the "not yet" dimension of an eschatological point of view.[59]

Citizenship is the currency that the city of God and the earthly city share within the mutual ground of the *saeculum*. Citizens of both cities seek peace;

however, as noted in the Introduction, in the earthly city peace is achieved through the imposition of one's own will by the exercise of force. For Augustine, the only true society and true peace exist in the city of God. With Aristotle, Augustine can say that humans are naturally social animals who find fulfillment in a polity of some kind. Against Aristotle, and much other political thought, he argues that the political societies we see around us, and thus the form citizenship takes in them, are neither natural nor fulfilling because they are fallen and oriented away from the true end of human beings – communion with God – and toward their own prideful, self-destructive ends. For Augustine, politics in the *saeculum* is about enabling a limited peace that is on the one hand shorn of messianic pretensions but on the other not given over to demonic despair.

At its minimum, political witness, on the basis of Augustine's framework, is about negotiating what is necessary for a tolerable earthly peace to exist within which the Gospel can be preached and which the city of God makes use of for a time. It is not an end in itself, but serves an end – communion with God – beyond itself.[60] As such, Augustine would be deeply suspicious of the idea of a Christian society (*pace* T. S. Eliot), any project of salvation or human fulfillment through politics, and alert to the temptation of rendering the prevailing hegemony as "natural" or ontologically foundational.[61] All political formations and structures of governance are provisional and tend toward oppression, while at the same time, whether it be a democracy or a monarchy, any political formation may display just judgments and enable the limited good of an earthly peace through the pursuit of agreed or common objects of love. Moreover, "The better the objects of this agreement, the better the people; and the worse the objects, the worse the people."[62] Thus, while existing on a spectrum, there is a difference between the Roman Empire and a band of brigands.[63] No political formation is neutral, but they can be better or worse rather than simply good or bad. As Markus puts it: "Being imperfectly just is not the same thing as being unjust."[64] Yet the peace of all earthly societies is different in kind from the just and certain peace of the true society found in the city of God.[65]

All of this raises a problem already hinted at. Augustine's account of the two cities coexisting in the *saeculum* is an attempt to emphasize the distinctness of the People of God as the true society while at the same time recognizing that these peculiar people not only share mutual ground with but also are often the same as those who are directed away from God. He achieves this through contrasting two spatial realms – two cities – as coexisting in a single time – the *saeculum*. However, the citizens of each city are inextricably interwoven and cannot be told apart until Christ returns.[66] Thus, over and above coexisting in time, they share mutual space. The question then arises as to whether this mutual ground allows for any common objects of love and thus a common life. John Milbank suggests that to posit the possibility of a common life is to fall into positing the kind of autonomous secular sphere already noted in Markus.[67] Yet, while alert to the dangers of this, it is not a necessary move. Indeed, quite the opposite is the case. As will be argued through the course of this book, forming common objects of love between the citizens of the two cities is a necessary condition of faithful witness to the Lordship of Christ over all things. Discovering and tending common objects of love is a precondition of forging the kind of multifaceted or "complex space" and "hazy" boundary between different forms of life and institutional arrangements, including church and state, that Milbank seeks. For Milbank this kind of complex space is vital in order that a "social" existence of many interlocking powers may emerge and thereby forestall, or at least hold in check, the formation of anti-Christic and idolatrous monopolies of power, whether they be ecclesial, political, or economic.[68] Thus common objects of love between the citizens of the two cities are a precondition of the kind of tolerable earthly peace that Augustine envisages. Alinsky's approach constitutes a means of both identifying and sustaining these common objects of love and upholding the kind of plurality of institutional and associational forms that constitutes the basis of a tolerable earthly peace.

A number of initial connections between Alinsky and Augustine can be made in light of what has already been stated. First, Augustine's account of the ambiguity and contingency of the structures and institutions within the *saeculum* as well as their tendency to pursue the *libido dominandi* correlates with Alinsky's understanding of the world as it is as distinct from the world as it should be. For Alinsky and Augustine, the world as it is, or earthly city, is a dynamic whereby even the best is corrupted and the just can never be quite sure they are doing the right thing. Like Augustine's conscientious judge, Alinsky's organizer must endure an "ever-gnawing inner uncertainty as to whether or not he is right."[69] Yet at the same time: " 'The fear of soiling ourselves by entering the context of history is not virtue but a way of escaping virtue.' "[70] Alinsky's quotation of Henry James serves as a summary of both their views:

"Life is, in fact, a battle. Evil is insolent and strong; beauty enchanting but rare; goodness very apt to be weak; folly ever apt to be defiant; wickedness to carry the day; imbeciles to be in great places, people of sense in small, and mankind generally unhappy. But the world as it stands is no narrow illusion ... we can neither forget it nor deny it nor dispense with it."[71]

However, while Augustine and Alinsky are political realists, they are not pessimists. For both there is a messianic horizon "ever beckoning onward" and challenging the corruption of the present age.[72] It is true to say that Alinsky, the agnostic Jew, conceives this horizon in less ontological terms than Augustine.[73] However, both draw direct influence from the Biblical prophetic tradition and what Walter Brueggeman calls a "hopeful imagination" that announces the possibilities of a state of peace and justice or *shalom* that renders contingent all present political and social arrangements.[74] The hopeful realism of Augustine and Alinsky is perhaps best summarized by Chambers who states: "The foundational conviction of the IAF organizing tradition is that it is the fate of human beings to exist *in-between* the world as it is and the world as it should be."[75]

Second, given the world as it is, for both Augustine and Alinsky, politics necessarily involves conflict.[76] However, as Charles Mathewes points out in relation to Augustine, it is a conflict over people's loves, thus it is a conflict over what binds people together in a public or common life.[77] Conflict, while inevitable in the *saeculum*, is not the fundamental condition or the sum total of human relations; they originated in loving gift and their promised end is harmonious difference in loving relations. And, as Eric Gregory argues, love, albeit often in distorted and self-destructive forms, is fundamental to political life.[78]

Third, despite Alinsky's rhetoric, Augustine and Alinsky's hopeful realism suggests a remedial rather than revolutionary approach to politics. Indeed, Alinsky-inspired approaches are often criticized for not being "progressive" or "radical" enough. This is an astute observation as both Augustine and Alinsky are anti-progressive, anti-utopian, and anti-ideological.[79] History does not bear within itself its own resolution and so while the order of things can be improved in incremental ways, there is no inherent direction to history: things will not always get better (or worse). The non-progressive nature of history means that a perfect or true order of things is not realizable within history, so any human system or ideology that claims to provide the means of bringing about this order is a denial of the fallen and contingent nature of historical existence. No political system is sacrosanct, all are but provisional and providential arrangements open to amelioration. Attempts to enable the world as it is to approximate more closely the world as it could or should be must work from historical experience and existing patterns of life. As already noted, for Alinsky, this is the only ground on which real change is possible. For Augustine, God in Jesus Christ deals with the world as it is and, in light of the Incarnation, history constitutes the crucible of divine–human relations and the eschaton the only true fulfillment of these relations. Attempts to overturn a political system in the name of an ideological blueprint or set of abstract principles will be inherently destructive as they are an attempt to step outside of history or circumvent historical conditions and thereby deny the goodness and the limits of creation reaffirmed in the Incarnation and falsely realize the eschaton by sinful means. As summarized in the community organizing maxim, "no permanent enemies and no permanent allies," Augustine and Alinsky refuse to make absolutist judgments on present political arrangements. Change and redemption are always possibilities and good and bad are present in all political systems.[80] To use Dietrich Bonhoeffer's categories, their political vision involves neither straightforward radicalism (which sees only the world as it should be and with legalistic zeal opposes working within the limits of a good but fallen creation) nor compromise (which places the ultimate beyond the bounds of daily life and reconciles itself to the world as it is).[81] Rather, Augustine and Alinsky envisage a kind of conservative-radical politics. The IAF organizer Michael Gecan expresses the nature of Augustine's and Alinsky's conservative radicalism, when he states:

> So leaders and organizers face a tough challenge: maintaining a conservative's belief in the value and necessity of stable institutions, along with a radical's understanding of the need for persistent agitation and reorganization. We are called to love, engage, and uphold our most cherished institutions, while watching them, questioning them, and pressing them to change, all at the same time.[82]

Gecan's comments can be related to families, workplaces, churches, and civic institutions, all of which are mutually constitutive domains in which we respond to the vocation to love God and neighbor.[83]

The link between a prudential politics, indwelling existing traditions, and a commitment to justice may seem counterintuitive. However, whether it is the work of either Sheldon Wolin or Alasdair MacIntyre, there exist extensive philosophical and historical accounts that warrant precisely the kind of conservative-radical politics that Alinsky advocates.[84] Yet the question for Wolin, MacIntyre, and Alinsky is where do the resources for "persistent agitation" come from? As I have argued elsewhere, theologically, one means of grace through which God furnishes us with the resources for the healing and renewal of our institutions and traditions so that they remain conduits of human flourishing is more often than not our encounter with strangers.[85] It is my contention that a basic condition for the health of this kind of conservative-radical politics is hospitality and a commitment to building a common life with others. It is through these that we encounter others not like us and with whom we disagree. Such encounters forestall "archaic" traditions from becoming idolatrous and oppressive repristinations of a dead faith. For Christians, this is part of what it means to live betwixt and between this age and the age to come, simultaneously within the earthly city and the city of God. Theologically, it is to make missiology central to ecclesiology. As set out in Jeremiah 29, a passage that is central to both Augustine's own political vision and the Jewish tradition out of which Alinsky emerged, in seeking the welfare of the city, even though it is Babylon, not only do we find our own welfare, but also we encounter God in new and surprising ways.[86]

The advocacy of hospitality should not be heard as a synonym for hybridity. As Romand Coles argues, advocacy of hybridity as an ethical-political orientation too easily disconnects itself from particular traditions and real differences, becoming what Will Kymlicka called "boutique multiculturalism."[87] In the contemporary context, it is also to conform to the spirit of capitalism that precisely demands the dissolution of particularity and the formation of liquid identities in order to aid capital flows. Hybridity is a way we can all come from nowhere and so be moved anywhere the market requires and by which any effective and affective political and social alternatives to its logic may be dissolved.[88] Community organizing is a way of honoring one's own tradition while at the same time hallowing others among whom one lives. It is a way of paying attention to others – through one-on-ones and testimony where vulnerability, anger, passions, and hopes are shared – and so stepping out of one's own limited perspective and enable new understanding to emerge. As Coles puts it:

> In this more responsive and receptive context, relationships are formed and deepened in which a rich complex critical vision of a community develops along with the gradual articulation of alternative possibilities. ... As different positions, problems, passions, interests, traditions, and yearnings are shared, through careful practices of listening, participants begin to develop increasingly relational senses of their interests and orientation in ways that often transfigure the senses with which they began. And as relationships deepen, bonds are formed that are more capable of enduring the rough and tumble of more-agonistic politics. These transformative effects are recorded in narratives that populate many accounts of IAF politics.[89]

To adapt a metaphor current in discussions of Scriptural Reasoning, community organizing is in relationship with and subsistent on *temples* – authoritative traditions of interpretation and practice – and *houses* – local, contextually alert places of worship and formation (such as a congregation) – but is itself a *tent*: that is, a mobile, provisional place where faithful witness is lived in conversation with other faiths and those of no faith.[90] Community organizing is a form of tent making where a place is formed in which hospitality is given and received between multiple traditions. Sometimes there are issues heard in the tent that can be collectively acted upon and some that cannot, but the encounter with others and their stories informs the sense of what it is like to live on this mutual ground, to dwell together in a given and shared urban space. The hearing of others' interests and concerns in the context of ongoing relationships and the recognition that everyone in the tent occupies the same mutual (not neutral) ground foster the sense that in each others' welfare we find our own.

It could be argued that recourse to the motif of hospitality, whereby one makes room for another, is an inherently patronizing way of organizing relations between strangers. There are a number of things to say in response to such a criticism. First, hospitality, as I have outlined more extensively elsewhere, is precisely a way of countering patronizing or excluding relations between strangers because it demands that the host become decentered and transform their understanding of themselves in order both to make room for and to encounter the other.[91] Second, hospitality refuses the political fantasy of neutral ground on which all may meet as equals: all places are already filled by someone and so some account of how to cope constructively with the asymmetries of power between "established" and "immigrant" groups is needed if a common good is to emerge.[92] Hospitality is a way of framing how such mutual ground can be forged in a context where the space – be it geographic, cultural, or political – is already occupied and no neutral, uncontested place is available. To reiterate the metaphor of temples, houses, and tents, the practice of hospitality, as conceptualized here, recognizes tent-like places to subsist off the prior life and work of temples. At the same time, the practice of hospitality ensures a relationship between temples and tent-like places so that the temples themselves do not congeal and ossify into domains of oppression, closed off from God and neighbor.

Christian Realism *Redivivus*?

At first sight the kinds of connections I am making between Augustine and Alinsky would suggest a direct affinity between Alinsky and Reinhold Niebuhr's "Christian realism." This would also make sense contextually as many Protestants who became directly involved in the IAF were influenced by Niebuhr. More specifically, from 1969 onward, Niehbuhr's work was used as part of the training of those seminarians and clergy who had been involved in anti-war and civil rights activism and then became involved in IAF.[93] Theologically, a number of commentators on the relationship between

Alinsky and Christian political engagement have seen Niebuhr as providing the clearest theological framework for justifying the uptake of Alinsky's approach by Christians.[94] However, I will contend that situating Alinsky within the framework of Niebuhr's Christian realism leads to a misconception of the kind of political witness that Alinsky's approach offers. The misconception arises because first, Christian realism occludes explicitly ecclesial forms of political engagement; second, it justifies the kind of liberal interest-group politics that Alinsky opposes; and third, its separation of power and love conceals how these are integrated in Alinsky's work.[95] There is more at stake, however, in drawing out the contrasts between Alinsky and Niebuhr than simply clarification. By drawing out the contrasts, the ways in which Alinsky's work is fruitful in addressing some of the central theological debates concerning the relationship between Christianity and contemporary politics can be identified.

The connections between Alinsky and Niebuhr's Christian realism are striking. Like Alinsky, Niebuhr was critical of liberalism and a great advocate of democracy. Niebuhr saw a direct affinity between Christianity and democracy and he was concerned to defend democracy as the best form of human government since it best accords with the historical reality of the human condition.[96] In *Moral Man and Immoral Society* (1932), Niebuhr argued that it is legitimate and reasonable to talk about the moral responsibilities of individuals, but it is quite another matter to talk about the moral responsibilities of social and political institutions like states. Individuals can have a moral sense, they are moral agents in that they can consider the interests of others, have a measure of sympathy for others and, by reason and education, develop with a degree of objectivity a sense of what justice means in a particular situation, even though their own interests may be involved. All these developments are more difficult for societies and social groups. These are less capable of employing rationality to determine action and restrain collective egoism and to comprehend the needs of others beyond the group in question, whether family, town, or nation. Any social analysis must be realistic in its assessment and to be realistic it must take account of self-interest and power relations (or in theological terms, original sin as it affects groups and, in particular, states).[97] The best that can be achieved in any social conflict is an equitable balance of power. Any attempt to apply the self-sacrificial or disinterested love that may characterize relations between individuals to relations between groups is not only impossible but also dangerous.[98] Likewise, appeals to disinterested or selfless love in politics as a motivation to change power relations (for example, for whites to grant equal rights to blacks in America) are sentimental idealism.[99] However, power itself is essentially neutral and can be used to realize either selfish interests or justice. For Neibuhr:

> The relations between groups must therefore always be predominately political rather than ethical, that is, they will be determined by the proportion of power which each group possesses at least as much as by any rational and moral appraisal of the comparative needs and claims of each group.[100]

Within this framework, Alinsky is simply advocating the formation of an interest group by the poor and disenfranchised so they can pursue power and thereby achieve a measure of justice.

For Niebuhr the primary role of the church is to present the Gospel and thereby enable both individuals and nations to discern the divine author of their life. Yet any talk of the church as holy or as a paradigmatic community of witness or as having its own politics is problematic for Niebuhr. While the love ethic that Christ's sacrificial death exemplifies is not a counsel of perfection but part of the structure of things, it cannot be lived in this age because of sin, thus the "law of love" stands on the "edge of history" not at its center.[101] Loving sacrifice may be possible between two people, but when more than that are involved self-love comes in. All attempts to set up holy communities are problematic because they fail to reckon with the true nature of human history. Thus any notion that the church might be an agent of sanctifying society or a leaven or have a unique pedagogic role is mistaken. The church qua church has no particular political responsibility other than to contribute, along with all other sectors of society, to the equal and just, if provisional, ordering of society. Any attempt to move beyond this constitutes both an over-realized eschatology and an intolerant and egoistic assertion of itself over others in the public domain. Thus the church, far from constituting an alternative society, is either a threat to the liberal democratic order, or it is subsumed to the demands of the liberal democratic order so that they share the same aim: the humanization of social, economic, and political life. In effect, the church becomes an adjunct to the prevailing social order in the name of maintaining a proximate justice.[102] It is at this point that the continuing legacy of Niebuhr can be seen in ongoing discussions of the relationship between Christianity and politics that tacitly subsume the church to either the needs of the prevailing political order or to an immanent project of humanization. Such an approach gives up any hope of the Spirit acting to irrupt anticipations and glimpses of the eschaton within the *saeculum* and renounces its vocation to bear witness to the world as it is in Christ within the world turned in on itself.[103] What Hauerwas calls Niebuhr's "pale theism" leads in effect to the deracination of the church as a social and political body in itself.[104]

On one reading, subsuming the church to the humanization of the social, economic, and political order is entirely in accord with Alinsky's attitude toward the church. There are numerous remarks and incidents to indicate that Alinsky had a somewhat instrumentalist approach to the churches he worked with. Yet Alinsky states that democracy is not an end in itself but the best means toward achieving the values of "equality, justice, freedom, peace, and all those rights and values propounded by Judeao-Christianity and the democratic political tradition."[105] For Alinsky there is a direct affinity between Christianity and his democratic vision. However, the affinity is not with Niebuhr's vision of interest-group politics but with the Christian democratic vision of Jacques Maritain; that is, with a vision of political life and of democracy in particular, as conversation about the common good.[106]

A Thomistic Democratic Politics?

Maritain identifies a direct link between his political vision and that of Alinsky. He comments in a letter to Alinsky concerning the latter's book *Reveille for Radicals*: "It reveals a new way for *real* democracy, the only way in which man's thirst for social communion can develop and be satisfied, through freedom and not through totalitarianism in our disintegrated times."[107] Bernard Doering points to key areas of synchronicity between Alinsky and Maritain's conception of Christian democracy.[108] They shared an emphasis on the centrality of the human dignity of the individual, the priority of the common good over particular goods, and the principle of subsidiarity. Alinsky's neighborhood councils were in a way the embodiment of Maritain's vision of a personalist and pluralist pattern of social, economic, and political life that was a precondition of true democracy.[109] This positive vision was built on a trust in the practical wisdom of ordinary people as against technocrats and ideologues.[110] This trust was coupled with the need to identify and work alongside the poor and marginalized, moving beyond charity and welfare paternalism. Yet at the same time, their opposition to injustice took as a given the ambivalence of the world and the sinfulness of human relations.[111] While Maritain chides Alinsky on his rhetoric of excess concerning the relationship between means and ends – Alinsky at times taking the posture of an out-and-out Machievellian – they basically agreed that in a fallen world it was a tragic necessity at times to resort to bad means for good ends.[112] The analogy here is with just war theory where the use of force is at times a moral imperative in order to truly love one's enemy and defend the innocent. However, Maritain pushes Alinsky to go beyond this and see a complementarity between what he advocates and the approach of Gandhi and Martin Luther King: that is, rather than constitute the use of bad means for good ends in exceptional circumstances, Alinsky's approach was more accurately the use of moral power to overcome evil.[113] The moral basis of this power is that it is relational and seeks to respond to others as ends not means, rather than unilateral and thereby instrumentalizing others as a means to a private, uncommon end. Lastly, both saw the need for prophetic figures that could awaken people from an unjust status quo. Such figures were not propagating the false messianism of political revolution, forcing the people to be free, but those who set out new visions that deepened and extended the justice and generosity of the existing political order.[114]

A point of connection that Doering does not note is the common concern for a more pluralistic body politic. It is this connection that has perhaps the greatest salience for contemporary political debates. Alinsky and Maritain advocate the need for a genuine communal plurality or "complex space" as a means of holding in check the centralizing and totalizing thrust of the modern market and state. Maritain argues for a genuine plurality and a corporatist conception of political or civil society (as distinct from the state). Maritain calls it "an organic heterogeneity in the very structure of civil society" whereby there are multiple yet overlapping "political fraternities" that are independent of the state.[115] Maritain distinguishes his account of a corporatist political society and economic life from fascist and communist ones that collapse market, state, and civil society into a single entity *and* from collectivist and individualistic conceptions of economic relations.[116] Crucially, civil society constitutes a sphere of social or "fraternal" relations that has its own integrity and telos but which nevertheless serves the defensive function of preventing either the market or the state from establishing a monopoly of power, thereby either instrumentalizing/politicizing social relations for the sake of the political order or instrumentalizing/commodifying social relations for the sake of the economy. Within this sphere there can exist multiple and overlapping and, on the basis of subsidiarity, autonomous forms of institutional life and association, forms that are not reducible to either a private or voluntary association.[117] Indeed, in contrast to his overall theological framework, Maritain's account of a corporatist body politic overturns the kind of divisions between public and private at work in, for example, Rawls and late-modern liberalism more generally. Alinsky's approach displays in practice what such a corporatist political life that nevertheless seeks to discern and uphold goods in common might consist of. Alinsky's approach offers an alternative imaginary to how a Christian democratic vision developed in Europe after World War II, aligned as it was with a turn to the state as both the sole keeper of the common good and as the primary or only means of addressing social and economic ills via legal regulation and welfare programs. As the totalizing logic of this alignment has come under increasing criticism, Alinsky's approach points to what a non-statist, decentralized, and pluralist Christian democratic vision might look like in practice.[118] Indeed, Alinsky seems to have understood community organizing as just such an alternative.[119] Within this alternative imaginary national politics is like an enclosed park into which there is public access and right of way but minimal involvement. By contrast, more localized, place-based forms of politics are like common land, providing the possibility of building genuinely public spaces of shared responsibility and cooperation and nurturing what Wolin calls "politicalness": that is, the "capacity for developing into beings who know and value what it means to participate in and be responsible for the care and improvement of our common and collective life."[120]

Maritain points the way to a deeper reading of Alinsky, one that refuses Alinsky's own contrarian self-descriptions. In a letter to Alinsky he states: "All your fighting effort as an organizer is quickened *in reality* by *love for the human being, and for God*, though you refuse to admit it, by a kind of inner *pudeur*."[121] And in a letter to a third party describing Alinsky he points out the inner theo-logic in Alinsky's work:

> Alinsky's methods may seem a little rough. I think they are good and necessary means to achieve good and necessary ends. And I know (this is the privilege of an old man) that the deep-rooted motive power and inspiration of this so-called trouble-maker is pure and entire self-giving, and love for those poor images of God which are human beings, especially the oppressed ones – in other words, it is what St Paul calls *agapé*, or love of charity.[122]

On Maritain's reading, in contrast to a Niebuhrian one, Alinsky does not subsume Christianity to a project of humanization nor does he refuse the possibility and necessity of neighbor love in political life. Rather, Alinsky's approach constitutes a means of upholding human dignity and a civic form of neighbor love that can find its fulfillment in communion with God.

It is at this point that we can see the full significance of Alinsky's approach emerge. It is a means of presenting a contradiction to the dynamics of totalizing power in the contemporary context. It should not be surprising that it emerged and has proved most relevant in urban contexts where the dynamics of monopolistic forms of power are felt most keenly. We can also see the worth of Alinsky's understanding of the relationship between Christianity and democracy. Christianity is neither a resource for a superordinate project of democratization or "progressive" politics nor is it necessary for Christians to subscribe to a version of Maritain's mediating "democratic secular faith."[123] Rather, both democracy and Christianity are bearers of practices and beliefs that uphold the dignity of persons and deliberation about common objects of love as the basis of an approximately just and generous political life. Both are means of contradicting the logic of commodification and instrumentalization at work in capitalism and technocratic managerialism. The link between Christianity and Alinsky's approach is best understood as what Oliver O'Donovan calls an "exploratory partnership" or John Howard Yoder calls a "holy experiment" that enables the expression, within the contemporary context of Western liberal polities, of faithful "political discipleship."[124] Community organizing as a form of democratic politics is a mode of action in which those charged with bearing witness to the Gospel do three things simultaneously: first, they act defensively to uphold or forge anew an institutional plurality that serves as a bulwark against the totalizing thrust of modern forms of economic and political power; second, they hold to account governing authorities so as to enable right or fit judgments to be made through a meaningful process of consultation and deliberation; and third, they act constructively, by forging public friendships and enabling the discernment of goods in common that form the basis of an earthly peace in which all, including Christians, may find their welfare. In short, it is a way for churches to relate acts of political judgment and realize obligations of neighbor love in the public sphere.

Reweaving Civil Society

William Cavanaugh argues that civil society is now subsumed to and serves the needs of the sovereign state. Institutions such as schools, prisons, unions, and churches discipline and educate their members so that they are compliant with and supportive of what is now the market-state.[125] Any attempt to posit civil society as a free space in which to forge communities of resistance is problematized by the co-inherence of state, economy, and civil society.[126] On Cavanaugh's reading, community organizing is not a means by which to forge alternative centers of power from the free space of civil society.[127] Rather, despite its own best efforts, it is simply a means by which to discipline the church and make it serve the needs of the market-state.[128] By contrast, for Cavanaugh:

> The Church gathered around the altar does not simply disperse and be absorbed into civil society when God's blessing sends it forth. The liturgy does more than generate interior motivations to be better citizens. The liturgy generates a

body, the Body of Christ ... which is itself a *sui generis* social body, a public presence irreducible to a voluntary association of civil society.[129]

Echoing the work of Hauerwas and the O'Donovans outlined in Chapter 1, Cavanaugh points to how conceiving the church as a constituent of civil society, even one that can provide resources to renew political life, forfeits Augustine's emphasis on the church as the primary community of Christians whose pattern of citizenship constitutes a truly public form of life.[130]

In response to Cavanaugh's critique of civil society as subsumed to the market-state, I am proposing that he is right to envisage the church as a public constituted by its worship life but that as precisely this it is the free or truly public space in which civil society can be re-formed.[131] It is from the church that contradictions to the dominant and oppressive dynamics of power may be forged, as is illustrated by Cavanaugh's own accounts of the COPACHI (Committee of Cooperation for Peace in Chile) and the Vicariate of Solidarity as well as the work of the Sebastián Acevedo Movement against Torture in Chile under Pinochet.[132] Where what it means to be human is threatened or undermined, it is the vocation of the church to witness to its proper form; that is, its form as established and reconciled to God in Christ. As Dietrich Bonhoeffer argued, "the space of the church is the place where witness is given to the foundation of all reality in Jesus Christ."[133] In times of crises the world seeks in Christ (as distinct from the church) the renewal of what it means to be truly human and thence truly social; that is, what it means to live with and for others acting responsibly and cooperatively. For Bonhoeffer, the crucified Christ has become the refuge, justification, protection, and claim for higher values and anyone who defends them. He states: "It is with the Christ, persecuted and suffering together with his church-community, that justice, truth, humanity, and freedom seek refuge."[134] It is not always acted upon or if acted upon often it is an ambivalent and painful process, yet for Christians, it is the prior experience of being the world reconciled in and through Christ that provides the church with the possibility of hosting the reemergence of a genuinely political space in which human dignity is upheld and common objects of love may be deliberated over and acted upon. Time and again, from Poland and East Germany under communism, to South Africa under apartheid and the Philippines under the Marcos regime, politics, framed in terms of democracy, has been hosted and nourished by churches.[135] As Maritain put it: "The cause of freedom and the cause of the Church are one in the defense of man."[136] On this reading, Alinsky and community organizing are an example of how those who seek to uphold human dignity and "higher values" seek shelter in Christ through relationship with the church and conversely, Christians learn in Babylon what they failed to learn in Jerusalem; that is, how to faithfully love God and neighbor.

Politics without Piety Is Pitiless; Piety without Politics Is Pitiful

For Maritain a crucial element of keeping the pluralistic body politic open and decentralized is its openness to God and a non-reductive anthropology (what he calls Christian humanism) that sees the *telos* of persons as fulfilled beyond any economic and political order. For Maritain, like Augustine, true freedom cannot be realized within a temporal realm. Yet as William Cavanaugh convincingly argues, Maritain's own theological conception of church–state relations closes off the temporal from the eschatological, downplaying the implications of the incarnation and spiritualizing the church. In short, Maritain's wider theology has much the same implication as Niebuhr's; that is, "Maritain does not allow the possibility that the Gospel may have its own bodily performances, its 'own politics,' its own set of social practices which are neither purely otherwordly nor reducible to some 'purely temporal' discourse."[137] By contrast, Alinsky's approach does allow for a "church practice of the political."[138] So if Maritain points to a deeper reading of Alinsky, Alinsky points to a way beyond Maritain.

It is arguable that a central feature of community organizing is its symbiotic and dialectical relationship with its constituent worshiping communities. Alinsky envisaged the formation of a broad-based federation of organizations. This federation works with the grain of the traditions and practices of its constituent institutions. At an empirical level this is how the relationship has developed in practice. Both Richard Wood and Mark Warren note how Alinsky-influenced groups made increasing use of religious language and symbols in public political settings after Alinsky's death.[139] For example, Wood notes the importance of prayer. He states:

> Prayer located the organizing process within the context of a reality transcending instrumentalist power politics. Prayer was the most visible marker communicating to new participants that this was not just another effort to exert power around narrow self-interests, but rather something linked to a broader vision of the common good and their own religiously grounded view of social justice.[140]

What has emerged through Alinsky's approach is a way for churches to overcome the privatization of religion in modern liberal politics (as outlined in Chapter 1). It enables churches to deploy their own language and symbols rather than having to translate them into some form of "public reason," subscribe to a mediating democratic creed, or adopt wholesale the languages of either "progressive" or "conservative" politics.[141] Wood points to how this works in practice, stating:

> Including prayer in public meetings prevents participants from easily compartmentalizing themselves into a "secular self" separate from their "religious self" enacted in other settings; instead, this creates a setting in which these often fragmented identities can be integrated and enacted publicly as "whole selves."[142]

There is a symbiosis between the structures of community organizing and that of the participating congregations. The community organizations Wood studied were entirely dependent on the prior social bonds, practices, and "moral-political teachings" of the churches involved.[143] In Wood's evaluation, it is these that provide the vision and motivation for and means of sustaining the political action.[144] However, the community organization and its political work are distinct and separate from the churches themselves.[145] Wood sees the community organization as providing a "buffering of the sacred core." He states: "The worship life of the community remains sacred ground, related to but autonomous from the pressures of engagement in the political system."[146] For Wood, Alinsky's approach represents a means by which the worship life of a congregation can bear witness to the wider social and political realities but without losing its character as worship. Theologically, the relationship between community organizing and worship ensures that the church is free to testify that the world is not its own; it is dependent on God rather than sustained by political and economic processes.

The structural dualism between congregation and community organization means that the worship life of the church constantly raises a question over the means and ends of the political engagement. This is institutionalized by constant ethical reflection on the organizing process at all levels.[147] Thus worship gives rise to the possibility of political ethics among participants in community organizing as politics is not all there is and politics is not invested with soteriological expectations. Put simply, if politics is all there is (for good or ill), then anything goes, but if there is an order over and beyond political life, then politics has an ethical ground and limit to which it is accountable. Bernd Wannenwetsch argues that the celebration of worship is not directed simply against this or that totalitarian regime; it is directed against the totalization of political existence in general. He states that worship "does not just interrupt labor and 'fabrication'; it also suspends political action in the world. In this way it affords a salutary limitation of sotierologically charged expectations addressed to politics."[148] Community organizing is as much in need of such a limit as any other form of political action.

There is always the danger in the relationship between churches and community organizing that worship becomes subservient to formulating effective public policy rather than forming the People of God and shaping their witness in the world. As Wannenwetsch points out, using worship as a political instrument ceases to see an act such as prayer as contributing its own meaning and dynamic.[149] Functionalized worship ceases to be the inner ground out of which the political action springs and to which the political action is accountable.[150] Instead, worship has been made subservient to its impact on society and reduced to a "resource" for the moralization of the world.[151] Such instrumentalization is a real and present danger in community organizing, but it is not a necessary consequence of it. On a theological reading, the point at issue here is the externality of the point of reference that enables change. As already noted in relation to Alinsky's conservative radicalism, a key issue is where the resources for critique and contradiction come from. For Christians, Scripture mediates the word from outside our immediate context (what Luther called the *verbum externum*), reorienting the church to the world in faithful, hopeful, and loving ways, ways that are in excess of any immanent possibilities. Ways that, nevertheless, conform to the eschatological order established in and through Jesus Christ. And in worship we are formed and empowered by the Spirit (the *verbum internum*) so that we may respond to this order faithfully, hopefully, and lovingly. Scripture reads our world as open to the eschatological horizon and in worship, through the Spirit, we are subjectively opened to these possibilities. To put it in terms of narrative theology: Scripture enables us to locate our story within God's story and thereby orient ourselves to the world faithfully.[152] Or as Bonhoeffer put it, in listening to Scripture we are "uprooted from our own experience and are taken back to the holy history of God on earth. ... What is important is not that God is a spectator and participant in our life today, but that we are attentive listeners and participants in God's action in the sacred story, the story of Christ on earth. God is with us today only as long as we are there."[153] In relation to the church, it is actively listening to Scripture, primarily in preaching and liturgy, which best alerts Christians to the constant temptation to instrumentalize both the church and its worship. Attention to the *verbum externum* alerts the church to the fact that it does not possess itself or manufacture its worship; rather, its inner or animating life and relationship with God is a gift to be received again and again and a covenant to be lived into rather than a state of being to be achieved. In relation to Christian involvement in community organizing, framing political actions in terms of Scripture inserts an important reminder that such action is not self-generated or self-subsisting but derived from the prior, originating power of God.

The above emphasis on Scripture in relation to community organizing is not just a conceptual point. Historically, a primary way in which community organizing, from Alinsky onward, is framed is in reference to Scripture. Warren notes how engagement with Scripture was central to revitalizing the work of IAF after Alinsky's death.[154] Ernesto Cortes, a key figure in the revitalization of IAF and the lead organizer in Texas, devised a training program for leaders that drew upon the stories of Pentecost and Sinai to frame the work of community organizing. Other key texts engaged with included Exodus, Corinthians, and Ezekiel's prophecy of the valley of the dry bones.[155] Wood notes how Scripture was a major source of reflection for the organizers and leaders he observed and how participants framed what they were doing in reference to Scripture.[156] Listening to and debating Scripture is often, though not always, a formative part of the preparation for political action. The outworking of this kind of reflection is seen in the names given to different projects resulting from IAF political actions in New York and Baltimore: for example, the Nehemiah homes – a project that builds affordable housing for low income families – and the Joseph Plan – a state strategy to set aside surplus funds during boom years to bolster threatened social services during leaner times.[157] Some groups directly shape their political action around their communal reflection on Scripture. This is not the case in all community organizations. The point at issue is that although listening to Scripture is not necessarily normative in community organizing, it has been a constitutive element in its development and is a focal practice for many groups. Moreover, this was the case right from its inception: in their reference to and reflection on Scripture, Cortes and others follow a precedent set by Alinsky, whose books are laced with biblical references and which envisage Moses and Paul as model organizers.[158]

There is then an act of double listening, or listening on two horizons simultaneously, that can and should form the faithful participation by churches in community organizing and which enables community organizing to form Christians in faithfulness.[159] As noted at the outset, listening to one's neighbors is a constitutive feature of the Alinksy approach to democratic politics and policy formulation.[160] We have also seen how listening to Scripture is a key way in which political action is framed within community organizing. I want to suggest that in terms of the involvement of the church, the act of double listening is crucial for how broad-based community organizing functions as a school of discipleship for Christians. The process of double listening constitutes training in how to hear and discern the address of God amid the earthly city. The theme of Divine address amid the earthly city will be developed in Chapter 4 in relation to the theology of ordinary politics; however, political action born out of listening to the stories and concerns of our near and distant neighbors (both Christian and non-Christian) and to Scripture can be a central feature of community organizing and when it is, this form of double listening constitutes a basis for why community organizing can be a form of faithful witness.[161]

For the church listening is *the* constitutive political act. Through listening and responding to the Word of God the church is assembled as a public body – the *ekklesia* – out of the world. In being called out, this body is then enabled, as Rachel Muers argues, to participate in God's hearing of the world, and so it can discern the truth of the world and respond accordingly.[162] The fulfillment of this time and the inauguration of the time to come in the risen and ascended Christ frees those in Christ to take the time to listen and thence act responsibly with and for others in conformity to Christ.[163] Politics can thereby cease to be tragic – it can become a realm of worthwhile and good action that relates to the ultimate – without having to become messianic.

The initiatory human response to the prior work of Christ is the act of listening to God and others. As Ambrose exhorts: "The law says: 'Hear, O Israel, the Lord thy God.' It said not: 'Speak,' but 'Hear.' … Be silent therefore first of all, and hearken, that thou fail not in thy tongue."[164] This initiatory act of listening forms the body of Christ. As Bonhoeffer puts it:

> The first service one owes to others in the community involves listening to them. Just as our love of God begins with listening to God's Word, the beginning of love for other Christians is learning to listen to them. God's love for us is shown by the fact that God not only gives us God's Word, but also lends us God's ear. We do God's work for our brothers and sisters when we learn to listen to them.[165]

For Bonhoeffer, listening with the "ears of God" is the necessary precursor to being able to proclaim the Word of God because those who do not listen to others, or who presume to already know what the other person has to say, will soon no longer listen to God.[166]

Listening is an act of faith that whatever the relation of difference (constructive) or sin (destructive) between oneself and another, Christ's life, death, and resurrection recapitulate and mediate a common world in which all may now participate. Just as God created us as one family, so now in Christ, we may be one again, sharing a common life with others on the cusp between creation and new creation. As Muers puts it: "In listening to someone, one also listens to discourse that locates her in a shared world; the act of listening intends the other as a participant in the making and discernment of meaning in this shared world."[167] Thus listening both presumes a common realm of shared action and meaning established in Christ and is an act that intends and embodies such a realm. As such, listening to God in worship and to others among whom one lives is what Wannenwetsch calls a "therapy for the hermeneutics of suspicion."[168] As Wannenwetsch points out, the hermeneutics of suspicion refuses a common world of meaning and action, locating the real meaning of something as hidden or as intending something other than what is actually said. The hermeneutics of suspicion is thereby anti-political because it undermines the possibility of acting together and discerning goods in common, positing a realm of only private or hidden interests. By contrast, listening is an act of trust in the words of others. Wannenwetsch states:

> Trust does not reduce the other person to mere behaviour, by hearing in his words only what we expected of them, in the light of our predetermined view of him (as right-wing, or left-wing, and so forth). It does not pin him down to a particular role, and does not degrade the political discourse to the mechanism of provocation-reaction. ... [T]rust leads to the movement towards consensus, to the common search for sustainable conditions of social life. It makes it possible for people to act together.[169]

Thus listening is not only the constitutive political act of the church but, in the contemporary context, is itself a primary form of faithful witness to the Christ-event within political life.

Against the interest groups politics schematized by Albert Hirschman's typology of exit, voice, and loyalty, Christianity inserts listening, an act that is neither withdrawal (as in exit), or assertion (as in voice), or commitment, obedience, or passivity (as in loyalty).[170] Rather, listening positions the church in relation to others, whether they are poor or powerful, as one of active contemplation that moves beyond seeing and appearing before others to epiphanic encounter. As a political act, listening overcomes the antinomy between the *vita activa* and the *vita contemplativa* that Hannah Arendt delineates by locating contemplation of God and others as the beginning point of public action.[171] Listening enables genuine dispute and deliberation about what is the shared good in this place for these people at this time as against the predetermination of what that good might consist of via some theoretical construction or the refusal of the possibility of such a shared good within the interest-based politics of either liberalism or identity politics.

Listening as an ecclesial-political act begins the process of identification by which we become neighbors to others as opposed to family members, strangers, or enemies. Being a neighbor is not a condition or state of being or pre-assigned role but a contingent and contextual relationship that requires listening to who is before one. Unlike such things as family, class, ethnicity, or gender, I cannot predetermine who is my neighbor. Neighbors have neither assigned social identities (e.g., father, sister, etc.) nor institutionally constructed roles (e.g., doctor, postman, information technology (IT) officer, etc.). Rather, as Wannenwetsch points out, the possibility of being a neighbor speaks of a freedom that transcends all natural ties and functional roles.[172] As the parable of the Good Samaritan indicates, on occasion the call of the neighbor supersedes prior commitments and demands, whether professional, religious, social, or political. We can encounter a neighbor in any one of our roles. Conversely, we have to constantly learn how to be a neighbor.[173] Listening, primarily in and through worship, but also in our encounters with strangers, is the curriculum of neighborliness.

As already suggested, listening, rather than simply being either active or passive, involves a process of active contemplation. Listening to others in order to hear them as neighbors and discern goods in common requires much hard work. It involves precisely the kind of organizing, mobilizing, and forging contexts of listening through such exercises as one-on-ones and listening campaigns that the Industrial Areas Foundation undertakes. Likewise, listening to scripture requires real labor, for exegesis, in its fullest form, is an ecclesial event rather than either a scholarly or individual undertaking. Something of the visceral nature of the work involved can be overheard in Augustine's sermons when he states: "I forgot how long I talked. Now the psalm is over, and I can tell from the stench in here that I have given too long a sermon!"[174] Or "Pay attention so that, in the name of Christ, we may be strong Christians. There is only a little of the psalm which remains. Let's not flag."[175] Augustine himself points to the need for such common work in the pursuit of understanding. At the end of a homily on Psalm 147 he contrasts the bodily fatigue of his congregation to the crowds flocking into the amphitheater. Pointing to the discipline and stamina of those who patiently study Scripture he asks: "If [those in the theater] had to stand so long, would they still be at their show?"[176] As Michael McCarthy notes: "Not only does the ecclesial performance of Augustine and his congregation frame [Augustine's] exegesis, but the practice of that exegesis itself forms the *ecclesia* in a way that is theologically significant." For McCarthy, following developments in ritual studies and J. L. Austin's speech-act theory, Augustine's actual practice of interpreting Scripture with his community makes the church: it generates an *ecclesia* at a distinct historical moment.[177] Whether sung or said antiphonally, the recitation of the psalms in the daily offices is another example of communally performed reception and interpretation.[178] Two further examples can be added to illustrate the point. The call and response tradition of preaching in African-American churches is a particularly dramatic enactment of exegesis as an ecclesial event, as is the Congregationalist pattern of each member bringing a word or testimony to the assembly. However, all acts of reading and interpreting Scripture communally should properly embody the same logic of mutually constitutive proclamation and reception and necessarily requires work on behalf of both readers and listeners or preacher and congregation together for the Word of God to be heard.[179]

The primary link between Alinsky's approach and the church is through worship, for in worship a people is formed who can trust the words of others and who have faith in the possibilities of common action with and for others. And if worship is one context in which we learn what it is to be a neighbor, wherever we are, whatever we are doing, and whoever is before us, then the kind of democratic politics envisaged by Alinsky is another. For it requires actively listening to and forming relationships with those not like us and with whom we disagree. It is a means by which we encounter strangers – sometimes as their guest and at other times as their host.[180] This guest–host dynamic has a very practical outworking: community organization meetings are held in churches, mosques, schools, and a wide variety of other settings.[181] Community organizing literally draws you out of what is familiar and invites those who are unfamiliar into your sacred spaces.[182] It is my contention that Alinsky's approach constitutes a form that Christian hospitality may take as it seeks the welfare of Babylon.[183] It is a form of common life by which we expose our loves to others and struggle for conversion, the conversion of ourselves so that we may encounter others as neighbors and thence genuinely love them rather than patronize, co-opt, or ignore them, and the conversion of others so that they may begin to know the world as God's good but fallen and now redeemed creation.[184]

What the reflection on listening in relation to community organizing has suggested is the centrality of listening to the formation of faithful political action. The assessment of community organizing in this chapter serves as a case study on what it might mean in practice to listen to others in order to discern who is your neighbor, what goods you might have in common with them, and how you might encounter God in relation with them. In addition, a case was made for the importance of listening to Scripture and the symbiosis of listening to others and listening to the voice of Christ speaking through Scripture. Community organizing has, at times, incorporated such a symbiotic process into its political action. However, at present I have simply pointed to the need and a rationale for listening to Scripture in relation to faithful political witness. Part of the next chapter constitutes a case study in what it might mean to listen to Scripture in practice in relation to a contested political issue, that of the duty of care to refugees. Its emphasis is less on how one might encounter the other in practice and more on how we discern the Word of God in order to recognize the other as our neighbor. A key issue touched on in this chapter but developed further in the next is the interrelationship between worship, Scripture, and faithful political action. Finally, the centrality of listening to the formation of faithful political action will be examined and developed further in the conclusion where its relationship with the formation of just judgments and neighbor love will be a key point of reflection.

Summary

The extensive engagement with Alinsky by way of Augustine and Maritain's conception of Christian democracy helps establish the terms and conditions of faithful political witness in the contemporary context and thereby how to resist the temptations confronting the church today. Alinsky's approach does not look to the state as a primary means of addressing the needs of the poor and the politically marginalized. Neither does it view the provision of human need as simply a response to pastoral or humanitarian concern. Determining need is always, in the first instance, a political judgment that requires organization and power for those whose need is to be cared for. A community organization is a means by which the economically poor and politically marginalized can address their situation rather than be made dependent on either state welfare or private charity, for such an organization enables them to forge a place from which to act in the political arena rather than simply be acted upon by state technocrats and paternalistic elites. Community organizing is a way of enabling the participation of ordinary citizens in the deliberations over shared resources. It envisages decisions over the distribution of resources as public and not ones that should be resolved in the first instance by either market-based mechanisms or technocratic, administrative solutions. Community organization thus seeks the restoration of democratic politics as the way to enable just judgments to be made in response to questions of distribution and the allocation of resources.

There is, however, a constant danger crouching at the door of Christian involvement in community organizing and other forms of democratic initiatives. Involvement can slip into a grooming of the church to envision itself first, as a voluntary society within a wider civil society, and second, as contributing to a superordinate project such as social cohesion, democratic renewal, or progressive politics. However, the link between Christianity and democracy is best understood as an exploratory and mutually disciplining partnership. Democracy finds resources from which it may be reconstituted as a form of "politicalness" that pursues justice for all the members of a particularly polity. Democracy within a context of religious and moral plurality provokes Christians to practice hospitality, demanding they move beyond relationships of condescension or co-option, and recognizing the civic realm as mutual ground within which goods in common can be discovered and acted upon. At the same time, as bearers of practices and beliefs that uphold the dignity of persons, Christianity and democracy are both means of contradicting the logic of commodification and instrumentalization at work in capitalism and the modern state.

To this day, much community organizing focuses beyond the needs of particular groups or sectional interests both by seeking changes to corporate and state policies and by reweaving social relationships through building links between institutions. Community organizing constitutes an explicit refusal of the politics of recognition, building as it does coalitions between incommensurable and divergent religious and civil society groups at the same time as forming a political space in which different groups can contribute to deliberation about goods in common, each in their own way. Alinsky's approach provides a process for discovering and acting upon goods in common, a process that works against the antagonistic logic of identity politics. A central way in which a politics of the common good is forged is the facilitation of listening to and forming relationships with those not like us and with whom we disagree. Community organizing is a means by which we encounter strangers – sometimes as their guest and at other times as their host. It is thus a form of tent making where a place is formed in which hospitality is given and received between multiple traditions. The hearing of others' interests and concerns in the context of ongoing relationship and the recognition that everyone in the tent occupies the same mutual ground fosters the sense that in each other's welfare we find our own. Thus, as a process for discovering and acting upon goods in common, community organizing works against the competitive dynamics and interest group politics of multiculturalism.

Sheldon Wolin, Alasdair MacIntyre, and William Connolly are among a slew of political philosophers who point to the need for some kind of local politics and a genuine communal and institutional plurality (or what Milbank calls the "advocacy of complex space") as a means of holding in check the centralizing and totalizing thrust of the liberal, capitalist, nation-state.[185] My argument is that the relationship between Christianity and

Alinsky's approach displays what such a corporatist and "complex" politics might entail within a postsecularist political context. However, from a Christian perspective, community organizing is best viewed as a political form of ascetic discipline that enables churches to resist the temptation to be either co-opted by the state, compete with other faith groups, or conform to the market. However, it is not the case that community organizing constitutes the *only* way of faithfully pursuing a just and generous political order. Rather, it provides a particularly generative and telling case study in the pitfalls and possibilities confronting Christian political witness in the contemporary context. Alinsky's approach is suggestive of ways and means of embodying faithful witness under present conditions. As a form of democratic politics it is a secular work – in the Augustinian sense – that does not demand that participants profess Christian truths; rather, as Maritain puts it: "It allows among its characteristic features a pluralism which makes possible the *convivium* of Christians and non-Christians in the same body politic."[186] What the assessment of community organizing unveils is that while the emerging relationship between church and state tends toward co-option, other, more constructive ways are available, ways that simultaneously allow the church to be the church, cooperate with religious others in pursuit of earthly goods in common, and contradict the totalizing tendencies of the market and the state.

So far it is the relationship between Christianity and contemporary politics at a local level that has been the primary focus. In the next chapter the focus will be on the conditions and possibilities of faithful witness at a national level but set within the context of global political developments.

Notes

1 www.industrialareasfoundation.org/iafabout/about.htm (accessed August 20, 2007). An IAF affiliate was set up in Sydney, Australia in 2007.
2 See Sanford D. Horwitt, *Let Them Call Me Rebel: Saul Alinsky – His Life and Legacy* (New York: Alfred Knopf, 1989). Horwitt does not focus on Alinsky's experience of Jewish life in Chicago, but Irving Cutler, in his study of the Jews in Chicago, draws out how important were traditions of self-organization in the Maxwell Street area where Alinsky grew up. However, by the time Alinsky left the University of Chicago, these were in rapid decline. Irving Cutler, *The Jews of Chicago: From Shtetl to Suburb* (Chicago, IL: University of Illinois Press, 1996).
3 Bernard Sheil, the Auxilary Roman Catholic Bishop of Chicago from 1928 to 1959, was a crucial figure when Alinsky was first developing his approach to community organizing (see Horwitt, *Let Them Call Me Rebel*). Ed Chambers,

who took over the running of the IAF after Alinsky's death, had been a Benedictine seminarian and spent time with Dorothy Day from the Catholic Worker Movement before joining Alinsky as an organizer (ibid., p. 326; for an autobiographical account of his theological training see Edward Chambers with Michael Cowan, *Roots for Radicals: Organizing for Power, Action and Justice* (New York: Continuum, 2004), pp. 91–4). This was not uncommon; many of the early organizers had a theological training, for example, Richard Harmon and Jeff Williams (Horwitt, *Let Them Call Me Rebel*, p. 398).

4   Both Sanford Horwitt's biography and studies of developments in community organizing since Alinsky's death (for example, Warren in *Dry Bones Rattling: Community Building to Revitalize American Democracy* (Princeton, NJ: Princeton University Press, 2001)) underline this point.

5   Saul Alinsky, *Reveille for Radicals* (New York: Vintage Books, 1969), p. 17.

6   Saul Alinsky, *Rules for Radicals: A Pragmatic Primer for Realistic Radicals* (New York: Vintage Books, 1989), p. 123.

7   Alinsky, *Reveille*, p. 50.

8   Ibid., p. 54.

9   Ibid.

10   Horwitt, *Let Them Call Me Rebel*, pp. 83–4.

11   For an account of how this worked in practice see Sanford Horwitt's account of the formation of the Back of the Yards Neighborhood Council amid the meat-packing district of Chicago and how Alinsky drew together the various ethnic groups and churches in that area. Horwitt, *Let Them Call Me Rebel*, pp. 56–76.

12   Understanding the life of the community involved, spending time observing and talking to local people in a kind of self-conscious ethnographic study, and drawing on demographic and other data to compile a profile of an area. Evidence for this is given in the extensive reports given by Alinsky and other organizers to the Archdiocese of Chicago in the Industrial Areas Foundation Archive, University of Illinois in Chicago Library, Special Collections.

13   Alinsky, *Reveille*, p. 135.

14   Ibid., 228. Alinsky, *Rules*, p. 59.

15   On this see Horwitt, *Let Them Call Me Rebel*, pp. 525–35; and Stephen C. Rose, "Saul Alinsky and His Critics," in *Citizen Participation in Urban Development. Vol. 1: Concept and Issues*, ed. Hans B. C. Spiegel (Washington, DC: NTL Institute for Applied Behavioural Science, 1968), pp. 162–83.

16   Ernesto Cortes develops the clearest articulation of this dimension of broad-based community organizing. Ernesto Cortes, "Reweaving the Fabric: The Iron Rule and the IAF Strategy for Power and Politics," in *Interwoven Destinies: Cities and the Nation*, ed. Henry Cisneros (New York: W. W. Norton, 1993), pp. 295–319.

17   For examples of this in practice see Michael Gecan's account of the Nehemiah Homes project and the Living Wage Campaign in Michael Gecan, *Going Public: An Organizer's Guide to Citizen Action* (New York: Anchor Books, 2002). Mark Warren notes how this kind of approach has been extended to

other health and educational initiatives in the USA. Warren, *Dry Bones Rattling*, pp. 259–60.

18 Alinsky, *Reveille*, p. 6. Elsewhere Alinsky uses the term "orderly revolution" to describe his approach. Ibid., p.198.

19 Sheldon Wolin, "Archaism, Modernity and *Democracy in America*," and "Tending and Intending a Constitution: Bicentennial Misgivings," in *The Presence of the Past: Essays on the State and Constitution* (Baltimore: John Hopkins University Press, 1989), pp. 66–81, 82–99. Wolin's work is a key reference point for many involved in community organizing. Ed Chambers goes so far as to describe Wolin as "America's finest political teacher." Chambers, *Roots for Radicals*, p. 125.

20 Sheldon Wolin, *Politics and Vision: Continuity and Innovation in Western Political Thought*, exp. edn (Princeton, NJ: Princeton University Press, 2004), p. 603.

21 Ibid., pp. 604–5.

22 For an account of this see Mark Santow, "Running in Place: Saul Alinsky, Race and Community Organizing," in Marion Orr, ed., *Transforming the City: Community Organizing and the Challenges of Political Change* (Lawrence, KS: University of Kansas Press, 2007), pp. 28–55.

23 See, for example, Alinsky's critique of anti-poverty programs that seek to address economic poverty without addressing the poverty of power. Saul Alinsky, "Behind the Mask," in *American Child: Which Way Community Action Programs?* 47.4 (1965), 7–9. Wolin is equally critical of welfarism, noting how it has become an enemy of democratic participation. Wolin, "Archaism, Modernity and *Democracy in America*," p. 79.

24 Alinsky, *Reveille*, p. 175.

25 Chambers, *Roots for Radicals*, p. 7.

26 Ibid., p. 200; p. 213.

27 Chambers, *Roots for Radicals*, p. 14.

28 However, community organizing is sometimes criticized for avoiding contentious subjects related to race, class, gender, and sexuality that might divide groups involved in the organization (see for example, Romand Coles, *Beyond Gated Politics: Reflections for the Possibility of Democracy* (Minneapolis, MN: University of Minnesota Press, 2005), p. 236). However, the issue for Alinsky is not one of how to avoid deep disagreements but how, amid such disagreements and incommensurable positions, one forges a common life and identifies goods in common. Disagreements are all too obvious in the contemporary context; what is difficult is the identification of connections that are neither commodities nor determined and mediated by the state. Moreover, as Wolin notes: "A society that agrees on some matters is more likely to accept policies dealing with more controversial subjects." Wolin, *Politics and Vision*, p. 59.

29 Alinsky, *Rules*, p. 21.

30 Alinsky, *Reveille*, p. 156.

31 See, for example, the parables of "Honest Joe," "Big Jim," and "Tycoon." Ibid., pp. 110–46.

32 Ibid., p.18. Although uncited by Alinsky, the text is Deuteronomy 32.41–42. These two quotations may seem contradictory. However, parallels can be drawn with two key motifs of God envisaged in the prophetic tradition of the Old Testament that are directly analogous: that of the Divine warrior-king who enacts his rule of justice and that of the Divine shepherd, pastorally leading his people out of captivity. See, for example, Isaiah 40.10–11.

33 We can note in passing that the combination of parable and rule as the primary mode of explication is closer to the genre of the Gospels than to political theory.

34 Romand Coles points to a central feature of Alinsky's trickster politics: it involves playing an "interest group liberal game" with an eye to cultivating a "radical democratic game." Alinsky is not proposing some kind of Niebuhurian interest- group politics, but a trickster politics that establishes a means through which divergent groups can be drawn into deliberating upon goods in common. Romand Coles, "Of Tensions and Tricksters: Grassroots Democracy between Theory and Practice," *Perspectives on Politics* 4.3 (2006), 547–61.

35 Alinsky, *Rules*, p. 128.

36 Ibid., p. 141.

37 For Alinsky the suggestion outlined here was often repeated, sometimes with the assertion that it had actually taken place. It seemed to function for him as a kind of paradigmatic story or parable that encapsulated his ethos.

38 Alinsky, *Rules*, p. 130. As Alinsky points out, the classic statement of polarization comes from Jesus: "He that is not with me is against me" (Luke 11.23).

39 There are parallels between Alinsky's work in the area of popular education and that of Paolo Friere. However, perhaps a closer parallel is between the political dramas that Alinsky's approach stages, dramas that redraw the official representation and organization of power, and the "forum theatre" of Augusto Boal. See Augusto Boal, *Theatre of the Oppressed*, trans. Charles and Maria-Odila Leal McBride (London: Pluto Press, 1979) and *Legislative Theatre: Using Performance to Make Politics* (London: Routledge, 1998).

40 *Bricolage* and de Certeau's distinction between tactics and strategies constitute the basis of his account of trickster politics as a response to powerlessness. Michel de Certeau, *The Practice of Everyday Life*, trans. Steven Rendall (Berkeley, CA: University of California Press, 1988), pp. 29–39.

41 Alinsky, *Rules*, p. 152.

42 It is this that distinguishes Alinsky from de Certeau for whom trickster politics only ever remains a form of oppositional subcultural resistance rather than opening up possibilities of a genuinely shared world of action. For a critique of Certeau on this point see Chapter 4.

43 Alinsky, *Rules*, p. 130.

44 For a discussion of the distinction between community organizing and social or protest movement see Chambers, *Roots for Radicals*, pp. 129–31; and Leo Penta, "Islands of Democratic Practice: Organizing for Local and Regional Power in the USA," Paper presented at the Biannual European Conference of the Inter-University Consortium for International Social Development in Cracow, Poland, September 24, 1999.

45   I am grateful for discussions with Hans Ulrich for helping to frame Alinsky's approach in this way.

46   O'Donovan, *The Desire of the Nations*, p. 215.

47   Warren, *Dry Bones Rattling*, p. 30–6.

48   Contrary to the continuity I outline, both Warren and key organizers within IAF have a more disjunctive reading, seeing a distinct shift from 1972 onward when Ed Chambers takes over the running of IAF. I maintain that what occurs is a process of consolidation, intensification, and a making explicit of elements already present with Alinsky rather than a new direction. For example, perhaps the most significant shift is seen to be the move to see religious institutions as more than instruments for mobilizing resources and instead to organize around their values (for example, see Warren, *Dry Bones Rattling*, p. 47). Yet, while Alinsky could be cavalier and rhetorically utilitarian about his relationship with churches, his correspondence with Jacques Maritain reveals a deep sympathy between his political vision and developments in Catholic social teaching, and a concern, for example, with how his work contributed to ecumenical relations. See his letter to Jacques Maritain, May 15, 1962 in *The Philosopher and the Provocateur: The Correspondence of Jacques Maritain and Saul Alinsky*, ed. Bernard Doering (Notre Dame, IN: University of Notre Dame Press, 1994), p. 89.

49   Quoted from J. Rick Altemose and Dawn A. McCarty, "Organizing for Democracy through Faith-Based Institutions: The Industrial Areas Foundation in Action," in Jill M. Bystydzienski and Steven P. Schacht, eds., *Forging Radical Alliances Across Difference: Coalition Politics for the New Millennium* (New York: Rowman & Littlefield, 2001), p. 135.

50   Chambers states that he innovated the "one-on-one" and the emphasis on the importance of listening and relationship building as central tools of organizing. Chambers, *Roots for Radicals*, pp. 44–9. It is perhaps fairer to say that Chambers systematized and rendered explicit something Alinsky was already doing.

51   For examples of how the relationship between tension and negotiation works in practice see Richard Wood, *Faith in Action: Religion, Race, and Democratic Organizing in America* (Chicago, IL: University of Chicago Press, 2002), pp. 43–9.

52   Evidence for this consensus is seen in the work of R. A. Markus who has recently changed his position so as to concur with O'Donovan's view that it is history rather than political authority that is neutral. See Robert Markus, *Christianity and the Secular* (Notre Dame, IN: University of Notre Dame Press, 2006), pp. 28–30, 51. There continues to be considerable divergence as to the scope for the legitimate role of political authority after Christ, a debate that hinges on the role of political authority in *paideia* or the cultural and moral formation of persons. Markus reads John Milbank as running counter to the consensus on the neutrality of the *saeculum* (ibid., p. 41). However, it seems that Markus conflates Milbank's understanding of the earthly city with his conception of the *saeculum*. Milbank's view of the earthly city as a realm given over to "unconditionally bad ends" is not inimical with viewing the *saeculum* as neutral; however,

it does place him at the opposite pole to Markus on the question of the role of political authority in relation to *paideia*. Milbank, *Theology and Social Theory: Beyond Secular Reason* (Oxford: Blackwell, 1993), p. 406.

53   This is to summarize what I take to be Oliver O'Donovan's reading of Augustine in *Desire of the Nations*.

54   For how Augustine's eschatology directly draws on Paul's eschatology, especially the Pauline account of the "principalities and powers," see Markus, *Christianity and the Secular*, pp. 14–17, 55–6.

55   Charles Mathewes, "Faith, Hope, and Agony: Christian Political Participation Beyond Liberalism," *Annual of the Society of Christian Ethics* 21 (2001), p. 140. The work of John Howard Yoder is one of the clearest articulations of this view, although he draws the same conclusion directly in reference to Pauline eschatology. John Howard Yoder, *The Politics of Jesus*, 2nd edn (Grand Rapids, MI: Eerdmans, 1994), pp. 134–61.

56   Markus, *Christianity and the Secular*, p. 37.

57   The implications of Markus's positing of the secular sphere as autonomous can be seen in his advocacy of Augustine as a proto-political liberal whose work foreshadows Rawls's concept of "overlapping consensus" (Ibid., p. 67–8). Yet a Rawlsian account inherently undermines the Augustinian conception of the city of God as the truly public and just society. Even though Markus recognizes that common objects of love between pagans and Christians can emerge in politics, faith is for the sacred sphere and the secular is for politics. Markus thus restates liberalism's public/private divide and thereby denies the possibility of the church constituting a public in and of itself.

58   One detects in Markus echoes of Richard Niebuhr's *Christ and Culture* and the positing of culture as a similarly ambiguous but autonomous sphere of relations in need of transformation. For a critique of Niebuhr on this point see: John Howard Yoder, "How H. Richard Niebuhr Reasoned: A Critique of *Christ and Culture*," in *Authentic Transformation: A New Vision of Christ and Culture*, eds. Glen Stassen et al. (Nashville, TN: Abingdon, 1996), pp. 31–90.

59   Eric Gregory, *Politics and the Order of Love: An Augustinian Ethic of Democratic Citizenship* (Chicago, IL: University of Chicago Press, 2008), p. 79.

60   Markus, *Christianity and the Secular*, p. 56. Markus states: "The agencies and institutions of society cannot serve to promote man's ultimate good; they serve only as means to turn human ferocity to the fostering of a precarious order, some basic cohesion which Augustine called 'the earthly peace.'" Ibid. Some political philosophers, most notably William Connolly, criticize this aspect of Augustine's work, especially the subordination all things to the love of God. For a defense of Augustine's eudaimonism and his conception of the "use" of the temporal political order see Charles Mathewes, *A Theology of Public Life* (Cambridge: Cambridge University Press, 2007), pp. 88–94; and Gregory, *Politics and the Order of Love*, pp. 324–62.

61   From the writing of Genesis as a alternative creation mythos to the *Enuma Elish* to the refusal to bow the knee to the Roman emperor as the Pantocrator to the

Barmen Declaration, it is a foundational political insight of Christianity to deconstruct and offer an alternative to any instance of *cosmopolis*; that is, the writing of the political order into the cosmic order so that a historically contingent form of political rule is inscribed with an immutable character and posited as inevitable and "natural."

62   Augustine, *City of God*, XIX, 24.

63   Augustine, *City of God*, IV, 4.

64   Markus, *Christianity and the Secular*, p. 44, although it is important to note that defining Augustine's conception of justice in the earthly city as "imperfectly just" is itself problematic. Augustine argues in *City of God* XIX, 23–7 that true justice does not exist without true piety. The implication of this is that knowledge of justice is not possible outside of knowledge and worship of God through and in Christ. Thus the order found in Rome or any other instance of the earthly city is not just. However, this does not mean that its order is wholly evil; it is an earthly peace. But this earthly peace should not be viewed as on a continuum with the just order of the city of God. For a detailed examination of Augustine's conception of the relationship between justice and the "justice" of the order found in the earthly city see: Robert Dodaro, *Christ and the Just Society in the Thought of Augustine* (Cambridge: Cambridge University Press, 2004), p. 27–114.

65   Augustine, *City of God*, XV, 21.

66   Ibid., XIX, 17.

67   Milbank, *Theology and Social Theory*, pp. 406–8.

68   Ibid., p. 408. See also John Milbank, "On Complex Space," in *The Word Made Strange: Theory, Language, Culture* (Oxford: Blackwell, 1997), pp. 268–92.

69   Alinsky, *Rules*, p. 11. For Augustine's account of the judge see *City of God*, XIX, 6.

70   Alinsky, *Rules*, pp. 25–6. Alinsky is here quoting Jacques Maritain, *Man and the State* (Washington, DC: Catholic University of America Press, 1998), pp. 62–3. For Maritain's theological account of the relationship between political ethics – or the relationship between means and ends in politics, the Incarnation, and the necessity of working within the conditions and possibilities of history – see *Integral Humanism: Temporal and Spiritual Problems of the New Christendom*, trans. Joseph Evans (New York: Charles Scribner's Sons, 1968), pp. 246–52.

71   *Rules*, p. 14. Augustine's somber picture of life in the earthly city is not Manichean. Rather, it must be held in tension with his account of the reality and beauty of earthly goods (for example, see *City of God*, XXII, 24). In addition to the quote from James, Alinsky also uses the metaphor of Yin and Yang to describe the conflict between good and evil and at times seems to suggest that good and evil are complementary (*Rules*, p. 15). However, his own activism and commitment to challenging evil so that it does not triumph would seem to contradict such a conclusion. Yet this ambiguity is not wholly alien to Christianity. Job and Ecclesiastes have similar ambiguities and it is even more pronounced in the early Patristic ransom theory of atonement.

72 Alinsky, *Rules*, pp. 14, 22.

73 A parallel can be drawn here with Derrida's "messianicity without messianism." Jacques Derrida, *Acts of Religion* (London: Routledge, 2002), p. 56. See also John D. Caputo, *The Prayers and Tears of Jacques Derrida: Religion without Religion* (Bloomington, IN: Indiana University Press, 1997).

74 Walter Brueggemann, *Hopeful Imagination: Prophetic Voices in Exile* (Philadelphia: Fortress Press, 1986), pp. 10–31. Brueggemann's account of the prophetic hopeful imagination draws directly on Jeremiah 29–30.

75 Chambers, *Roots for Radicals*, p. 22. As will be outlined in Chapter 4, to live "in-between" is the normative condition of the Christian life.

76 Augustine, *City of God*, XII, 28; Alinsky, *Rules*, p. 59. See also Chambers, *Roots for Radicals*, pp. 31–4.

77 Mathewes, "Faith, Hope, and Agony," p. 137. See also Mathewes, *A Theology of Public Life*, pp. 274–6.

78 This is succinctly summarized in Gregory's account of the "Augustinian story." Gregory, *Politics and the Order of Love*, pp. 21–2. See also Chambers, *Roots for Radicals*, pp. 27–31.

79 As Markus notes, the basis of this in Augustine is his eschatology which constitutes the negation of ideological and utopian programs. R. A. Markus, *Saeculum: History and Society in the Theology of St Augustine* (Cambridge: Cambridge University Press, 1970), p. 173.

80 Totalitarian political systems, for example, Nazi Germany, would seem to be the obvious exception to this claim. Yet even here, a distinction must be made between the evil of the system as such and the political life present within it which was multifarious rather than monolithic or consistently evil throughout. As Scripture testifies, within the total depravity of Sodom and Gomorrah good was a possibility and good people existed, and beyond that, Nineveh is capable of repentance. We must not be like Jonah and suffer a failure of imagination and sympathy by first limiting the sovereignty, power, and mercy of God, second, refusing to believe that repentance is possible even in the most unlikely candidates, and third, defining others, even evil or repugnant others, as outside a common humanity. For an exploration of these themes in the book of Jonah see Jacqueline Lapsley, " 'When Mercy Seasons Justice': Jonah and the Common Good," in *In Search of the Common Good*, eds. Patrick Miller and Dennis McCann (London: T&T Clark, 2005), pp. 41–57.

81 As Bonhoeffer points out, both constitute forms of hatred of the world because both refuse the possibility of change and redemption. Dietrich Bonhoeffer, *Ethics*, trans. Reinhard Krauss et al., ed. Clifford Green. Vol. 6, *Dietrich Bonhoeffer Works* (Minneapolis, MN: Fortress Press, 2005), pp. 153–7.

82 Gecan, *Going Public*, p. xix.

83 There is an explicit echo here of Bonhoeffer's reconfigured Lutheran account of the mandates. Bonhoeffer, *Ethics*, pp. 388–408. Family, work, church, and government are here understood as those distinct yet mutually constitutive and co-inhering spheres of life and responsibility in which humans discover, respond

to, and play with the different ways in which creation is an occasion for communion with God and others. This theme of the vocation to love God and neighbor will be developed further in Chapter 4 in relation to the discussion of ordinary politics.

84 Alasdair MacIntyre, "Politics, Philosophy and the Common Good," in *The Macintyre Reader*, ed. Kelvin Knight (London: Polity Press, 1998), pp. 235–52; Karl Polanyi, *The Great Transformation: The Political and Economic Origins of Our Time*, 2nd Beacon Paperback edn (Boston, MA: Beacon Press, 2002). For how Alinsky's approach intersects with Polanyi see Maurice Glasman, "Alinsky, Abraham and Aristotle," unpublished paper.

85 Bretherton, *Hospitality as Holiness: Christian Witness Amid Moral Diversity* (Aldershot: Ashgate, 2006), esp. chs. 4 and 5.

86 O'Donovan, *Desire of the Nations*, pp. 83–8. Even though cooperation between empire and the People of God was possible, O'Donovan emphasizes how in Jeremiah, the subsequent development of the prophetic tradition, and in the Gospels, the People of God are neither to see the rule of empire as compatible with the rule of God nor to view the coexistence of Israel and Babylon as a permanent condition. Quite the reverse, a central dynamic in both the Prophets' and Jesus' ministry is the refusal of empire's own deluded self-descriptions and pointing to the instability and transitory nature of all forms of political authority and rule other than God's.

87 Coles, *Beyond Gated Politics*, p. 65. My advocacy of hospitality is analogous to Cole's own conception of "receptive generosity."

88 Luc Boltanski and Eve Chiapello, *The New Spirit of Capitalism*, trans. Gregory Elliot (London: Verso, 2006).

89 Coles, *Beyond Gated Politics*, p. 222.

90 Ben Quash, " 'Deep Calls To Deep': Reading Scripture in a Multi-Faith Society," in Andrew Walker and Luke Bretherton, eds., *Remembering our Future: Explorations in Deep Church* (Milton Keynes: Paternoster Press, 2007), pp. 114–17. For a wider account of Scriptural Reasoning see David Ford and C. C. Pecknold, *The Promise of Scriptural Reasoning* (Oxford: Blackwell, 2006).

91 For a full account of hospitality see Bretherton, *Hospitality as Holiness*, especially ch. 5.

92 Some hospitality is reciprocal: each hosts the other in turn. However, the practice of hospitality is more often than not undertaken in a situation where one party is in a position of strength and the other in a position of vulnerability or weakness. There may be forms of reciprocity but undergirding it is an asymmetry of relationship. This points to the insight of Georg Simmel, who in his essay *The Stranger* noted that the stranger is not one who is geographically distant from us; that is to be in a situation of non-relation (Georg Simmel, *The Sociology of Georg Simmel*, trans. Kurt H. Wolff (New York: Free Press, 1950), pp. 402–8). Strangers are those with whom we share the same space but who are different from us. They are constituted by a coordination of simultaneous nearness and distance. Hence, as Simmel points out, the European Jews were

the paradigmatic stranger. However, this is now the situation of everyone in plural, liberal democratic polities wherein multiple modernities coincide. We encounter strangers (be they people of other religious traditions, of different cultures) in schools, hospitals, political institutions, and even in our households. Two temptations seem to beset members of liberal polities when they meet the stranger. First, we can objectify the other, creating a form of abstract relationship by which to manage and coordinate relations between generalized others in order that we never really meet concrete others. This is, in effect, what Rawls's conception of public reason does. Second, we are tempted to take advantage of our strength as an opportunity to exclude (as nationalists do) or demand some form of tribute (as those who demand assimilation do). By contrast, a Christian account of hospitality, while often not practiced, does demand making room for the vulnerable other a priority and hold open the possibility of a new form of life emerging through the interaction.

93 Horwitt, *Let Them Call Me Rebel*, p. 531.
94 Rose, "Saul Alinsky and His Critics," pp. 173–80; Jay MacLeod, *Community Organising: A Practical and Theological Appraisal* (London: Church Action, 1993), pp. 9–10; Dennis A. Jacobsen, *Doing Justice: Congregations and Community Organizing* (Minneapolis, MN: Augsburg Fortress, 2001), p. 40; Stephen Hart notes that alongside Catholic social thought and liberation theology, community organizing builds on the work of Niebuhr: Stephen Hart, *Cultural Dilemmas of Progressive Politics: Styles of Engagement Among Grassroots Activists* (Chicago, IL: University of Chicago Press, 2001).
95 There is an unaddressed issue of the morality of Alinsky's approach. It must suffice to say Alinsky is neither Niebuhrian nor a utilitarian. A full analysis of Alinsky's trickster politics, one that encompasses an assessment of his conceptions of power, self-love, and his account of the relationship between means and ends will be developed in due course. A related dimension of Alinsky's political ethics is his conception of self-interest and whether pursuit of self-interest can be tied to pursuit of the common good. This issue is examined in Chapter 4 in relation to fair trade as a form of political consumerism.
96 His appreciation of democracy is best summarized in his famous *aperçu*: "Man's capacity for justice make democracy possible; but man's inclination to injustice makes democracy necessary." Reinhold Niebuhr, *The Children of Light and the Children of Darkness* (London: Nisbet & Co., 1945), p. xiii. See also Reinhold Niebuhr , "Democracy, Secularism, and Christianity," in *Christian Realism and Political Problems* (London: Faber and Faber, 1953), pp. 99–100. For Alinsky's own statement on the synchronicity of Christianity and democracy see Alinsky, *Rules*, p. 12.
97 For a critique of Niebuhr's conception of original sin and the lack of realism in his social ethics see John Milbank, "The Poverty of Niebuhrianism," in *The Word Made Strange*, pp. 233–54.
98 Niebuhr does envisage there being a direct relationship between sacrificial love and justice. In a reply to his critics, he states, "I have spent a good part of my life

validating the love ethic as final on the one hand, and trying to prove on the other hand that it must and can include all the discriminate judgments and commitments which we may broadly define as commitments in the cause of justice." However, he continued to maintain that while sacrificial love, mutual love, or self-interest and justice were related (sacrificial love being the fulfillment of the latter), sacrificial love remained irrelevant to thinking about the collective life of humans. Reinhold Niebuhr, "Reply to Interpretation and Criticism," *Reinhold Neibuhr: His Religious, Social and Political Thought*, eds. Charles Kegley and Rober Bretall (New York: MacMillan, 1956), p. 450.

99   Reinhold Niebuhr, *Moral Man and Immoral Society: A Study in Ethics and Politics* (New York: Scribner, 1932), p. 253.

100   Ibid., p. xxiii.

101   Reinhold Niebuhr, *The Nature and Destiny of Man: A Christian Interpretation*, 2 vols. (New York: Scribner & Sons, 1941–3), vol. 1, p. 298.

102   Niebuhr himself admits that while he had a growing appreciation of the value of the church as a "community of grace" where "life is kept open for the final word of God's judgment to break the pride of men," this was only ever a "growing appreciation," one immediately tempered by a fear of what comes from the egoism of the church. Niebuhr, "Reply to Interpretation and Criticism," p. 437.

103   For more extensive theological critiques of Niebuhr see Robert Song, *Christianity and Liberal Society* (Oxford: Clarendon, 1997), pp. 76–84; and Stanley Hauerwas, *With the Grain of the Universe: The Church's Witness and Natural Theology* (London: SCM Press, 2001), pp. 113–40. Even if one follows the more positive assessment of Neibuhr's work offered by Langdon Gilky, the role of the church is still minimal. Langdom Gilkey, *On Neibuhr: A Theological Study* (Chicago, IL: University of Chicago Press, 2001).

104   Hauerwas, *With the Grain of the Universe*, p. 122.

105   Alinsky, *Rules*, p. 12.

106   It should be noted, however, that Maritain's own conception of the relationship between the church and state is itself highly problematic. The thrust of the critique of Maritain's conception of the church in relation to the state is that he tends to spiritualize the church as a social body and thereby underemphasize the extent to which the church is itself a polity or *res publica* that forms and socializes human bodies in ways that are very different to those of the modern nation-state. As Cavanaugh puts it: "[T]he key difficulty with Maritain's project is that he makes the Christian community the repository of purely supernatural virtues which stands outside of time, and thus interiorizes and individualizes the Gospel. Because he has sequestered political virtue from any direct habituation in Christian community, the state becomes that community of habituation, the pedagogue of virtue." William Cavanaugh, *Torture and Eucharist: Theology, Politics and the Body of Christ* (Oxford: Blackwell, 1998), p. 195. For the full extent of Cavanaugh's penetrating critique see William Cavanaugh, pp. 177–202. See also Daniel Bell, *Liberation Theology*

after the End of History: The Refusal to Cease Suffering (London: Routledge, 2001), pp. 46–50.

107 Doering, *The Philosopher and the Provocateur*, p. 20.

108 Doering, "Introduction," *The Philosopher and the Provocateur*, pp. xi–xxxviii.

109 Maritain, *Man and the State*, pp. 22–3; *Integral Humanism*, pp. 162–76.

110 Doering, "Introduction," pp. xxii–xxiii.

111 *Integral Humanism*, pp. 108–111.

112 Maritain, *Man and the State*, pp. 54–75. Cavanaugh is particularly critical of Maritain on this point. At a practical level he thinks Maritain justifies the state suspending the rule of law in certain circumstances, thus opening the way to the legitimate use of torture. Theologically he understands it to be based on a mis-reading of Aquinas's understanding of the relationship between nature and supernature. Cavanaugh, *Torture and Eucharist*, pp. 181–7.

113 Doering, "Introduction," pp. xxxvi–xxxvii.

114 Maritain, *Man and the State*, pp. 139–46.

115 Maritain, *Integral Humanism*, pp. 163, 171.

116 Ibid., pp. 169–71, 186–95. A parallel distinction is made by Pius XI in *Quadragesimo Anno*, #94–6 as way of distinguishing a Christian corporatist vision of politics from fascist ones. On the Christian account, corporatist and personalist forms of civic association and economic organization are precisely a means of preventing the subsuming of all social relations to the political order. For a critique of modern Catholic social teaching, and of *Quadragesimo Anno* in particular, as giving too much ground to fascism and of needing far closer attention both to socialism and medieval forms of complex or gothic space see Milbank, "On Complex Space," pp. 268–92. An alternative to both Milbank's and Maritain's conception of corporatist politics and complex space can be derived from a recovery of a Calvinist covenantal tradition of democratic politics. However, the articulation of such an approach and how it compares with both Roman Catholic and contractarian conceptions of democratic politics awaits development beyond the scope of this book.

117 The term subsidiarity is itself problematic and needs to be used with care. As Oliver O'Donovan points out, when understood as a way of protecting the integrity and relative autonomy of parts in relation to an overarching and integrating whole, then the totality of the whole always assumes an overriding, or even totalizing claim in its movement toward an all-embracing unity. O'Donovan, *The Ways of Judgment* (Grand Rapids, MI: Eerdmans, 2005), p. 259. Thus, the need for Maritain and Catholic Social thought more generally to distinguish itself from Mussolini's fascism on this score is not incidental, but a problem intrinsic to the conceptualization of subsidiarity itself. O'Donovan's alternative proposal is to think of society not as a composite of constituent parts, each with their own subsidiary integrity, but as a sphere of spheres which connect not at their edges but at their center, "like a multitude of leaves finding a common source in a single stem." He goes on to say: "A society ... exists

simply as the coherence in which the spheres of communication flourish in relation to each other." Ibid., p. 253. A fruitful point for further comparison is between O'Donovan's proposal and that of William Connolly and others for a rhizomatic as against an arboreal pluralism; i.e., one where parts relate along a common stem, each with their own roots, as opposed to one where each part is subordinated to and an outgrowth of a common root.

118　See, for example, the critical comments by John Paul II of what he calls the "social assistance state" in *Centesimus Annus*, #48. Sheldon Wolin develops a more comprehensive critique of the liberal welfare state in relation to his problematic notion of "inverted totalitarianism" (Wolin, *Politics and Vision*, pp. 591–5). Wolin argues that in contrast to fascism and communism (which it developed in opposition to) where the population is mobilized in order to serve the state, within an inverted totalitarian state the population is depoliticized and demobilized via the mobility of money, goods, and people (ibid., p. 554). For Wolin, inverted totalitarianism is the paradigmatic form of "postmodern power" in that it is at once concentrated and disaggregated, combining centrifugal and centripetal forms of power (an example of the former is the formation of fragmentary identity interest groups; and an example of the latter is the power of large business corporations). Part of the problem with Wolin's account is that it precludes any possibility of constructive politics.

119　In a memo addressed to Rt Rev Msgr John O'Grady for Dominico Cardinal Tardini, Cardinal Secretary of State, Vatican City dated August 27, 1959 Alinsky outlines how his approach represents a better way of relating church to politics and addressing the concerns and needs of the urban poor than the current strategies undertaken by the Roman Catholic Church in Italy. He is particularly critical of the Church's over-alignment with the Christian Democratic Party. In the memo, Alinsky frames broad-based community organizing as the most effective way of diminishing the influence and rise of communism, citing his experience in the Back of the Yards Neighborhood Council as evidence for what he says. Box 9, file 128, Industrial Areas Foundation Archive.

120　Sheldon Wolin, "Contract and Birthright," in *The Presence of the Past*, p. 139. The priority of local politics over national politics is a question of degree. Local politics is the *primary* not the only arena of Christian political witness. Engagement in local politics is a precondition of faithful witness in other arenas at a national and global level. We learn at a local level what it means to tend goods in common, a learning that we then take to other contexts, most notably our concern for those many miles distant who are poorer and more afflicted than ourselves. Local politics is never an end in itself but situated within a horizon of cosmopolitan concern. Alinsky, *Reveille*, p. 167. A fuller account of the theological basis of the Christian cosmopolitan vision sketched here, and how it contrasts with both nationalism and a rationalist cosmopolitanism, is developed in Chapter 3 in relation to debates about immigration and refugees.

121 Doering, *The Philosopher and the Provocateur*, p. 105. This is a recurrent theme in Maritain's response to Alinsky. He writes in a letter to the Ford Foundation (May 27, 1951): "I am writing this on a personal basis because I have known Saul Alinsky for about 10 years and because I admire and love him as a great soul, a man of profound moral purity and burning energy, whose work I consider the only really new and really important democratic initiative taken in the social field today, and whose natural generosity is quickened, though he would not admit it, by genuine evangelical brotherly love." Box 12, file 179, Industrial Areas Foundation Archive. It was not just Maritain who made this connection, as the following quote from a letter (dated December 3, 1959) from Monsignor John O'Grady, then secretary to the National Conference of Catholic Charities, to the Cardinal-elect Most Rev. Albert G. Meyer, Archbishop of Chicago, puts it: "I am glad to know that you are showing a richly deserved appreciation of the kind of work that Saul Alinsky has been doing for some twenty years in the Back-of-Yards Neighborhood Council, and in more recent years throughout the country. There is hardly any other person who has been more helpful to me in developing a truly Christian point of view in regard to Catholic Charities in the United States than Mr Alinsky." Box 47, file 668, Industrial Areas Foundation Archive.

122 Ibid., p. 109.

123 Maritain, *Man and the State*, pp. 108–14. O'Donovan criticizes Maritain's conception of a "democratic secular faith" on the basis that it stymies the presentation of the Gospel to the state (*Desire of the Nations*, p. 219). Maritain is assiduous in reiterating the importance of presenting the Gospel to political authorities and reiterating how the Gospel is the basis for a truly human political life. However, O'Donovan's criticism does point to a real problem with Maritain's proposal: that is, his account of a democratic secular faith is akin to Rawls's conception of public reason in that it sets up a mediating discourse to which all must conform and thereby forestalls genuine political deliberation to which all may contribute each in their own way. William Cavanaugh notes that despite Maritain envisaging the "democratic secular faith" and human rights in general as inspired by the Gospel, the implication of Maritain's approach is to banish the Gospel from public discourse. Cavanaugh, *Torture and Eucharist*, p. 187.

124 O'Donovan, *Desire of the Nations*, p. 220. John Howard Yoder, "The Christian Case for Democracy," in *The Priestly Kingdom: Social Ethics as Gospel* (Notre Dame, IN: University of Notre Dame Press, 1984), pp. 151–71. There is a perhaps surprising overlap and parallelism between the arguments for democracy and involvement in democratic politics given by Yoder and O'Donovan. Both see democracy as a historically contingent and fallen political form of rule, but one that has a certain moral rhetoric and demands certain virtues with which the church can engage and which echo certain ecclesial imperatives, notably freedom of speech. For an outline of O'Donovan's

discussion of the benefits of democracy see O'Donovan, *The Ways of Judgement*, pp. 178–80.

125 Cavanaugh, *Theopolitical Imagination*, p. 77.

126 William Cavanaugh, "Killing for the Telephone Company: Why the Nation-State is Not the Keeper of the Common Good," in Patrick Miller and Dennis McCann, eds., *In Search of the Common Good* (London: T&T Clark, 2005), pp. 310–32.

127 Cavanaugh develops his critique of civil society explicitly in response to Harry Boyte's conception of community organizing and Boyte's application of his conception to Roman Catholic schools in the USA: Cavanaugh, *Theopolitical Imagination*, pp. 63–9. For Boyte's own engagement with community organizing see Sara M. Evans and Harry C. Boyte, *Free Spaces: The Sources of Democratic Change in America* (New York: Harper & Row, 1986); Harry C. Boyte, *Commonwealth: A Return to Citizen Politics* (New York: Free Press, 1989); Harry C. Boyte, *Everyday Politics: Reconnecting Citizens and the Public Life* (Philadelphia, PA: University of Pennsylvania Press, 2004).

128 Cavanaugh, *Theopolitical Imagination*, p. 79.

129 Ibid., p. 83.

130 Ibid., p. 84.

131 For an extensive account of how and why the public life of the church is constituted by its worship see Bernd Wannenwetsch, *Political Worship: Ethics for Christian Citizens* (Oxford: Oxford University Press, 2004), pp. 146–59.

132 Cavanaugh, *Torture and Eucharist*, pp. 264–81.

133 Bonhoeffer, *Ethics*, p. 63.

134 Ibid., p. 346. For an exposition of the link between discipleship and citizenship in Bonhoeffer see Stefan Hauser, "The Cost of Citizenship: Disciple and Citizen in Bonhoeffer's Political Ethics," *Studies in Christian Ethics* 18.3 (2005), pp. 49–69.

135 For an account of the intrinsic relationship between Christianity and democratic change in Poland under Communism see David Herbert, *Religion and Civil Society: Rethinking Public Religion in the Contemporary World* (Aldershot: Ashgate, 2003), ch. 7. For an account of the subsequent capitulation to neo-liberalism see Maurice Glasman, *Unnecessary Suffering: Managing Market Utopia* (London: Verso, 1996). Glasman draws a contrast between the post-totalitarian reconstruction of Germany after the Nazis and that of Poland after communism, charting how democratic governance of the economy that drew directly on Christian democratic practices was abandoned in Poland but central to Germany's prosperous and stable development. It should also be noted that in parallel with the abandonment of Christian democratic thinking by the political classes of Poland, the Polish Roman Catholic authorities have also abandoned it. In its stead, they have frequently resorted to heavy-handed interventions in parliamentary proceedings, in electoral processes, and in public debates, and pursued their sectional interest in defense of institutional power.

On East Germany see John Burgess, *The East German Church and the End of Communism* (Oxford: Oxford University Press, 1997). On South Africa specifically see John De Gruchy, *The Church Struggle in South Africa*, 2nd edn (Grand Rapids, MI: Eerdmans, 1986) and on Africa more generally see Paul Gifford, *The Christian Churches and the Democratization of Africa* (Leiden: E. J. Brill, 1995).

136 Maritain, *Man and the State*, p. 187.

137 Cavanaugh, *Torture and Eucharist*, p. 181.

138 Ibid., p. 180.

139 Wood, *Faith in Action*, p. 140; Warren, *Dry Bones Rattling*, p. 42.

140 Wood, *Faith in Action*, p. 167.

141 There is thus an implicit rejection of the kind of restraints placed upon religious actors by most contemporary accounts of political liberalism, in particular that of John Rawls. For a summary and critique of Rawls's position on the role of religion in politics see Chapter 1.

142 Wood, *Faith in Action*, p. 167.

143 Ibid., pp. 70–1. My own ongoing empirical research into the work of London Citizens seems to confirm this.

144 Ibid., pp. 180, 199–213.

145 It is also important to note that Wood's study underscores the fact that different congregations, with different religious cultures and traditions, will have different and variable forms of involvement in community organizing and politics more generally. As Wood notes: "To suggest that religious culture in some generic sense is a fruitful cultural base for democratic organizing is thus far too simplistic. As in the case of secular cultural forms, some versions of religious culture bring the kind of interpretive resources necessary for vigorous engagement in the democratic public arena, and other versions of religious culture have a paucity of such resources." Ibid., p. 257.

146 Ibid., p. 72.

147 Ibid., p. 192.

148 Wannenwetsch, *Political Worship*, pp. 127–8.

149 Ibid., pp. 27–8.

150 For example, Dennis Jacobsen describes a political action in Milwaukee where a community organization staged a "pray-in" at the county courthouse in relation to a measure to reduce provision of treatment programs for drug addicts. Coping with the effects of drug trafficking and addiction was a major issue for churches in the inner cities of Milwaukee. In Jacobsen's account of the action the tactic itself was not simply framed by prayer, but used prayer as a political instrument. Jacobsen, *Doing Justice*, pp. 36–7.

151 Wannenwetsch, *Political Worship*, p. 35.

152 Stanley Hauerwas, *The Peaceable Kingdom: A Primer in Christian Ethics* (Notre Dame, IN: University of Notre Dame Press, 1983), p. 27.

153 Dietrich Bonhoeffer, *Life Together*, ed. Geffrey Kelly, trans. Daniel Bloesch and James Burtness, *Dietrich Bonhoeffer Works, Vol. 5* (Minneapolis, MN: Fortress Press, 1996), p. 62.

154   Warren, *Dry Bones Rattling*, p. 59.

155   Ibid., pp. 59–60.

156   For a description of this in practice see Wood, *Faith in Action*, pp. 60–5. In the estimation of Wood "participants use religious language and symbols to construct a counterhegemonic vision of citizenship." Ibid., p. 188.

157   Gecan, *Going Public*, p. 138. The organizer Michael Gecan named the Nehemiah homes project specifically in response to a sermon preached by Jonny Ray Youngblood on Nehemiah and the project itself developed out of listening to the stories and situation in East Brooklyn. Samuel Freedman, *Upon This Rock: The Miracles of a Black Church* (New York: Harper Perennial, 1993), pp. 331–2.

158   Alinsky, *Rules*, pp. 89–91. Alinsky quotes Exodus 32 and then interprets Moses as a trickster outmaneuvering God as he negotiates with God to have mercy of the people.

159   The notion of listening on two horizons simultaneously is indebted to the work of Hans-Georg Gadamer. Following Gadamer, it is important to note that the act of listening is inherently a historically located act that involves listening to the reception of Scripture within the tradition of Christian doctrine and practice. These pre-understandings or "preconceptions" constitute a regulative grammar for the interpretation of scripture (Hans-Georg Gadamer, *Truth and Method* (London: Sheed & Ward, 1981), p. 358). Thus in relation to the reception of Scripture it is not the case that one simply listens directly to Scripture in some literalist or ahistorical fashion, nor can one move immediately from the interpretation of Scripture to the contemporary context bypassing the reception of Scripture in the wider Christian tradition. Rather, listening to Scripture involves listening within a "cloud of witnesses" or body of believers in which the historically formed and contextually situated tradition of doctrine and practice enables both reception and discrimination in the process of listening. However, the outcome of this act of listening to the word from outside, under the guidance of the Holy Spirit, could well be to disrupt and reorient the settled tradition of belief and practice, and open out new understanding and direction. Likewise, the fusion of two horizons does not itself issue forth in an answer about what to do; rather, it is a process of discernment that guides, purifies, and disciplines our practical reason to the point where, as Oliver O'Donovan puts it, we are "free to engage in clear-sighted deliberation leading to decision." Oliver O'Donovan, "What Kind of Community is the Church?" *Ecclesiology* 3.2 (2007), p. 192.

160   For how the listening process directly relates to the formulation of concrete policy proposals see Wood, *Faith in Action*, pp. 40–1. On the importance of listening to Alinsky-style democratic politics see Coles, *Beyond Gated Politics*, pp. 217–22 and for congregational renewal that draws on the Alinsky approach see Michael Gecan, *Effective Organizing for Congregational Renewal* (Skokie, IL: Acta Publications, 2008), pp. 7–8. By way of example, London Citizens runs what it calls "Listening Campaigns" as a way of identifying common issues among its members in relation to which all the membership can organize.

161 My argument here goes beyond the advocacy by Yoder for the centrality of listening to Scripture as part of fostering and celebrating what he called "relative democratization" which can constitute a prophetic ministry of the church as a "servant people in a world we do not control." Yoder states: "In the Christian community, where the Word of God is proclaimed, all should be free to speak and all should listen critically (1 Cor. 14). If that is the way divine truth is to be articulated in the words of our world, then those who have learned those skills of listening critically and speaking prophetically should be able as well to apply them to debates about human justice." However, beyond just listening to Scripture, I contend that there is also the need to listen to strangers, although it is fair to say that Yoder's theology *in toto* would support such a move. Yoder, "The Christian Case for Democracy," p. 166.

162 Rachel Muers, *Keeping God's Silence* (Oxford: Blackwell, 2004), p. 99.

163 Drawing on Barth's discussion of God's patience, Muers states: "Listening can be described as the act of 'giving time' to allow the other's own possibilities for new speech to emerge – possibilities that are themselves in some sense given in and through the act of listening. The ideas that God is patient, or that God 'waits for' creation could, it would seem, allow the silence of God that grants responsibility to the world to be understood as coterminous with God's salvific action." Ibid., pp. 94–5.

164 Ambrose, "On the Duties of the Clergy," in *Nicene and Post-Nicene Father, Second Series*, vol. X, trans. H. De Romestein, eds. Philip Schaff and Henry Wace (Edinburgh: T&T Clark, 1989), p. 2. Ambrose directly locates listening and "active silence" to faithful witness and the building up of the church.

165 Bonhoeffer, *Life Together*, p. 98. Interestingly, Mike Gecan draws on this very quote to emphasize the importance of listening to organizing and the renewal of institutions, locating one-to-one meetings as a practice that fosters the art of listening. Gecan, *Effective Organizing for Congregational Renewal*, p. 8.

166 Ibid., pp. 98–9. For Bonhoeffer, the practice of confession best embodies the importance of listening because it positions Christians toward each other and toward the world as forgiven sinners: that is, as those who have been freed to serve and bear with each other and their neighbors from a position of humility and hope. Ibid., pp. 108–16.

167 Ibid., p. 67.

168 Wannenwetsch, *Political Worship*, p. 293.

169 Ibid., p. 307.

170 Albert Hirschman, *Exit, Voice, and Loyalty: Responses to Decline in Firms, Organizations, and States* (Cambridge, MA: Harvard University Press, 1970).

171 Hannah Arendt, *The Human Condition* (Chicago, IL: University of Chicago Press, 1998), pp. 7–17.

172 Wannenwetsch, *Political Worship*, p. 233.

173 Ibid., p. 232.

174 Augustine, *Enarrationes in psalmos*, Psalm 72.34. Quoted from and translated by Michael McMcarthy, "An Ecclesiology of Groaning: Augustine, the Psalms, and the Making of the Church," *Theological Studies* 66 (2005), p. 28.

175   Augustine, *Enarrationes in psalmos*, Psalm 93.24. Quoted from ibid., p. 38.

176   Augustine, *Enarrationes in psalmos*, Psalm 147.21. Quoted from ibid. p. 25.

177   Ibid., p. 25. On the relationship between meaning making and performance in ritual see Catherine Bell, *Ritual: Perspectives and Dimensions* (Oxford: Oxford University Press, 1997) and Roy Rappaport, *Ritual and Religion in the Making of Humanity* (Cambridge: Cambridge University Press, 1999). On speech-acts see J. L. Austin, *How to Do Things with Words*, 2nd edn (Cambridge, MA: Harvard University Press, 1975).

178   As McCarthy notes: "The activity of reciting and reflecting on the psalms tends to 'enact' or produce their meaning. Yet, taken within a theological horizon, such 'enactment' forms part of the sacramental and ecclesial efficacy of the Word." McMcarthy, "An Ecclesiology of Groaning," p. 37. On this see also Bonhoeffer, *Life Together*, pp. 53–8.

179   In advocating this it can be argued that I am following the pattern that Paul set out in 1 Corinthians, and enacted in the letter and its reception itself, for how wisdom from the Spirit comes to be imparted to the church in which each member is a constitutive part of the body (see especially 1 Cor. 2, 4, 12, and 14).

180   The encounter with strangers is at the heart of how we encounter God in new ways. In Hebrews, amid an exhortation to lead a righteous life, we are told "not to forget to entertain strangers, for by so doing some people have entertained angels without knowing it" (Heb. 13.2). There is the suggestion here that strangers may be the bearers of God's presence to us. But angels are scary, off-putting, and threatening and "entertaining" them involves demands on our time and resources (e.g., Abraham, Gen. 18:2–15), and may involve threats to our family and livelihood (e.g., Lot, Gen. 19), deep personal struggle (e.g., Jacob, Gen. 32.24–30), incomprehension or shock (e.g., Mary, Luke 1.27–35), and we will not necessarily agree with what they have to teach us (e.g., Zechariah, Luke 1.8–20). Nevertheless, such troublesome encounter is often the primary arena of our encounter with God. To shy away from it, as if proclaiming that the Gospel has nothing to do with learning from strangers, is to turn our backs on transformative encounter with God. The dynamics whereby the church encounters God in the stranger is developed more fully in the discussion of bare life as gift, judgment, and promise in Chapter 3.

181   Romand Coles outlines the importance of this kind of "geographical traveling" to democratic politics. Coles, *Beyond Gated Politics*, pp. 223–5.

182   Such a guest–host dynamic is central to the faithful following of Jesus Christ who was simultaneously the guest of a hostile world and its gracious host welcoming those who are far off. For the importance of the guest–host dynamic in the Gospels and to Christian witness see Bretherton, *Hospitality as Holiness*, pp. 135–8.

183   The account developed here has strong parallels with the account of the relationship between Christianity and radical democracy given by Hauerwas in conversation with Romand Coles. Stanley Hauerwas and Romand Coles, *Christianity, Democracy, and the Radical Ordinary: Conversations between a*

Radical Democrat and a Christian (Eugene, OR: Cascade Books, 2007). See especially Hauerwas's Augustinian reading of Yoder in "A Haunting Possibility: Christianity and Radical Democracy" (paper presented at Villanova University, October 27, 2006), pp. 17–30.

184　On politics as conversion see Mathewes, "Faith, Hope and Agony," pp. 140–2.

185　MacIntyre, *Dependent Rational Animals*; Wolin, *Politics and Vision*; and William Connolly, *Pluralism* (Durham, NC: Duke University Press, 2005); Milbank, "On Complex Space," p. 271.

186　Maritain, *Integral Humanism*, p. 206.

3

National
*Christian Cosmopolitanism, Refugees,
and the Politics of Proximity*

Introduction

The previous two chapters presented a critique of the liberal capitalist nation-state. This chapter extends this critique but also seeks to take seriously the nation-state as an arena of law and order. Following on from Augustine's understanding of the *saeculum*, and the importance of an earthly peace, the nation-state cannot be dismissed as monolithically bad. Nation-states do maintain an earthly peace, which can be better or worse rather than wholly good or bad. The status of the liberal, capitalist nation-state as an instance of Babylon should never be underestimated; however, there is still a need to think constructively about the nation-state as an arena of earthly friendship and peace. This chapter seeks to open up avenues for such theological reflection. Its central focus is an assessment of the contribution of churches to the question of how to value national identity and the nation-state through a case study of responses to immigration and the treatment of refugees.

The issues of immigration and asylum are key ones in the USA and Europe and bring to the fore questions about the relationship between identity, citizenship, and the rule of law. Moreover, assessment of debates on the political limits of migration is pivotal to understanding contemporary politics as it highlights the changing conditions of politics, as political authority within a nation-state has to reckon with contemporary patterns of globalization. Following Georgio Agemben's characterization of refugees as "bare life," this chapter argues that refugees unveil a deep contradiction in contemporary patterns of political sovereignty. In response this chapter develops an account of Christian cosmopolitanism as an alternative to, on the one hand, overly protectionist visions of the nation-state, and on the other, abstract accounts of liberal cosmopolitanism that call for borderless states. This Christian cosmopolitan vision forms the basis for distinguishing between economic migrants and refugees and identifying constructive ways of prioritizing the needs of those seeking entry to the Western states. At the same time, the theological vision of hallowing bare life is set out as a way of framing a response to all those who are rendered beyond the rule of law and placed in a state of exception by policies related to migration, refugees, and responses to terrorism. The chapter closes with an assessment of the practice of sanctuary, with a particular focus on the US Sanctuary movement, as a paradigmatic means by which the church has hallowed bare life.

Theological Politics and the Liberal Democratic Response to Refugees

In debates about appropriate ethical and political responses to refugees in liberal democratic polities, three key issues emerge. The first is the very definition of a refugee. The second is whether refugees should receive a priority of attention and resources as compared with the claims of economic migrants. The third is whether governments owe a greater duty of care to existing members than to those who exist beyond its formal boundaries. Directly related to this last issue is the question of whether borders and a defined territory are themselves moral.[1]

i. Definitions and the priority of refugees

There is some debate about how to define who and what is a refugee and how this contrasts with related terms, notably, the term "economic migrant." The most accepted definition is given in the 1951 UN Convention on Refugees. This states that a refugee is:

> A person who is outside his/her country of nationality or habitual residence; has a well-founded fear of persecution because of his/her race, religion, nationality, membership in a particular social group or political opinion; and is unable or unwilling to avail himself/herself of the protection of that country, or to return there, for fear of persecution.[2]

There are several things to notice about this definition. In the contemporary context the close interrelation between violent political conflict and severe economic and social disruption makes it difficult to distinguish between refugees and economic migrants. Technically, refugees move to save their lives and economic migrants move to improve their economic and social prospects. However, most migration – of which refugees are a sub-category – involves "mixed motives" stimulated by a variety of economic, social, and political "pull" and "push" factors.[3] Yet the UN Convention is specific. As Gil Loescher points out:

> The key criterion determining refugee status is *persecution*, which usually means a deliberate act of the government against individuals, and thus excludes victims of general insecurity and oppression or systematic economic deprivation, and people who have not crossed national frontiers to seek refuge.[4]

Thus a refugee must be outside their country of origin and without the protection of their government. This excludes internally displaced persons and those moving because of forced migration (either because of social, economic, or political disruption or low-intensity conflicts which exacerbate such disruption). The Convention is also individualistic in its assumption, requiring that the individual personally must face persecution. For example, someone who moves because of civil war or famine is not covered by the Convention and so cannot, according to the UN Convention, be granted refugee status. For these reasons a number of other, broader definitions are currently operative. Notable among these are those of the Organization of African Unity and of Sweden, both of which widen the focus to include victims of generalized states of violence and events which severely disrupt public order such as natural disasters.[5] Some, for example, Andrew Shacknove, seek to broaden the definition even further so as to include all those whose basic needs are not protected by their state.[6] However, as Matthew Gibney comments, we should "resist the temptation to define all threatened peoples as 'refugees.' There are other ways of drawing attention to the plight of people in need of protection and assistance than lumping them into a single amorphous category."[7] At a certain point, if the definition of who qualifies for refugee status is too broad then it becomes meaningless. While there is much to be said for broadening the definition to take account of contemporary geo-political realities, the crucial point to keep sight of is that, in order to be of any normative or practical use, the definition needs to be able to distinguish the moral status and claims of refugees from other categories of those in need in order that the appropriate forms of care can be given and the specific need met.

The qualitative difference between refugees and, for example, destitute economic migrants or those caught up in environmental catastrophes arises from the primarily political cause of their placelessness.[8] By implication, this affirms the trajectory of the UN Convention but widens it to include those rendered placeless due to both civil war and political policies deliberately designed to cause de-territorialization such as forced collectivization. For example, those dislocated because of the tsunami in 2004 or the 2005 famine in Niger are not refugees but destitute and in need of various forms of direct assistance. While there is a political dimension to these events, political authority was not the causal factor. Those rendered placeless by ongoing warlordism in Liberia or Afghanistan are refugees even though their life may be economically sustainable. It is the political basis of their placelessness that, I want to argue, is the defining feature of a refugee. This means that the primary need of the refugee is, as Gibney puts it, "the security of a new state within which to reside,"[9] as distinct from social welfare, economic investment, access to education, or some other good.

It is vital to properly locate the status and need of refugees and asylum seekers in order to make sense both of subsequent debate about the duty of care to refugees and to identify how best to help them.[10]

ii. The duty of care to near and distant neighbors

If the primary need of refugees is for a new polity, this immediately raises the questions of whether the political authority of any given state has a greater duty of care to its existent members than to nonmembers who make a claim to participate in its jurisdiction and protection. Thus, to state the obvious, the need of refugees may be for a new polity, but it does not necessarily follow that all polities have a duty of care to refugees.[11] The fulfillment of the refugees' need is dependent upon a duty of care being recognized by another polity. Two issues related to this are whether border controls are moral and whether proximity has moral implications. In this section the agency of refugees themselves is deliberately bracketed in order to examine the moral and political responsibilities of the "host."

Liberal utilitarians and deontologists argue that liberal democracies, in principle, owe an equal duty of care to all humanity and, by implication, that borders should, in principle, be open. Representative of these two approaches are the utilitarians Peter and Renata Singer, and the deontologists Michael Dummett and Joseph Carens. The Singers argue that immigration policy in general and refugee policy in particular should give equal consideration to the interests of all those affected, and where the interests of different parties conflict, priority should be given to those with the most pressing claim.[12] Michael Dummett argues that the requirements of justice are such that "all states ought to recognize the normal principle to be that of open borders, allowing all freely to enter and, if they will, to settle in, any country they wish."[13] Joseph Carens extends the logic of John Rawls's original position to include humankind as a whole.[14] On this basis he argues that free movement is essential for the realization of an individual's other liberties and thus should be considered as a basic human right, with open borders a direct implication of this right.[15]

Gibney provides a telling critique of the inconsistencies at work in each of these arguments, but he overstates the extent to which these writers argue for open borders per se.[16] None of these writers argue for completely open borders and all recognize limits to freedom of movement and how this freedom can conflict with other rights which may necessitate its legitimate restriction. The continuance of borders and the need to balance the duty of care to existing members with the duty of care to all humans qua humans is emphasized by the fact that none of them argue for world government. Rather, they should be characterized as liberal internationalists or what Seyla Benhabib calls "cosmopolitan federalists"[17] who, while universalistic or cosmopolitan in outlook, hold that intermediary political entities – which necessarily includes the nation-state – are the means through which the good of humanity is best served. However, proximity has little or no moral bearing upon their conclusions.[18] It is also difficult, on the basis of their arguments, to say whether the claims of refugees should receive priority over those of destitute economic migrants. A contrast can be drawn with the work of Gibney and Michael Walzer.

Walzer notes how entrance policy goes to the heart of political sovereignty and the ability of a community to sustain a common life.[19] He argues that the primary duty of care that members of a political community owe to each other is the communal provision of security and welfare.[20] Central to this provision is the need for community itself which inherently involves culture, religion, and politics.[21] Maintenance of security and welfare, which inherently involves maintenance of the community itself, justifies entrance policies. In relation to refugees, the provision of security and welfare gives rise to a conflict: what refugees need is a new state; however, the very thing they need cannot be exported, but takes historical and determinate form in particular places.[22] Thus, should the numbers of refugees ever threaten the provision of security and welfare, there is a strong case for refusing entry of the refugees.[23]

Like Walzer, Gibney sees entrance policies as a site of conflicting moral claims.[24] For Gibney, the needs of refugees should be privileged over and against the claims of other foreigners in need of help.[25] However, the claims of refugees must be balanced against the need for states to protect the institutions and values of the liberal democratic state.[26] Gibney goes on to argue that "liberal egalitarian principles can only be realized in communities where relations amongst citizens are characterized by solidarity and trust, relations which develop over time and can be jeopardized by large, short-term changes in membership."[27] Gibney proposes a "humanitarian principle" for adjudicating between the rival claims of citizens and refugees. This principle holds that "states have an obligation to assist refugees when the costs of doing so are low."[28] In concert with liberal utilitarians and deontologists, this principle recognizes the duties that arise from membership of a single human community, but specifies that priority be given to those in greatest need; that is, refugees. It recognizes also that, at times, other values and interests may need priority which may in turn lead to the exclusion of refugees, including asylum seekers already present within the borders of a given state.[29]

In contrast to liberal utilitarians and deontologists, Gibney and Walzer do attempt to give some account of how to order the duty of care to refugees in relation to the duty of care to existing members. They do this by a minimal account of the common good of liberal democracies.[30] However, neither Gibney nor Walzer gives an account of how the common good of liberal democracies finds its fulfillment beyond itself in some higher good or in the good of humanity. Thus, if the likes of the Singers, Dummett, and Carens underemphasize the value of the common life of a nation, Gibney and Walzer maroon that common life, making of it a self-subsisting good and thereby over-investing it with significance.

Within the multifarious strands of the Christian tradition there is a common teleology which orders the good of a particular community as being fulfilled in the good of humanity which is itself fulfilled in communion with God.[31] The work of Augustine and Aquinas represents two of the most notable examples of this common teleology. For example, Augustine states:

> Therefore, for as long as this Heavenly City is a pilgrim on earth, she summons citizens of all nations and every tongue, and brings together a society of pilgrims in which no attention is paid to any differences in the customs, laws, and institutions by which earthly peace is achieved or maintained. She does not rescind or destroy these things, however. For whatever differences there are among the various nations, these all tend towards the same end of earthly peace. Thus, she preserves and follows them, provided only that they do not impede the religion by which we are taught that the one supreme and true God is to be worshipped.[32]

In relation to Aquinas, Mary Keys notes that: "The social and civic inclination that gives rise, on Aquinas's account, to political life also points beyond the polis, or any political society, for its fulfillment in a universal or fully common good."[33] Calvin expresses this teleology in the following way:

> I deny not that the closer the relation the more frequent our offices of kindness should be. For the condition of humanity requires that there be more duties in common between those who are more nearly connected by the ties of relationship,

or friendship, or neighborhood. And this is done without any offence to God, by whose providence we are in a manner impelled to do it. But I say that the whole human race, without exception, are to be embraced with one feeling of charity: that here there is no distinction of Greek or Barbarian, worthy or unworthy, friend or foe, since all are to be viewed not in themselves, but in God.[34]

Following Calvin, a modern exponent of this teleology is Karl Barth in his treatment of the relationship between near and distant neighbors.[35] The basic contours of this teleology are succinctly summarized in *Gaudium et Spes* when it states:

Citizens must cultivate a generous and loyal spirit of patriotism, but without being narrow-minded. This means that they will always direct their attention to the good of the whole human family, united by the different ties which bind together races, people and nations.[36]

For the purposes of this chapter, this common teleology will be represented by two deliberately diverse and disparate figures: Dante Alighieri and Wolfhart Pannenberg.

In Dante's *Divine Comedy* we find an example of how, from Augustine onward, the local and universal horizons of Christian mission and ecclesiology were integrated. The cosmic history of the body of Christ may only be appropriated and entered into through the particularity of one's local language (Dante writes in the vernacular) and one's local political community (the history and destiny of Florence are a central preoccupation of the work); but that history is set within a wider imperial Roman history, and finds its fulfillment in cosmic salvation history. Thus, the local is not absolutized or made an end in itself; instead, it is the necessary beginning point for the pilgrim's journey that culminates in communion with God and redeemed humanity.[37]

The Christian cosmopolitanism of Dante's *Divine Comedy* and its subsequent development from the early modern period onward must be distinguished from its rationalist rival.[38] Both are deeply influenced by Aristotle, Stoicism, and notions of the *ius gentium* and natural rights. However, in the development of the former (witnessed in the likes of Vitoria, Saurez, and Grotius), rather than a world government or "empire," there is a commonwealth of nations, Christian or otherwise, that can seek a common good of nations and which ultimately finds its *telos* beyond itself in the communion of all humans together with God.[39] In the latter (witnessed in the likes of Montaigne, Jean Bodin, Locke, Liebniz, and eventually coming to fulfillment in Bentham and Kant), *pietas* is not teleologically ordered to the love of humanity, but is subsumed within it: that is, love for humanity precedes and has priority over love of one's immediate neighbor.[40] This latter view is best summarized by Liebniz's statement that: "I am indifferent to that which constitutes a German or a Frenchman because I will only the good of all mankind."[41] The concomitant of this rationalist cosmopolitanism was natural religion expressed in the genre of tracts known as the *Catéchèse de humanité*; for example, the Encyclopedist Saint-Lambert's *Catéchèse universelle* that instructed the public in their rights and duties as a brotherhood of mankind, an allegiance that the Enlightenment philosophers believed preceded any other familial, religious, or regional loyalty.[42] In short, *pietas* for humanity is understood as overriding the respect that is owed to one's particular community or to God. It is the rationalist cosmopolitan tradition that informs the work of Singer, Dummett, and Carens and those who call for open borders.[43]

A Christian cosmopolitanism also contrasts with Walzer and Gibney who see the common life of a nation or particular group as an end in itself. Wolfhart Pannenberg argues that the cultivation of a distinctive national life must be subordinated to the concern for an international order of justice and freedom.[44] However, this order can only begin in particular communities which then form unions with other nations of which Pannenberg cites the European Union as a good example. However, like nations themselves, such unions:

> Should be orientated beyond their own bounds towards the idea of an order of justice and peace that should one day include all humanity, that is, not only the world of our friends but also our present enemies. Thus this sequence of specific unions, which must have their beginnings in the internal political life of each people that is involved ... points toward the universal goal of a peaceful world that encompasses all mankind.[45]

It is the comprehensive goals of regional and then world peace that "determines the boundary between the justifiable cultivation of distinctive national features and nationalistic exaggerations."[46] It should be noted that, like Augustine, Pannenberg conceives world peace as a wholly provisional, political, and penultimate form of peaceableness that is in no way equivalent to the peace of God.[47] Thus, in contrast to Walzer and Gibney, there is no inherent or necessary conflict between the duty of care to refugees and the duty of care to existing members. Rather, the duty of care to refugees must be ordered in relation to pursuit of the common good which itself must be ordered in relation to the universal and cosmic good of humanity. The true end of humans lies in neither the family, nor a particular culture, nor a nation, nor in some kind of worldwide polity or universal society, but in the city of God: that is, a true commonwealth in which all may participate together with God.

Within a Christian cosmopolitan framework, the telos of humanity is neither a return to an original state of blessing nor a movement beyond the materiality of creation. Rather, it is a movement, via differentiation and development through history, to an eschatological fulfillment of creation. Unlike the rationalist cosmopolitans whose Platonic, protological teleology posits a return to a undifferentiated "humanity," a properly theological cosmopolitanism must incorporate the fulfillment of humanity via differentiation into particular sodalities of persons that involve differences of language, kinship, and territoriality and a myriad of other aspects of creation. For without discrete identities that take up and play with creation in particular ways through history there can be no interplay of persons in communion. However, this is not to say that all patterns of differentiation are good. There can be false and destructive patterns of binding and loosing creation; that is, humans can be set apart and bound together in ways that are oriented to chaos and nothingness rather than eschatological fulfillment.[48] Nationalism constitutes one such false form of binding and loosing. Diversity in unity of relationship to God is the way in which creation is to be properly ordered; without some account of this relationship, any attempt at unity, whether national or global, will constitute a "totalitarian project to centralize, homogenize and control."[49]

The loss of the above, or for that matter, any teleological framework renders debate about the ethics of refugee policy incoherent because there is no way to integrate or reconcile the moral claims of citizens and refugees. The absence of such a teleological framework means that rational deliberation about the just treatment of refugees is at best occasional and at worst wholly absent so that the interests of the strong – the existing members of a polity – tend to prevail over the interests of the weak.

The plight of refugees brings to the fore many of the salutary features of liberal, capitalist nation-states in comparison to other political regimes. Yet it is clear that the current refugee policies adopted by most liberal nation-states are morally problematic: they favor the strong over the weak. The crucial point at issue in relation to the formulation of a just and generous refugee policy goes back to Augustine's account of what constitutes a true *res publica*. For Augustine, it is the ends or loves of the polity that form the basis of its common life. Thus the difference between the earthly city and the city of God rests in their different ends or objects of love.[50] An earthly city cannot be a true *res publica* because the nature of its loves means that it can never be a truly harmonious society; rather, it always involves individual and group competition and hostility. For Augustine, the politics of any instance of the earthly city is about negotiating what is necessary for a tolerable earthly peace to exist within which the Gospel can be preached and which the heavenly city makes use of for a time. The earthly city is not an end in itself, but serves an end – communion with God – beyond itself. The role of political authority is to establish the conditions for human flourishing through the promulgation and enforcement of law.[51] Liberal democracies *are* good in so far as they provide a limited peace. However, as the treatment of asylum seekers makes clear, they have made an end in and of themselves and their common lives are based on objects of love – notably, individual and collective self-fulfillment and autonomy – that inherently tend toward hostility to friendless strangers. They tend toward hostility to friendless strangers because the pursuit of such goods directs us away from the just and generous consideration of the needs of others. Yet, on a conception of the polity within the Christian tradition, there should be no necessary incompatibility between welcoming refugees and pursuit of the common life of the polity.

As previously argued, the primary or defining need of the refugee is political; it is the need for a stable arena of law and order. This need coincides with how, for the most part, the Christian tradition, following Augustine, conceives the defining purpose of a polity, whether it be a city-state, a nation-state, or a confederation of states. Within the Christian political tradition, it is neither territory, nor ethnic/linguistic homogeneity, nor economic power that defines the political identity of a society, even though each of these contributes toward it.[52] Rather, as Joan Lockwood O'Donovan puts it, after the advent of Christ's kingdom, "we can discern the defining aspect of the earthly nation to be the concrete rendering over time of legal justice, that is, the ongoing practice of judgment conducted through the medium of law."[53] Thus the need of the refugee coincides with the raison d'être of the polity. The just political judgment to be made in relation to refugees is at what point the inclusion of more refugees threatens to destabilize any given arena of law and order and not, as so many other responses to refugees suppose, the point at which either territorial integrity, ethnic or cultural homogeneity, or economic power is threatened. Nevertheless, attention to territory, culture, and economics will properly and necessarily be factors in the deliberation process. It is just that they should be neither primary nor determinative.

It may be objected that to make the criterion of exclusion the point at which law and order becomes untenable is simply to make law and order an end in itself, something that, in the shadow of the totalizing thrust of modern political and economic power, sounds like a license to justify anything.

This is not the intention of this argument. Neither is it the intention of this argument to justify the "securitization" of refugee policy. Current approaches to security as part of the "war on terror" seem to militate against concern for legal process and the rule of law. To make law and order the criterion for exclusion is simply to draw out the logic that it can hardly be moral to will the destruction of that which is the very basis of the remedy sought. It is also to recognize that no single polity is responsible for all refugees. As is actually the case, the provision of asylum necessarily involves all nations. At the same time, there is an urgent need for further attention to how the burden of care is currently distributed, both between North and South and between Western liberal nation-states.

The above discussion of the purpose of an earthly polity points toward an inherent contradiction in the modern liberal democratic nation-state, a contradiction which greatly magnifies the suffering of refugees. It is a contradiction on which Hannah Arendt and Georgio Agamben are the most perceptive commentators. Inherent in the justification and legitimation of modern, liberal, democratic nation-states is the upholding of individual or human rights. Yet, these rights are extended only to members of the nation-states and not, despite the rhetoric, to humans qua humans.

The previous chapter postulated that the relationship between Christianity and democracy was best understood as an exploratory partnership in which each enabled the other to fulfill its own best insights. One way in which Christianity enables democracy to overcome its limitations is by contradicting the sectarian logic of democracy. The rights of citizens within a democracy are always tied to a particular *demos*.[54] They are not universal but require particular loyalties. Democracy inherently excludes or, at least, does not accord equal value to those who are not part of the *demos*. Contrary to popular perception, nationalism and democracy are natural bedfellows. Whether the "nation"/people is constituted by *jus sanguinas* (as it was in Germany)[55] or *jus solis* (as it is in France), there is a limit to who is included in "We, the people." Liberalism and Christianity both have a cosmopolitan outlook and seek to universalize these rights, both incorporating within democracy, and rendering democracy accountable to, transcendent norms. However, as already noted, liberalism does this at the expense of the particular, subsuming the particular to the universal. By contrast, Christianity's cosmopolitan vision universalizes the particular loyalties fostered in democratic politics by ordering the particular in relation to the universal. The liberal democratic nation-state is an uneasy amalgam in which the universalism of its liberalism undermines and corrodes the necessary particularity of its democracy and vice versa. Within Christianity, particularity is constitutive of universality or, as it is more properly called, catholicity. The city of

God is the place where differences are reconciled in harmony.⁵⁶ As Kristen Deede Johnson puts it: "United in Christ, differences of nationality and culture cease to be divisive without thereby ceasing to exist."⁵⁷ The body of Christ, in the power of the Spirit, bears witness to this harmony and through its catholicity contradicts the exclusionary logic of democratic nation-states (an example of this dynamic in practice will be explored later in relation to the practice of sanctuary).⁵⁸ The response to refugees by liberal nation-states draws out the tensions between their liberalism and their democracy but also illustrates how a Christian cosmopolitan vision acts as a contradiction to this tension.⁵⁹

Refugees as Bare Life

There are numerous studies that point to how, within the current context, refugees are labeled, stigmatized, and made scapegoats so that they can be dehumanized and abstracted, and empathy toward them diminished.⁶⁰ Crossing borders and transgressing the maintenance of boundaries, refugees bring into view the contested and contingent nature of national limits and identities. Asylum seekers are literally matter out of place. They do not conform to the established order, and cannot be domesticated; thus, they emerge as "dirt" or pollution in need of purification from the social body.⁶¹ Such dehumanizing processes allow for a grotesque inversion in perception whereby the vulnerability and powerlessness of asylum seekers is masked and instead, they are seen as a force of nature capable of "swamping" a country like some human tsunami.

These social processes are mirrored in politics and law. Around the world, refugees and asylum seekers are increasingly stripped of what little political and legal rights they had. Some examples from North America and the European Union will suffice to illustrate this. In the 1994 case, Sale vs. Haitian Centers Council, the United States Supreme Court ruled that it was a violation of neither US domestic nor international law to interdict Haitian boats before they reached US territorial waters and return them to Haiti without assessment of their asylum claims.⁶² Effectively, this puts an end to the principle of *non-refoulement*. On the back of the public furor following the revelation that one of those involved in the 1993 bombing of the World Trade Center in New York was in the process of applying for refugee status, the 1996 Illegal Immigration Reform and Immigrant Responsibility Act was signed by Bill Clinton. This reasserted political control over asylum and introduced a system of "expedited removal" that gave immigration officers the authority to remove "improperly documented aliens" arriving in the USA "without further hearing or review."[63] In 1999, in a ruling that set an ominous precedent, the Eleventh Circuit Court of Appeals determined that aliens held at Guantánamo Bay "had no legal rights under the domestic law of the US or under international law" because those rights were only available to persons on US territory.[64]

In the Europe Union, the 1990 Schengen Accord established a common set of restrictive policies with regard to those coming into the signatory states. The most significant of these was that refusal of asylum in one country meant refusal of asylum in all of them. Geddes notes that Schengen created a buffer zone and displaced the burden of dealing with immigrants and the dilemma of control outside the jurisdiction of the states of Western Europe. It allows EU states to uphold the commitment to the 1951 UN Convention and maintain civil rights for members while achieving illiberal asylum policies via diverting the problem to countries less concerned with human rights. For as Geddes puts it: "Externalization allows members states to pursue domestic migration policy objectives by other means."[65] The flouting of the UN Convention on Refugees is not restricted to Europe and America. Gaim Kibreab notes that in most of Africa the principle of *non-refoulement* is a dead letter.[66] In terms of the application of the 1951 UN Convention, Caroline Moorehead points out that "The Refugee Convention is in the odd position of being the only major human-rights treaty that is not externally supervised – all other key UN human-rights accords have some mechanism to ensure the states are held accountable for what they have signed up to."[67]

Denuding asylum seekers of their legal rights is not a new phenomenon. It directly mirrors the process of denaturalization and denationalization undertaken by European states after World War I. Beginning with France in 1915, which denaturalized citizens of "enemy origin," it culminated in the 1935 Nuremberg Laws which divided Germans into those citizens with full rights and those without political rights.[68] This legislation resulted in a situation of mass statelessness and formed the background to the "Final Solution."[69] Making this link is not to imply that Western liberal democracies are about to ship refugees off to extermination camps. However, it does draw out how, like the Jews under the Nazi regime, we encounter refugees as those whose human face is locked away in the iron mask of stereotype and stigma and who are without political rights. They are, to use Georgio Agamben's phrase, reduced to "bare life."

Agamben develops the ancient Roman legal category of *homo sacer* and relates it to both the Jews under the Nazis and contemporary refugees. The *homo sacer* was someone who, though human, could be killed with impunity or without the charge of homicide but could not be sacrificed to the gods nor submitted to sanctioned forms of execution.[70] The *homo sacer* was naked or bare life, neither simply *zoe* or natural life nor *bios* – a participant in a particular form of life.[71] Rather, the *homo sacer* exists in a zone of indistinction, life exposed to death, life that is excluded or banned from participation in both the divine and human community. It is as bare life that refugees raise their most pressing moral claim and unmask the deep contradictions at work in modern political regimes.[72]

Hannah Arendt was the first to see clearly how refugees unveil a self-contradiction at the heart of modern politics. Arendt argues that in the new, secular, emancipated societies of modernity humans were no longer sure of their social and human rights which "until then had been outside the political order and guaranteed not by government and constitution, but by social, spiritual and religious forces."[73] A consensus emerged that human rights needed to be invoked whenever individuals needed protection "against the new sovereignty of the state and the new arbitrariness of society."[74] Yet the question of human rights became inextricably blended with the question of national emancipation so that the individual could only be protected as a citizen. Agamben points out that the ambiguity between human rights and citizenship is implicit in the 1789 French "Declaration of the Rights of Man and Citizen." He states: "It is not clear whether the two terms *homme* and *citoyen* name two autonomous beings or instead form a unitary system in which the first is always already included in the second."[75] (The same tension can be seen at work in the UN Declaration of Human Rights.) In theory humans were supposed to bear rights simply by membership of humanity. However, as Arendt notes:

> The conception of human rights, based upon the assumed existence of a human being as such, broke down at the very moment when those who professed to believe in it were for the first time confronted with people who had indeed lost all other qualities and specific relationships – except that they were still human. The world found nothing sacred in the abstract nakedness of being human.[76]

Refugees should have been precisely those to benefit from inborn and inalienable rights. Their treatment by nation-states, both after World War II and today, demonstrates that the opposite is the case. For all the talk about global human rights regimes and deterritorialized or disaggregated forms of citizenship, the individual still depends upon a sovereign state for the upholding of their legal status.[77] Arendt concludes: "It seems that a man who is nothing but a man has lost the very qualities that make it possible for other people to treat him as a fellow-man."[78] Thus, the very thing that justifies and legitimates a liberal democratic nation-state – the upholding and protection of human rights – proves incapable of upholding and protecting at the greatest point of need. Refugees both unveil the inherent link between nativity, nationality, and human rights and represent its crises because, as a mass phenomenon, they cannot be assimilated to this order. Agamben states: "The refugee must be considered for what he is: nothing less than a limit concept that radically calls into question the fundamental categories of the nation-state, from the birth-nation to the man–citizen link."[79] Yet, at the same time, Arendt's and Agemben's analyses point to the importance of the nation-state.

The liberal democratic nation-state represents a form of precisely what the refugee needs: a stable arena of law and order. Advocacy of the kind of local politics outlined in Chapter 2 is never enough because such local politics cannot constitute a sufficiently robust or extensive realm of earthly peace. That said, a globalized version of "complex space" in which nation-states are an important constitutive part is conceivable and increasingly plausible. Hedley Bull, in his influential book on international relations, *The Anarchical Society*, gives an account of what he calls a "neo-medieval order." His account is suggestive of what such a complex international society might entail. Bull argues that prior to the emergence of the international system after the Treaty of Westphalia (1648), Christendom was organized through multiple layers of sovereignty: authority was shared among rulers, the vassals beneath them, and the Pope and the Holy Roman Emperor above.[80] Bull postulated that an equivalent form of organization, in which multiple governments share authority over a geographical area, might be possible today.[81] Such an order is plausible because: first, governments are becoming increasingly interdependent in economics, technology, and even defense; second, the United Nations, other international institutions, and transnational corporations (TNCs) play an increasingly important role in world politics; and third, nongovernmental organizations, social movements, transnational and diasporic communities with multiple loyalties, and developments in telecommunications technology enable a "globalization from below." However, as will be argued in the next chapter, these kinds of developments, while conducive to limiting the totalizing thrust of modern state and economic power, are not well adapted to do it. While a complex international order is emerging, the nation-state is still a determinative part of world politics and crucial for upholding a liberal constitutional-legal order and the civil and political freedoms that such an order enables. Indeed, the plight of refugees confronts over-enthusiastic rhetoric about a global civil society or de-territorialized citizenship with the stark realities of modern power and unveils the ongoing need for liberal constitutional-legal orders within bounded territories.

Bare Life and the Limits of Humanitarianism

Part of the response to the crisis of sovereignty that refugees represent is to separate humanitarian concern from politics and thus maintain refugees as bare life, excluded from the political community and exposed to death at every turn. According to its statute, the actions of the office of the United Nations High Commissioner for Refugees (UNHCR) are not to be political. Its mission is solely humanitarian and social.[82] Yet the primary need of a refugee is political: it is for an arena of law and order. For Agamben, the separation of humanitarian concern from political action means that humanitarian organizations "maintain a secret solidarity with the very powers they ought to fight."[83] The most pointed example of this was the upholding of the neutrality of the International Committee of the Red Cross and its refusal to comment on the actions of Nazis, despite knowing about the concentration camps. In the UK, this distinction simultaneously makes plausible and obscures the perverse inversion of sympathy whereby the general populace demonstrate great compassion to those suffering abroad, giving millions of pounds to fund humanitarian aid, while showing great hostility to those same suffering faces when they are more proximate strangers. However, while Agamben's critique is right in relation to the response to refugees, it is more problematic as a critique of humanitarianism in general.

The questions of in what contexts humanitarian action alone is appropriate and whether humanitarian action should or should not be politicized are separate from the question of what, in general, constitutes the appropriate response to refugees. As I have argued, the need of a refugee is for an arena of law and order rather than for food, education, or some other good. The provision of shelter, food, and water (or what might be called immediate pastoral care) to those affected by natural disaster or the ravages of war may be all that is possible, or even appropriate, in particular contexts. Such provision is a means of recognizing another as a human, as one who is the same as me, and thereby communicating that they are not rejected, abandoned, or forgotten but exist in a common world. Pastoral or humanitarian care is only ever a temporary and modest response to life in the earthly city. The problem with only responding in a humanitarian as opposed to a conscious way that addresses structural issues is that questions of justice are unaddressed, so that while the symptoms may be ameliorated, the causes of the problem are at best ignored and at worst legitimated or colluded with. However, the making of such care itself into a political instrument undermines it through instrumentalizing the one cared for and subordinating the simple act of care to a superordinate political goal. In the nineteenth century this superordinate project was European imperialism; in the contemporary context, humanitarianism has come to be seen as a means of inaugurating a rationalist cosmopolitan vision of world peace.[84] A case in point is the contrasting strategies of Live Aid in 1985 – which simply sought to raise money to provide immediate aid – and its subsequent incarnation as Live8 in 2005 – which was linked to the explicitly political and somewhat messianic "Make Poverty History/ONE" campaign. Similarly, while some agencies like Médecins Sans Frontières eschew a neutral stance but are solely focused on providing humanitarian relief, other agencies, for example, Oxfam, go beyond that and are now as much advocacy and human rights organizations as aid agencies. The inverse of this instrumentalization is the political justification of war as "humanitarian intervention," for example, in Kosovo, East Timor, and more controversially in the second Gulf War; the deliberate targeting of aid agencies in militarized conflict, for example, the bombing of the UN headquarters in Iraq in 2003; and the militarization of the delivery of aid itself, for example, its use by NATO forces as part of the military strategy in the conflict in Afghanistan from 2001 onward. Nevertheless, pastoral care can only ever be the first word and never the last word when responding to a situation of great need that has a directly political dimension. For example, the provision of care to internally displaced persons amid an ongoing civil war or within an oppressive regime may be all that is possible in the first instance. A good example of this is the provision of humanitarian assistance to those affected by the cyclone in Burma in 2008. Yet it is incumbent upon churches to act in such a way so as to identify and address the causes of the conflict or oppression rather than just the symptoms. However, these are different moments, are probably best undertaken by different people, and humanitarian action should not be confused or elided with political action. Yet, even given the problem of the instrumentalization of pastoral care, it is crucial that the primarily political nature of the needs of refugees be kept to the fore and neither occluded by their representation solely as a humanitarian need nor marginalized by economic, territorial, cultural, or, more recently, security concerns. Any such move makes the refugee an exception, albeit a permanent exception, who can be dealt with outside of the rule of law.[85]

Hallowing Bare Life: A Doxological Response

It is the identification of how refugees are rendered as bare life that points to how the church can makes sense of its own duty of care to refugees and move beyond humanitarian concern. Making sense of its own duty of care, and how that care contrasts with the dominant ways in which refugees are treated in the contemporary context, necessitates a consideration of the relationship between worship and Christian witness, as it is worship that constitutes the church as a *res publica* or social and political body in itself and contradicts how we are formed into a public life shaped by dynamics driven by the state or market.[86] If it is the dynamics of the nation-state that renders refugees as bare life, it is the dynamics of worship, and in particular listening to Scripture and prayer, that serve as a preliminary preparation for encountering the refugee as a neighbor.

This section builds on the discussion of the relationship between Scripture, worship, and political action outlined in Chapter 2. It constitutes a case study in how new vision may emerge from the active listening to Scripture and the reception and performance of Scripture in public prayer – in this case the Lord's Prayer – in relation to a contested political issue. Unlike in the previous chapter, the emphasis is less on how one might encounter the other in practice and more on how we discern the Word of God in order to recognize the other as our neighbor. So the focus here is on a particular practice of worship, although the Sanctuary movement is discussed as an example of a form of earthly political action equivalent to community organizing.

As suggested in the Introduction, in order that we may deliberate upon what justice and faithfulness require, our conceptions of ourselves in relation to God and others must undergo a deepening moral conversion. As Benedict XVI puts it: "If reason is to be exercised properly, it must undergo constant purification, since it can never be completely free of the danger of a certain ethical blindness caused by the dazzling effect of power and special interests."[87] As the primary means through which to listen to the Word of God, reading and hearing Scripture constitute training in how to envision the world in relation to God and neighbor. As Dodaro argues, for Augustine, the difficulty of interpreting Scripture is itself a means of training humans in how to hear God. He notes that for Augustine, God "forces the mind to unravel the meaning of obscure biblical symbols or ambiguous passages referring to justice with difficulty; in doing so it is freed from fixed, erroneous patterns of thought and drawn into a deeper understanding of justice as a mystery."[88] For Augustine, reading Scripture is primarily a figural process that invites the reader into ever-deeper readings of the world and the discovery of it as an order of love to be delighted in of itself.

Crucial to reading the world as an order of love is the inculcation of humility that comes through the labor of listening to Scripture within the context of worship. Within Augustine's theology humility is a central Christian virtue and the antidote to pride.[89] As John Rist puts it, for Augustine:

> Humility is honesty about the human condition, and it is on the basis of that honesty, that willingness to face the facts, that man's moral and spiritual regeneration has to be founded. Humility is thus the companion of love of God just as pride is the companion of love of self.[90]

Humility is the prerequisite for true self-knowledge; that is, knowledge of oneself in relation to God and neighbor. Without humility self-love dominates and so truly loving and just relations are not possible. Thus without humility there can be no true social or common life, only competing, private interests. In listening to Scripture in worship, paradigmatically enacted in saying the Lord's Prayer, the church stands properly before its Creator, and standing properly before its Creator, may stand in right relationship with each other, knowing these others as fellow creatures (and not as competitors or rivals), for the sake of whom they each must live and in whom they may delight as fellow creatures and subjects of God's redemptive love.[91]

In light of the link between reading Scripture, humility, and worship, we can begin to make sense of how listening to Scripture and prayer are a preparation for meeting refugees as neighbors. In prayer we enact a Christian cosmopolitan orientation to the world. For in prayer we move from the local and particular to the universal, we turn out from self to God and thence to neighbor. In prayer the Christian community is oriented beyond the ties of kinship, place, and polity, as well as the boundaries of possible action, to include all those in need of God's help. As Wannenwetsch puts it: "Under the conditions of creatureliness, neighborliness in the sense of direct action on our neighbor's behalf is limited. But in its own, priestly form of action, the praying community intercedes 'for all men' in a way in which anticipates the eschatological dissolution of these limitations."[92] As such, prayer is a preparation for public life as in prayer all are included in the common world of those in need of God's help and mercy, including our distant neighbors in lands far off, our enemies, and even the seemingly invulnerable such as the emperor or president.

The saying of the Lord's Prayer in particular performs the universality of the body of Christ for it manifests the church's diachronic and synchronic unity in Christ. For as an act of worship the Lord's Prayer is a truly catholic form of worship. Not only is it shared by all denominations, including non-sacramental Christian churches such as the Salvation Army, but all Christian communities, in all parts of the world, from the very origins of the church have also practiced it. Moreover, as an act of prayer, unlike the Eucharist, it is not restricted to occasions of gathered worship but can be said in all times and in all places. Thus its universality is both temporal and spatial.

The co-inherence of reading Scripture, listening to God, practices of worship, and the social and political being of the church in the saying of the Lord's Prayer make it paradigmatic for understanding the relationship between listening to the Word of God and the ability to make increasingly just, wise, and faithful political judgments. The Lord's Prayer, said as an act of either individual or communal prayer, is simultaneously a performance of Scripture and a reconstruction and performance of the world as addressed by God. In the prayer we discover alternative repertoires or scripts for envisioning the world to those of the dominant hegemony. In the Lord's Prayer, the church as a body hears and performs the world as a place that is open to the transformative love of God and neighbor.

Hallowed Be Thy Name

The involvement of churches with refugees should be characterized as the hallowing of bare life. The hallowing of bare life is intrinsic to the command to hallow the name of God (Exod. 20. 1–7). As Karl Barth argued, the second clause of the Lord's Prayer – "Hallowed be thy name" – carries within it the declaration that God establishes God's name. Yet, in the call to hallow the name of God there is also the permission and command for the church to stand against the "twilight and ambivalence that characterizes our present" by bearing witness to the glory of God and making known "the promise of morning without evening."[93] To hallow the name of God involves us in standing against that which desecrates God's holy name.[94] The rendering of creatures as bare life constitutes just such a desecration.

The verb "to hallow" has two definitions. The first is to call or summon with shouting. The second is to make holy and sanctify or to bless a thing so that it is under the protection of a deity. The response of the church to refugees encompasses both of these definitions: it summons forth bare life from exclusion into a public or common life by abiding with refugees as persons able to express themselves within and act upon a common world; and it names refugees as creatures called by God to participate as persons in divine communion. The hallowing of God's name sets the pattern for how the church is to hallow bare life and involves recognizing bare life as gift, as judgment, and as promise. In articulating how the church is to recognize bare life as gift, judgment, and promise I will spell out the Christian cosmopolitan vision that should shape a Christian understanding of how to value political life in nation-states.

i.   Bare life as gift

To hallow something means recognizing the irreducible worth of what is before one. To hallow a name is to recognize a person and value that person's "external self-outworking and self-expression in relation to all other beings."[95] To hallow one with a name is to identify someone who is free to act in and of herself, who is not simply a passive recipient, but someone who brings herself to expression in the world (either potentially, actually, or latently). A person with a name is one who is differentiated, distinct, and deserving of honor that is their due. Barth identifies hallowing the name of God with glorification and transfiguration. Barth takes these to mean the overcoming of "all misunderstanding and obscurity concerning someone and to set forth and display his true being openly and clearly" so that he may be known "distinctly and unmistakably as the one he really is."[96] To hallow one made in the image of God, imaging being understood in relational terms, involves this same dynamic of overcoming misunderstanding and obscurity. Thus, within discussions of refugees and asylum seekers we are to avoid characterizing them as passive subjects. Rather, they are persons with a name possessing their own complex agency and motivations. Echoing the dynamics of broad-based community organizing, the church's duty of care to refugees must involve creating places for the recognition and expression of their ability to act on their own behalf.

In hallowing the name of God we recognize both the otherness of God and that God is intimately related to us. The One we hallow is named to us as Father. Thus, the two dimensions of divine personal being – otherness and relation – are encompassed in the prayer. Likewise, if hallowing bare life involves recognizing another person with a name who is distinct and other, it also involves recognizing relationship as constitutive of creaturely personhood.[97] Each of us is like all other humans, a creature of God. Yet this sameness is only ever experienced in the particularity of creaturely relations – that is, we are not God-like, everywhere all at once. Rather, to be human is to exist in the properly created limits of time and space. Relations between particular creatures necessarily involve limits and points of exchange at both an individual and communal level. There is, in effect, a proper moment of resistance and conflict in all human relations as these limits are encountered and lived through. Such limits form the basis and pattern of the relations of gift and reception that constitute creaturely personhood in the image of God. Concentric circles of sociality thus constitute creaturely personhood in the image of God. However, the dynamics of neighbor love within these concentric circles of sociality are not like ripples in a pond, becoming weaker and weaker the further they move away from an animating center. As suggested in Chapter 2, the call to respond to an other as one's neighbor disrupts such a linear or sequential logic and may entail, for example, greater intensity of devotion to distant neighbors than to family members.

The concentric circles of sociality are not dissolved by the Spirit-responsive dynamics of neighbor love. Instead, the particularity that neighbor love demands ensures that each aspect of the sociality that constitutes us as persons in the image of God is ordered in relation to each other. These dynamics involve a threefold pattern whereby while we are the same as all other creatures, we are more like some persons than others and we are also like no other person; each person is unique. The dynamics of neighbor love ensures that due attention is given, within the created limits of time and space, to each part of this threefold structure. The call to respond to an other as neighbor at times attends to what we share with them as fellow creatures, at other times to what we share within a common culture or kinship group, and at other times to an other's dissimilarity and uniqueness; for example, in response to loving the severely disabled. This basic threefold structure of human being is at once assumed and affirmed in the incarnation of Jesus Christ, the one who is truly human. Jesus is human; Jesus is unique; and Jesus, as a historical person, is more like some than others. Hospitality toward refugees (or any vulnerable stranger), as a form of neighbor love, integrates all aspects of the above threefold pattern of interpersonal relationships. To welcome the other is to recognize one who is the same as me. Yet to welcome the other is to be in a place of welcome, to be at home and thus in relationship with others who are more like me than the "stranger" who is welcomed. However, to truly welcome another is to welcome one who is like nobody else, affording them the concrete respect that communicates recognition of their unique particularity.

Relations of gift and reception constitute personhood in the image of God.[98] As already stated, such relations necessarily involve particularity, limit, and points of exchange. The particularity of creatures is, to a large extent, constituted by their place; that is, their social, economic, political, and historical location in creation. As John Inge argues, Scripture, and preeminently the Incarnation, emphasizes that places are "the seat of relations or the place of meeting and activity in the interaction between God and the world" and are thus fundamental to human being.[99] The interrelationship between personhood and the dense fabric of place – that refugeehood represents the rupture of and asylum represents the gift of – suggests the necessity of borders to relations of gift and reception. A sense of place and the existence of borders resist the homogenizing collectivism and abstraction of a cosmopolitan egalitarianism (whether liberal, capitalist, or communist) that would make everyone the same and thereby eradicate the possibility of gift-exchange. The parable of the Good Samaritan, a frequent reference point in philosophical discussions of the duty of care of refugees, is instructive here.[100]

The parable of the Good Samaritan is often read as justifying a universalistic ethic of unconditional love.[101] However, while the parable suggests that aid knows no boundaries – all may be counted as neighbors – the extension of solidarity is particular: care is given by one person to another. Proximity and location are directly relevant: the Good Samaritan responds to one he finds nearby, not some generalized "Other" who exists nowhere and everywhere. The one in distress is presented as a fleshly body to be hosted through costly personal involvement. To abstract or objectify this particular body and so pass on by without encountering them is a sin. Moreover, that the Samaritan comes from a particular place that has a particular relationship to the hearers of the story and the other characters in the parable is central to its dramatic force. Oliver O'Donovan notes: "It is essential to our humanity that there should be always foreigners, human beings from another community who have an alternative way of organising the task and privilege of being human, so that our imaginations are refreshed and our sense of cultural possibilities renewed."[102] The parable explicates, among all its hearers, both ancient and modern, precisely how someone from another place can renew our false constructions of what neighbor love consists of. As the parable suggests, while the church must uphold the worth of places as intrinsic to personal relations, it must also recognize that all our human constructions of place are under judgment.

ii. Bare life as judgment

Christianity affirms that although the above threefold pattern of relations between humans is good, it is fundamentally disrupted by sin. The proper moment of resistance between individuals and human sodalities – be they families, kinship groups, or nations – is marked by destructive rather than generative conflict. Miroslav Volf characterizes such conflict as exclusion. Through an exegesis of Genesis 1, Volf notes that God separates the "formless void" and binds together certain elements. Creativity involves separating and binding together (i.e., difference and relationship). Exclusion is the process by which the proper separation and connections that God establishes are exploded and imploded. Exclusion is destructive of creation because, first, it cuts good connections, breaking down interdependence, so that the other emerges as an enemy; and second, it erases separation, not recognizing the other as someone who, in his or her otherness, belongs to the pattern of interdependence. The other then emerges as an inferior who must be either assimilated or subjugated to me. Volf states: "Exclusion takes place when the violence of expulsion, assimilation, or subjugation and the indifference of abandonment replace the dynamics of taking in and keeping out as well as the mutuality of giving and receiving."[103] Volf distinguishes exclusion from differentiation. Exclusion is the false setting of boundaries and the exploding of proper ones, pushing creation back to chaos. Differentiation is that which maintains generative boundaries and patterns of relationship. Hallowing bare life and hospitality of strangers upholds differentiation while countering exclusion.[104] However, given the sinful nature of human relations there is no reason to suppose that our hospitality will not be quarrelsome and contentious. The issue is whether human hospitality toward others, for the most part, reinforces exclusion or upholds a creative differentiation.

Just as the hallowing of God's name reorients the community of prayer to God, so the hallowing of bare life reorients the church's existence, calling into question patterns of sedentary exclusivity. Refugees, like the fetus and the suffering-dying, call us to recognize bare life as human life worthy of respect and to be afforded dignity as a potential or existent participant in a particular human community. Refugees call us to extend public friendship and question our limits as to whom we recognize as persons; that is, whom we include in the relations of gift-exchange in a particular place and whether our response to the boundaries between ourselves and another is generative or destructive. In short, hallowing bare life presses a universal or, more specifically, an eschatological horizon upon particular loyalties and concerns. The primary moral claim of the refugee is the claim to personhood through the restoration of their ability to express themselves within and act upon a common world. Yet, our response to refugees unveils our propensity to retreat and withdraw in order to protect "our" property or "our" way of life, thereby turning place from gift to possession and rendering refugees as bare life. Our response to refugees unveils the deeply embedded economy of scarcity and equivalence that informs Western society. It is an economy that refuses the possibility of a generative, over-abundant eschatological future and conforms to the logic of fate rather than faith. The emphasis in current refugee policy on deterrence rather than prevention is indicative of such fatalism.[105]

John Milbank suggests that Jesus can be characterized as a *homo sacer*.[106] On this reading, Jesus unmasks the exclusionary violence and self-justification at work in human society. Analogous to how the church is to receive Jesus and so repent and turn away from its participation in systems and structures of sin and "idolatrous security," refugees, as *homo sacer*, decenter and disrupt our sedentary lives and our refusal to live as pilgrims within the earthly city.[107] Conversely, we should be wary of over-valorizing exile, diasporic existence, and mobility. Refugees point to the importance of home, place, and territory – their need is precisely for these things – and so they call into question the "postmodern beatification of the nomad."[108]

iii. Bare life as promise

The hallowing of bare life involves trusting that we will see God's kingdom come and his will be done on earth as it is in heaven. "Hallowed be thy name" is an expression of eschatological hope for that time when God will be all in all.[109] The Lord's Prayer as a whole can be read as a summons to live according to the kingdom of God. The gift of kinship with God that is established in Christ is the beginning of a new community whose pattern of life is set out in the Prayer. This new community generates new forms of solidarity. Wannenwetsch notes how the formation of the *ekklesia* overcame the antinomies of *polis* and *oikos* to form a hybrid, the *oikos-polis*.[110] The new political space that was the church refigured all existing social relations. Women, slaves, and children, who were previously excluded from the public political realm, are now addressed as citizens.[111] Men, the only ones who had political agency, and who in their homes were the *paterfamilias*, are now asked to identify themselves as brothers to slaves, women, and children.[112] As Galatians 3 suggests, ethnic, sexual, political, and economic differences do not count when it comes to being included as a citizen in the city of God; and as the Gospel of Matthew puts it, it is "whoever does the will of my Father in heaven [who] is my brother and sister and mother" (Matt. 12.50). The hallowing of bare life involves just such a refiguring of social relations in the contemporary context.[113] Churches throughout the world have, for the most part, been at the forefront of arguing for the political rights of refugees, providing sanctuary, visiting them in detention centers, and trying to overcome their dehumanization in contemporary debates. A good example of this is the Sanctuary movement in North America that built relationships between North Americans and Central Americans; led to extensive ecumenical cooperation; at a local level it forged new relationships between Hispanics, African-Americans, Native Americans and White/Anglos, Jews, Christians, and agnostics, and "liberal" and "conservative" believers; and, despite its predominantly male

leadership, placed women in prominent roles in the public sphere.[114]
As Hilary Cunningham notes:

> [The Sanctuary movement] bonded people together in a novel social group
> recasting the way in which they perceived and experienced themselves as
> "church." In redefining what a "church" was, the participants of the Sanctuary
> movement profoundly reconstituted their social reality and their place within it.
> This process of "articulation" altered the ways in which the individuals identi-
> fied themselves vis-à-vis their families/kin groups, their denominational churches,
> their nation/government, and, ultimately, the international community.[115]

The new forms of public friendship that emerge through the hallowing of
bare life necessarily involve a two-way reconfiguration. Openness to the
other involves changing the status quo in order to accommodate the otherness of the other. Likewise, the "guest" must adapt and change as they, with
their host, together seek communion with God. As José Martín, an organizer in the San Francisco refugee community, comments in relation to his
experience of receiving help from the Sanctuary movement: "We are the
guests and the North Americans are the hosts, but they share in the pilgrim-
age that we are on."[116] This is to spell out the dynamics of gift-exchange and
mutual learning within the normative practice of Christian hospitality.
However, such mutual transformation necessarily involves loss as the familiar and what counts as "home" is renegotiated. In order for new forms of
friendship to emerge, a process of grieving is necessary as both guest and
host emigrate from the familiar.[117] Such grieving is the prelude to the formation of shared memories; an interdependent identity narrative; and a new
place emerging that both guest and host can call home. Without any account
of loss and grief, racist politics and an exclusionary nostalgia gain legitimacy and so the promise of bare life is never fulfilled.[118]

In relation to all of the above, it must be remembered that the hallowing
of bare life is not a call to be overwhelmed by what cannot be done. Christian
eschatology is neither utopian nor idealistic. We are not to fret that we are
not gods. We can only take little steps operating within the world as it is;
that is, within the framework of opportunities and possibilities open to us.
The church cannot solve the refugee problem and it cannot present itself as
the bearer of a solution to the complex interplay of factors that result in
huge numbers of refugees. Yet, as Karl Barth notes, "Measured by whether
it is analogous or not to the hallowing of God's name for which we pray, a
supposedly great step might be a fairly small one. Measured by the same
criterion, a supposedly little step might really be a very big one."[119] Stories
of five thousand fed from a few loaves and fishes, of mustard seeds turning

into great trees, of new life gestated in crucifixion and death should open our eyes to the reality that, within an economy of grace, small steps can bear manifold fruit.

Sanctuary: The Practice of Hallowing Bare Life

An example of just such a small step bearing manifold fruit and of hallowing bare life in practice is the US Sanctuary movement. The movement was a response to what was perceived as the immoral and illegal deportation of Central American refugees from countries with regimes supported by the US government, in particular Guatemala and El Salvador.[120] The movement was inaugurated in March 1982 by the public declaration of sanctuary by Southside Presbyterian Church in Tucson, Arizona. Cunningham, in her ethnographic and historical study of the movement, notes that at its height in 1986–7 it spanned Mexico, the United States, and Canada, involved more than four hundred congregations (including synagogues), and claimed between sixty and seventy thousand participants.[121] The primary activity of the movement was to develop an "underground railway" and network of support and "safe houses" for those seeking asylum, self-consciously reminiscent of the abolitionists prior to and during the American Civil War.[122] The Reagan–Bush response to those fleeing persecution in brutal regimes in such places as Chile and El Salvador was to deny that they were refugees and class them as illegal aliens and economic migrants. This policy was highly selective as those seeking to claim asylum from persecution under communist regimes were actively encouraged and supported by the then US administration.[123] The church groups sought to uphold the tradition of offering asylum to the persecuted and the unbiased application of the legal obligation stemming from the 1980 Refugee Act and the incorporation of the UN protocols on refugees into US law in 1968.[124]

At its origin, the decision of provide sanctuary came out of a process of listening to both Scripture and the needs of vulnerable strangers simultaneously. Susan Coutin, in her ethnography of the movement, records how pastors of six congregations located near the University of California were holding a weekly Bible study on the lectionary readings that were the basis of their sermons. At the same time, in response to the murder of Archbishop Romero, and other high-profile incidents, the Bible study group started to read about deportations and human rights abuses in Central America. In response they began to consider whether the tradition of sanctuary could be applied to Central American refugees. It was at this point that church leaders in Tucson contacted them and asked whether they would house undocumented Central

Americans. Meanwhile, in Tucson, some involvement with Central American refugees led members of the Tucson Ecumenical Council to consider whether they might offer sanctuary to those seeking asylum and under threat of deportation.[125] In preparation for a vote by the congregation at its annual general meeting on whether to make the church a sanctuary for refugees, Southside Presbyterian Church undertook two months of Bible study meetings and reflection on US immigration laws.[126] The centrality of Scripture to the self-definition of the movement is suggested by the use of Scriptural references in what Coutin terms the "religious humour" that abounded in the movement.[127] For example, the number of the hotline that sanctuary workers established during the trial of eleven of their co-workers was 1-800-LEV-1933, after Leviticus 19.33, a verse that was a key inspiration for the movement.[128] A process of listening to Scripture and the testimonies of refugees continued to be a key part of the development and motivation of those involved in the movement.[129]

The provision of Sanctuary was a self-consciously ecclesial act, its work viewed as a form of ministry and framed within explicitly theological discourses. Symbolically, this was enacted at the first public declaration of sanctuary to the government and the media by a march from downtown Tucson to Southside Church where an ecumenical service was held to mark the occasion.[130] It was articulated at a theoretical level in, for example, the work of Jim Corbett, one of the key early leaders in Tucson, who drew on his Quakerism and Liberation theology in order to frame the provision of sanctuary and the activities in support of the refugees as a way of forming an ecumenical and Covenantal (i.e., involving Jews and Christians) base community through which "the beneficiaries of violence are entering into active community with the violated."[131] Likewise, the East Bay Sanctuary Covenant group conceptualized their work as an ecclesial act whereby different Christian and Jewish congregations covenanted to act together for a common purpose.[132] Institutionally, the commitment to the ecclesial basis of sanctuary led the Tucson-based groups to resist what in Chapter 1 was identified as a process of institutional isomorphism whereby church responses copy state forms. They insisted that the provision of sanctuary remain a congregationally based activity rather than a bureaucratically and nationally organized endeavor where individual rather than communal action would become more important.[133] In terms of governance, church-based forms of deliberation and authorization were seen to provide sufficient legitimacy to act in the face of either ambivalent or absent legal authorization.[134] As one pastor comments, reflecting on the process by which his congregation came to a decision about whether to provide sanctuary or not: "Their reasoning was based on Christian hospitality. We decided that we had always helped people before on the basis of human need, and that we'd never asked anyone for their I.D.s or green cards."[135] In other words, the status of the refugee before God was prior to the status ascribed to them by the state.[136] As an action of the church qua church, sanctuary was understood as inherently contesting the actions of the state. Sister Darlene Nicgorski makes this explicit in her defendant's statement at her trial for people smuggling. Addressing the Judge, she stated:

> You and only you, Judge Carroll, can still make a difference. You have the authority and power. Many have prayed for your conversion, hoping you would see the light of truth and life. You by your sentence can add your YES to the God of Justice and Life and therefore your NO to the Caesar who wants to use his money, power, and law to silence the witnesses of its policies in Central America. I do not ask for myself but ask because it will be a symbol of the change of your heart and herald of hope to Central America.[137]

As the movement developed, significant divisions emerged between the "Chicago" and "Tucson" wings.[138] The Chicago Religious Task Force on Central America (CRTF) was an advocacy group formed in response to the murder of four American churchwomen in El Salvador in 1980 and was primarily led by former Catholic missionaries. It drew more narrowly on Liberation theology than the Tucson wing.[139] In the first instance, it approached members of the Tucson group about becoming involved.[140] Subsequently, the Tucson group invited them to provide a coordinating and advocacy role for the growing numbers of congregations involved in the provision of sanctuary. The CRTF framed the action as a form of civil disobedience with the overtly political objective of changing US foreign policy. This was played out in the fact that CRTF wanted to restrict the underground to Central Americans fleeing right-wing violence and repression. In contrast, the Tucson-based group envisioned their actions as a form of "civil initiative" designed to uphold the laws the US government was violating.[141] Moreover, the Tucson group self-consciously resisted the instrumentalization of the refugees and the subordination of the church to a prior political project.[142] Jim Corbett, a central figure in the Tucson group states:

> The Sanctuary covenant community that has formed in Tucson could never assimilate into such a movement because we provide Sanctuary for the persecuted regardless of the political origins of their persecution or of their usefulness in promoting preconceived objectives. We are convinced that whenever the covenant community's decision to stand with the oppressed is understood to mean it must place itself in a subordinate alignment with any creed, ideology, hierarchy, platform, armed force, or party, its prophetic role is betrayed

and its reconciling role is abandoned. We disagree with any interpretation of Sanctuary that would shape it selectively into a factional instrument.[143]

Coutin notes how participants in the Tucson wing distanced themselves from what they saw as conventional political activism, which they associated with dogmatism, factionalism, and the pursuit of class-based interests rather than the common good, and, echoing Corbett's remarks, understood what they were doing as prophetic rather than narrowly political.[144]

As the discussion in Chapters 1 and 2 would suggest, it is the Tucson group who were the more faithful witnesses. Moreover, in relation to the argument of this chapter, the offer of sanctuary was precisely an upholding and extension of the rule of law to those rendered bare life by the liberal nation-state and the calling forth of a more consistent application of the liberal constitutional-legal order over and against its subversion by the then government.[145] Like community organizing, the actions of the Tucson group held to account the governing authorities so as to arouse or call forth just judgment on a contested political issue. And again, like churches involved in community organizing, they acted constructively by extending bonds of neighbor love to vulnerable strangers so as to establish a common world of meaning and action.[146]

In addition to seeking to enable right judgment and extending the bonds of neighbor love, the Tucson group's action, like community organizing, sought to forge anew an institutional plurality as a defense against the totalizing thrust of modern state power. This can be understood best in reference to how the practice of sanctuary as a way of hallowing bare life harks back to the medieval practice of sanctuary and the complex space of overlapping and multiple jurisdictions within Christendom. The Christian practice of sanctuary drew explicitly on the Hebrew scriptures (e.g., Exod. 21:12–14; Num. 35:6–34; Deut. 4:41–43) and became a key institutional means for the protection of the falsely accused, limiting blood feuds and ensuring mercy and due process for fugitives.[147] Through Canon law it also incorporated and greatly extended elements of the existing rights of asylum at pagan temples in Roman law.[148] However, a key point of contrast with the prior Roman practice was that even the guilty could seek refuge and thereby find absolution.[149] For example, Augustine justifies the provision of sanctuary even to the guilty on the basis that it echoes God's forgiveness of the wrong-doer through enabling penitence and the reception of grace.[150] The first formal recognition of church sanctuary comes in the Theodosian Code (AD 392). The Theodosian laws suggest the usage of churches for asylum prior to their legal authorization, the laws seeking to regulate some aspects of existing practice.[151] Gervase Rosser notes that in its Christian articulation sanctuary was not only vested in holy places but in holy people as well.[152] In its earliest forms sanctuary was a practical expression of the church's peace, acting as a peaceable zone of exception mitigating the severity of violent rule by both kith and king within the *saeculum*.[153] Sanctuary complemented the Peace and Truce of God movements that, from the tenth and eleventh centuries onwards, sought to limit violence in feudal society. For example, Rosser delineates how sanctuary functioned to enable a suspension of violence in disputes and open a space for negotiation and peaceful settlement.[154] However, the provision of sanctuary did not simply enable a nonviolent means of dispute resolution. As Trisha Olson puts it: "Undergirding all forms of dispute resolution was the entrenched belief that the proper gesture, given in the proper manner, and properly accepted could restore what wrongdoing had destroyed."[155] Penitential rites were thus a constitutive part of the process of resolution and repair.

Through the emergent practice of sanctuary, from late antiquity to the late medieval period, the church contradicted the movement toward monarchical consolidation of power.[156] From the outset the question of who granted the right of sanctuary – the church, the king, or local custom – was fiercely contested, the provision of sanctuary being a site of vehement negotiation that marked the shifting boundary between political and ecclesial sovereignty and their mutual relationship with place-bound practices and social norms.[157] What is clear is that the provision of sanctuary, in all its different modes and legal formulations, represented both a limitation on the sovereign power of the king and an alternative arena of jurisdiction to secular power.[158] Its demise in England in the early modern period was part of the centralizing and homogenizing thrust of the developing nation-state.[159] William Ray states that by 1486: "The courts were prepared to go to whatever lengths necessary to limit the privilege and discredit proven sanctuaries so that the political aims of the government would be advanced. The fact that sanctuary had been a heretofore untrammelled right of every English subject seemed to have mattered little."[160] As Rosser notes, according to most writing on the subject, its decline is not lamented but viewed as part of the proper triumph of the modern secular state over priestly privilege.[161] In England it was officially abolished by statute in 1624.[162, 163] However, although abolished as a formal legal procedure, it continued as a recognized right and custom.[164] For example, the right of sanctuary continued to exist at the Abbey of Holyroodhouse until 1880.[165] In an ironic twist, the church's right to provide sanctuary remained part of Roman Catholic Canon law until 1983 – the very point at which it was being rediscovered in the USA as a way of marking the church as a *res publica* or public body, constituted by its worship, that bore witness to the relative value of earthly sovereign power.

The practice of sanctuary, as a specific form of Christian hospitality, is the therapy or antidote for anyone rendered bare life under the totalizing thrust of the state. As a practice, it witnesses to the claim that after Christ divine law holds sway and all must eventually come to judgment before Christ the King – both accused and accuser, king and subject, outlaw and law-maker, violated and violator – and all may be forgiven in and through Christ. Agamben does not take account of this in his account of *homer sacer*. For the church, the Christ-event constitutes a ban of *homer sacer*. For example, Olson outlines how it was the duty of every man in eleventh-century England to pursue an outlaw, ravage his lands, burn his house, and hunt him as prey for he was a *caput gerat lupinum* – a friendless man, *werewolf*, wolf-man – in other words, he was bare life.[166] Yet at the same time, the right of sanctuary and liturgical processes of giving satisfaction provided a countervailing injunction to enable the possibility of forgiveness and reconciliation if the proper sacrifice was made.[167] Thus, for example, William I's charter for Battle Abbey, in keeping with ancient custom dating back to the sixth-century reign of Ethelbert, King of Kent, states that "if any thief or homicide, or anyone other guilty [person] flee from fear of death to this church, let him in no way be hurt, but let them all be freely discharged."[168] So in contrast to the outlaw who could be killed with impunity, the sanctuary fugitive and abjurer was under the protection of the Church and as long as they kept to certain conditions, they could not be harmed.[169] As Jordan puts it: "The fundamental outcome of sanctuary was the saving of the lives of vulnerable people."[170] Theologically, if Christ is King, then no earthly sovereign or community has the power or right to utterly exclude or make an exception of anyone from the status of a human being. The church is to witness to this and sanctuary is one such means of faithful witness.

The formal provision of sanctuary created political spaces through which the church could emphasize an individual's relation to and status before God in a way that was independent of the state and the community.[171] Like all forms of hospitality, it is open to abuse and there is much evidence to suggest that it was abused. Nevertheless, despite this, sanctuary was a form of public action that bore witness to how a person's status as criminal, outlaw, or political subject was relativized and limited by their status as one who is created, fallen, and redeemed by God. The practice of sanctuary was not necessarily a form of dissent or opposition to the crown. Indeed, the sovereign often reinforced and upheld the privilege of sanctuary as the example of chartered sanctuaries indicates. However, sanctuary did limit sovereign power and represented an alternative arena of jurisdiction, and the question of who could or could not claim sanctuary was a site of contestation between church and state. Thus the practice of sanctuary conforms to the O'Donovans' conception of Christendom as outlined in Chapter 1; that is, it was a measure that embodied the assumption that ecclesial and political authority share a joint responsibility for the formation of an earthly peace and enabling judgment, with the judgment of the church taking the form of proclamation of the Gospel (in this case via the practice of sanctuary) and the judgment of political authority being limited to the arena of coercive human legal and political judgment.

Summary

This chapter constitutes an assessment of the contemporary debate on the duty of care to refugees and presented a theological response to this debate. The needs of the refugee are distinct from those of the economically destitute or those displaced due to natural disaster. They are political. The needs of refugees being for a new polity means that in relation to migration, refugees are the most vulnerable because their needs cannot be met in any other way except by inclusion in a new polity. Thus, in relation to policies of admittance, they should receive priority even over destitute economic migrants (although distinguishing between the two is often difficult in the contemporary context). Others, with other needs, can be aided by a variety of different means. Indeed, churches should call on governments to emphasize the needs of refugees over and against current policies which favor certain types of skilled economic migrant yet are increasingly restrictive toward asylum seekers. Policies which favor those who make an economic contribution over those whose need is for a new polity is, on this account, immoral and raises larger questions about what ends any given polity seeks: that is, is it a community that seeks justice or simply a way of organizing economic competition?

As should be clear from the preceding argument, I am not proposing the provision of sanctuary as an appropriate response to economic migration. However, there are various proposals for the regularization of undocumented, long-term economic migrants that are wholly consistent with what I have argued for here. One such example is that developed by the Citizen Organising Foundation (COF), an umbrella for broad-based community organizing in the UK. The basic tenet of the proposal is the following: "We believe that those who have been here for four or more years should be admitted to a two-year pathway to full legal rights ('leave to remain') during which they work legally and demonstrate their contribution to UK economy and society." The detailed proposal retains a proper attention to place and the moral licitness of borders; it balances the duty of care to existing citizens with the need to prevent migrants being rendered bare life; and it seeks to reestablish the rule of law and uphold the liberal legal-constitutional order through ensuring that those rendered outlaws by government inaction and deliberate policy are enabled to become law-abiding citizens.[172]

Refugees, by definition, need a relatively stable and just regime of law and order. As relatively stable and just regimes of law and order, liberal democracies are called upon to provide asylum. However, a question thus arises about how to reconcile a duty of care to refugees with the ongoing duty of care to existing members of liberal democracies. Debates about how to respond to this question appear irresolvable because contending parties lack any teleology by which to make a just judgment between different claims. On a Christian account of political authority there is no necessary conflict between welcoming refugees and the pursuit of the common life of a polity. There is, however, a need for just and generous political judgment. Such a judgment is possible only when the pursuit of the goods of a particular polity are ordered to the good of humanity as a whole and the common good of humanity is itself ordered in relation to communion with God. The tragedy of the contemporary context is that, despite their best intentions, liberal democratic polities render refugees as bare life, life exposed to death at every turn. Conversely, refugees unveil how humans possess rights only when they are counted as participants in a nation-state – whether as citizens or as putative citizens. The response of the church must be to move beyond the antinomies of humanitarian concern and political exclusion and refuse to link inclusion of the most vulnerable in a common life with participation in a nation-state.[173] Refusing to see refugees as an exception, churches must overcome the exclusion of refugees by abiding with them as persons able to express themselves within and act upon a common world. Such action can be characterized as the hallowing of bare life. Hallowing bare life involves being open, first, to the dignity of refugees as those who are subjects of Divine justice and forgiveness, irrespective of their citizenship status; second, to how refugees disrupt patterns of idolatrous security; and third, to how they call the church to witness to the in-breaking reign of God. The witness of the Sanctuary movement is a concrete example of what, within particular circumstances, hallowing refugees looks like in practice.

The first two chapters outlined a critique of the nation-state and emphasized local forms of corporate politics as the primary arena of faithful witness. This chapter has extended the critique of the nation-state while at the same time seeking to value the nation-state as an arena of law and order that represents exactly what a refugee needs. Yet it is exactly this need that is increasingly withheld from refugees, as other goods such as security or economic advantage are valued over and above the rule of law at both a national and international level. At a national level, especially in relation to issues such as immigration and asylum, the witness of the church is to be directed to upholding the rule of law and extending that rule to those whose need is greatest. If this chapter has sought to value the limited, earthly good of the liberal democratic nation-state within a wider Christian cosmopolitan vision, the next chapter moves beyond the nation-state to consider the conditions and possibilities of faithful witness within the context of globalized economic relations.

Notes

1 Related issues, not directly addressed in this chapter, are: first, the morality of deterrence and prevention policies that aim to reduce the numbers of asylum seekers arriving in a country; second, the ethics of detention centers; third, the ethics of dispersal policies which isolate refugees from fellow countrymen and whether these contravene a fundamental aspect of what it means to be human (i.e., the ability to express oneself in relationship with others); and fourth, the question of what can be expected or required of refugees when they are participants, whether temporary or permanent, of a given, "host" society (i.e., the duties of "guestship" and residence).

2 For a history of the origins and development of the international refugee regime see Gil Loescher, *Beyond Charity: International Cooperation and the Global Refugee Crises* (Oxford: Oxford University Press, 1993), pp. 11–128.

3 Loescher, *Beyond Charity*, pp. 16–17, 141.

4 Ibid., p. 6.

5 For the OAU definition see Myron Weiner, *The Global Migration Crises: Challenges to States and to Human Rights* (New York: HarperCollins College Publishers, 1995), p. 188. Since 1997, in addition to the grounds for recognition given in the UN Convention, Sweden has recognized a well-founded fear of capital or corporal punishment; protection from non-state persecution (civil war, external conflict, or environmental disaster); and a well-founded fear of persecution because of gender or sexual orientation. Andrew Geddes, *The Politics of Migration and Immigration in Europe* (London: Sage, 2003), p. 110.

6 Andrew Shacknove, "Who is a refugee?" *Ethics* 95.2 (1985), pp. 274–84.

7 Matthew Gibney, *The Ethics and Politics of Asylum: Liberal Democracy and the Response to Refugees* (Cambridge: Cambridge University Press, 2004), p. 8.

8 It should be noted, however, that the line between political policy and natural disaster is not hard and fast. The work of Amartya Sen calls into question quite how "natural" many natural disasters are. See, for example, Amartya Sen, *Poverty and Famines* (Oxford: Clarendon Press, 1981).

9 Gibney, *The Ethics and Politics of Asylum*, p. 9.

10 For the purposes of this chapter an *asylum seeker* is someone who is fleeing persecution in their homeland, has arrived in another country, made themselves

known to the authorities, and exercised the legal right to apply for asylum under the UN Convention. It should be noted that it is not technically possible to seek asylum illegally. Passage from a country of origin into another country may be illegal, but, once in the UK, anyone may legitimately claim asylum under current legislation. A *failed asylum seeker* is someone whose asylum application has been turned down and is awaiting return to their country of origin. In UK law, "failed asylum seekers" are entitled to appeal and remain until a final decision has been made. The Home Office recognizes other reasons why it may not be able to remove someone from the UK immediately, ranging from illness and imminent childbirth to refusal by the country of origin to accept the person back without documentation or if it is not safe for unsuccessful asylum seekers to return. For any of these reasons they may be granted leave to stay. An *illegal immigrant* is someone who has arrived in another country, intentionally not made him or herself known to the authorities, and has no legal basis for being there.

11   Likewise, the right to emigration does not entail a right to immigration in another country. On this see Michael Walzer, *Spheres of Justice: A Defence of Pluralism and Equality* (New York: Basic Books, 1983), pp. 39–40; and Gibney, *The Ethics and Politics of Asylum*, p. 68.

12   Peter and Renata Singer, "The Ethics of Refugee Policy," in *Open Borders? Closed Societies? The Ethics and Political Issues*, ed. Mark Gibney (Westport, CT: Greenwood Press, 1988), p. 121–2.

13   Michael Dummett, *On Immigration and Refugees* (London: Routledge, 2001), pp. 26–7, 80.

14   Rawls himself does not develop the "original position" in this way. For his critique of a global original position see Rawls, *The Law of the Peoples*, pp. 82–3, 119–20. Rawls argues that boundaries are a necessary feature of political association (pp. 38–9). In his account of the "Law of the Peoples" he sees the right of self-determination and the preservation of a particular way of life as goods in and of themselves, advocating a "proper patriotism" (pp. 111–12). By implication the preservation of these goods necessitates admission policies and, within his account of distributive justice, priority should be given to existing members of a given country, with inequality between peoples dealt with on a society-to-society basis rather than an individual basis (pp. 115–19). For a critique of Rawls's argument, especially Rawls's account of a "people," see Seyla Benhabib, *The Rights of Others: Aliens, Residents and Citizens* (Cambridge: Cambridge University Press, 2004), pp. 74–114. Benhabib presents a parallel argument to Carens, focusing on individual rights in international relations rather than organizing such relations on a society-to-society basis.

15   Joseph Carens, "Aliens and Citizens: The Case for Open Borders," *The Review of Politics* 49.2 (1987), pp. 251–73. However, more recently, Carens has shifted his position, arguing that the right to move freely across borders is not absolute and that there can be justifiable reasons for restricting it. Joseph Carens, "A Reply to Meilaender: Reconsidering Open Borders," *International Migration Review* 33.4 (1999), pp. 1088–9.

16 Gibney, *The Ethics and Politics of Asylum*, pp. 65–76.

17 Benhabib, *The Rights of Others*, pp. 220–1.

18 See, for example, Martha Nussbaum, "Patriotism and Cosmopolitanism," in *For the Love of Country: Debating the Limits of Patriotism*, ed. Joshua Cohen (Boston, MA: Beacon Press, 1996), pp. 12–17.

19 Walzer, *Spheres of Justice*, p. 62.

20 Ibid., p. 64.

21 Ibid., p. 65.

22 Ibid., p. 49.

23 Walzer argues that while all humans owe each other mutual aid, political membership is a distributive good that is necessarily distributed unequally.

24 Gibney, *The Ethics and Politics of Asylum*, p. 82.

25 Gibney, *The Ethics and Politics of Asylum*, p. 84.

26 Ibid., p. 83.

27 Ibid. This argument, however, can be applied to what any polity, whether liberal democratic or not, holds to be a good.

28 Ibid., p. 231.

29 Ibid.

30 Such an account intrinsically recognizes the situated or embedded nature of a liberal account of the good life.

31 For accounts of the deep Scriptural and doctrinal logic that this teleology draws on, see O'Donovan, *The Desire of the Nations: Rediscovering the Roots of Political Theory* (Cambridge: Cambridge University Press, 1996), pp. 66–73; Jon D. Levenson, "The Universal Horizon of Biblical Particularism," in Mark Brett, ed., *Ethnicity and the Bible* (Leiden: E. J. Brill, 1996), pp. 143–69; and Nigel Biggar, "The Value of Limited Loyalty: Christianity, the Nation, and Territorial Boundaries," in David Millar and Sohail Hashimi, eds., *Boundaries and Justice: Diverse Ethics Perspectives* (Princeton, NJ: Princeton University Press, 2001), pp. 38–54; Luke Bretherton, "Valuing the Nation: Nationalism and Cosmopolitanism in Theological Perspective," in Stephen Holmes, ed., *Public Theology in Cultural Engagement: God's Key to the Redemption of the World* (Milton Keynes: Paternoster, 2008), pp. 170–96.

32 *City of God*, XIX, 17. As Neville Figgis argues, against the aggregations of empire, Augustine favors an international order of small states. Augustine states: "If men were always peaceful and just, human affairs would be happier and all kingdoms would be small, rejoicing in concord with their neighbors. There would be as many kingdoms among nations of the world as there are now houses of the citizens of a city." (*City of God*, IV, 15). John Neville Figgis, *The Political Aspects of S. Augustine's "City of God"* (Gloucester, MA: Peter Smith, 1963), p. 58. Augustine's Christian cosmopolitanism can be situated within his overarching conception of love as beginning "at home" and extending outwards. On this see Eric Gregory, *Politics and the Order of Love: An Augustinian Ethic of Democratic Citizenship* (Chicago, IL: University of Chicago Press, 2008), pp. 356–7.

33 Mary M. Keys, *Aquinas, Aristotle, and the Promise of the Common Good* (Cambridge: Cambridge University Press, 2006), p. 117.

34 John Calvin, *Institutes of the Christian Religion*, trans. Henry Beveridge (Grand Rapids, MI: Eerdmans, 1983), II. viii. 55.

35 Karl Barth, *Church Dogmatics: The Doctrine of Creation* vol. III part 4, trans. A. T. Mackay et al. (Edinburgh: T&T Clark, 1961), pp. 309–23.

36 *Guadium et Spes*, #74.

37 Theologically, Dante is a deliberately ambiguous or borderline figure given that in his more explicitly political writing (most notably in *De Monarchia*), he divorces human fulfillment from its fulfillment in communion with God such that it becomes an autonomous end. On this see Oliver O'Donovan and Joan Lockwood O'Donovan, *From Irenaeus to Grotius: A Sourcebook in Christian Political Thought 100–1625* (Grand Rapids, MI: Eerdmans, 1999), pp. 413–14, 423–4.

38 After Dante and Marsilius of Padua, the theological vision of the church as the concrete embodiment of the universal commonwealth in which each particular nation moved beyond itself into divine and human communion was eclipsed by the thrust for an autonomous, "natural" universal human community. In short, what we see in the contrast between Dante's *Commedia* and his *Monarchia* are the rival strands of the cosmopolitan tradition: one theological, the other rationalist.

39 There is a strand of Christian political thought that justifies empire, for example, Eusebius. Even here, empire is framed as a fulfillment of the local where the local is part of a hierarchy of rule rather than simply being overridden. Within modern theology, arguments for world government were put forward by Jacques Maritain. As already noted in Chapter 2, his work informs much contemporary Catholic social thought, in particular *Pacem in Terris*. However, for the most part, the tradition equates world government with oppressive empire or the "beast" of Revelation. For a critique of Maritain and *Pacem in Terris* see Joan Lockwood O'Donovan, "Subsidiarity and Political Authority in Theological Perspective," in Oliver and Joan Lockwood O'Donovan, *Bonds of Imperfection: Christian Politics, Past and Present*, Oliver and Joan Lockwood O'Donovan (Grand Rapids, MI: Eerdmans, 2004), pp. 225–45.

Although qualified by the recognition in *Pacem in Terris* that the common good of a nation cannot be absolutized or separated from the good of the entire human family and in *Centesimus Annus* (1991) of the priority of civil society over and against the state, there is an absence in modern Catholic social thought of any substantive critique of the liberal nation-state as an arena in which the common good can be deliberated and acted upon. What is required is the incorporation of something like Alasdair MacIntyre's Thomist account of local politics and his critique of the nation-state. In relation to Catholic social teaching, MacIntyre's work specifies what it might mean, outside of a commitment to the liberal nation-state, to declare: "The Church's commitment on behalf of social pluralism aims at bringing about a more fitting attainment of the common good and democracy itself, according to the principles of solidarity, subsidiarity and justice." (Pontifical Council of Justice and Peace, *Compendium of the Social Doctrine of the Church* (London: Continuum, 2004), p. 210). More generally, MacIntyre's account of local politics outlines why local as opposed to national politics is necessarily the primary arena of Christian political witness. For a more extensive account of MacIntyre's conception of local politics and how it relates to a critique of the nation-state see Bretherton, *Hospitality as Holiness*, pp. 95–101.

40 *Pietas* denotes the reverence and concern for that to which one owes the possibility of one's own development, be it God, one's family, city, or country.

41 Quoted from Thomas Schlereth, *The Cosmopolitan Ideal* (Notre Dame, IN: University of Notre Dame, 1977), pp. xxiv–xxv. For a review of the different approaches to international relations and schemes to bring world peace set out by Enlightenment philosophers see ibid., pp. 90–125.

42 Ibid., p. 90. Martha Nussbaum's advocacy of "cosmopolitan education" can be seen as a contemporary equivalent of this kind of project. Nussbaum, "Patriotism and Cosmopolitanism," pp. 12–17.

43 See, for example, Teresa Hayton, *Open Borders: The Case Against Immigration Control* (Sterling, VA: Pluto Press, 2000).

44 Wolfhart Pannenberg, *Ethics*, trans. Keith Crim (Philadelphia, PA: Westminster Press, 1981), p. 147.

45 Ibid., p. 148.

46 Ibid.

47 Ibid., p. 151–74.

48 On this see Miroslav Volf, *Exclusion and Embrace: A Theological Exploration of Identity, Otherness, and Reconciliation* (Nashville, TN: Abingdon Press, 1996), pp. 57–98.

49 Ibid., p. 226.

50 *City of God*, XIV, 28.

51 Oliver O'Donovan, "Government as Judgment," in *Bonds of Imperfection*, pp. 207–4.

52 Joan Lockwood O'Donovan, "Nation, State and Civil Society in the Western Biblical Tradition," in *Bonds of Imperfection*, p. 287.

53 Ibid., pp. 286–7.

54 On this see Chantal Mouffe, *The Democratic Paradox* (London: Verso, 2000); and Seyla Benhabib, *The Rights of Others*, pp. 43–8. Benhabib, while noting the particularity and territoriality of democracy and how this sets up a conflict with the universalist claims of human rights, argues that it is resolvable in the contemporary context via new modalities of political agency involving multiple democratic iterations within a cosmopolitan federalist structure. This would give rise to what she calls a "disaggregated" as opposed to a unitary conception of citizenship (ibid., pp. 171–81). However, she seriously underestimates the nature of the conflict between democracy and the universalism of human rights, envisaging the conflict as simply a material rather than a formal one.

55 In 1999 Germany changed its *jus sanguinis* laws to include elements of a *jus soli* policy so that those not of German descent but born in Germany could become German citizens.

56 Augustine, *City of God*, XIX, 17.

57 Johnson, *Theology, Political Theory, and Pluralism: Beyond Tolerance and Difference* (Cambridge: Cambridge University Press, 2007), p. 181. For a fuller account of how Augustine relates particularity and universality see ibid., pp. 176–85.

58 As will be seen in Chapter 4, this reorientation is not only social but also temporal.

59 Use of the term "contradiction" should be understood in terms of the formal definition of the term given in Chapter 2.

60 See, for example, David Morley, *Home Territories: Media, Mobility and Identity* (London: Routledge, 2000); and Paul Statham, "Understanding Anti-Asylum Rhetoric: Restrictive Politics or Racist Publics?" in Sarah Spencer, ed., *The Politics of Migration: Managing Opportunity, Conflict and Change* (Oxford: Blackwell, 2003), pp. 163–77.

61 On this see Mary Douglas, *Purity and Danger: An Analysis of the Concept of Pollution and Taboo* (London: Routledge, 1966).

62 Gibney, *The Ethics and Politics of Asylum*, p. 163.

63 Ibid., p. 164

64 Ibid., p. 163. There is, of course, a direct parallel between the denuding of refugees of legal rights and the treatment of suspected terrorists after the bombings of September 11, 2001.

65 Geddes, *The Politics of Migration and Immigration in Europe*, p. 127. A parallel process of externalization is seen in relation to the "rendition" of terror suspects.

66 Gaim Kibreab, "Revisiting the Debate on People, Place, Identity and Displacement," *Journal of Refugee Studies* 12.4 (1999), p. 402.

67 Moorehead, *Human Cargo: A Journey among Refugees* (London: Vintage, 2006), pp. 35–6.

68 Georgio Agamben, *Means Without End: Notes on Politics*, trans. Vincenzo Binetti and Cesare Casarino (Minneapolis, MN: University of Minnesota Press, 2000), pp. 16–17.

69 Georgio Agamben, *Homo Sacer: Sovereign Power and Bare Life*, trans. Daniel Heller-Roazen (Stanford, CA: Stanford University Press, 1998), p. 132.

70 Ibid., p. 103.

71 Ibid., p. 90.

72 The contrast between the situation of refugees, whose physical bodies are exposed to death at every turn, and that of transnational corporations, those most abstract and ethereal of bodies, is instructive. While refugees are systematically denied or stripped of their international rights, TNCs are afforded more and more international legal protection. On this see B. S. Chimni, "Globalization, Humanitarianism, and the Erosion of Refugee Protection," *Journal of Refugee Studies* 13.3 (2000), 243–63.

73 Hannah Arendt, *The Origins of Totalitarianism* (San Diego, CA: Harcourt Brace Jovanovich, 1951), p. 291. For a parallel critique of human rights see Alisdair MacIntyre, *After Virtue: A Study in Moral Theory*, 2nd edn (London: Duckworth, 1994), where he famously argues that rights which are alleged to belong to human beings as such, divorced from some substantive account of the good, are a fiction "and belief in them is one with belief in witches and in unicorns." Ibid, p. 69.

74 Arendt, *The Origins of Totalitarianism*, p. 291.

75 Agamben, *Homo Sacer*, pp. 126–7.

76 Arendt, *The Origins of Totalitarianism*, p. 299.

77 This is a point that the exhortations of *Pacem in Terris* regarding refugees failed to grasp. *Pacem in Terris* (1963), #103–6.

78 Arendt, *The Origins of Totalitarianism*, p. 300.

79 Agamben, *Homo Sacer*, p. 134.

80 Hedley Bull, *The Anarchical Society* (London: MacMillan, 1977), p. 245.

81 Ibid., p. 246. Jeffrey Isaac argues that just such a vision of a complex international order informs Hannah Arendt's understanding of the proper relationship between politics, human freedom, and international order. He states: "The 'lost treasure' of the revolutionary tradition is, for Arendt, the model of an associational politics that exists beneath and across frontiers, shaking up the boundaries of the political and articulating alternative forms of allegiance, accountability, and citizenship." Isaac, *Democracy in Dark Times* (Ithaca, NY: Cornell University Press, 1998), p. 95.

82 Agamben, *Homo Sacer*, p. 133.

83 Ibid. For a critique of Agamben's account of the split between humanitarian concern and political action see Volker Heins, "Georgio Agamben and the Current State of Affairs in Humanitarian Law and Human Rights Policy," *German Law Journal* 6.5 (2005), pp. 845–60.

84 See David Rieff, *A Bed for the Night: Humanitarianism in Crises* (London: Vintage, 2002), pp. 31–120.

85 On the centrality of the "state of exception" to modern sovereignty and contemporary politics see Agamben, *Homo Sacer*, pp. 15–29.

86 The claim that worship constitutes the church as a public draws on Wannenwetsch's study of how within the primitive church worship was the public life of the congregation by which it simultaneously overcame classical antinomies of public and private, *oikos* and *polis*. Bernd Wannenwetsch, *Political Worship: Ethics for Christian Citizens* (Oxford: Oxford University Press, 2004), pp. 146–59.

87 *Deus Caritas Est*, #28.a.

88 Robert Dodaro, *Christ and the Just Society in the Thought of Augustine* (Cambridge: Cambridge University Press, 2004), p. 135. Dodaro notes that: "Augustine wonders, for example, what effect the narrative about the woman caught in adultery (Jn 8:3–11) might have if read and pondered by a magistrate about to condemn a convicted criminal to death. How do the dialectical

elements of Jesus' response to the Pharisees and scribes invite the judge to revise his own concept of justice in the light of the deeper wisdom behind the divine justice?" Ibid.

89 *City of God*, XIV, 13.

90 John Rist, *Augustine: Ancient Thought Baptized* (Cambridge: Cambridge University Press, 1994), p. 190.

91 Michael Banner, "Who Are My Mother and My Brothers?: Marx, Bonhoeffer and Benedict and the Redemption of the Family," in *Studies in Christian Ethics* 9.1 (1996), p. 17.

92 Rist, *Augustine*, p. 342.

93 Karl Barth, *The Christian Life: Church Dogmatics IV, 4, Lecture Fragments*, trans. Geoffrey Bromiley (Grand Rapids, MI: Eerdmans, 1981), pp. 175, 182.

94 Ulrich Luz notes that "hallowed be thy name" denotes both the sanctification of God's name by God himself (Lev. 10.13; Ezek. 36.22; 38.23; 39.7) and the sanctification of God's name by humans which intrinsically involves following God's commands and the pursuit of holiness (Exod. 20.7; Lev. 22.32; Isa. 29.23). Ulrich Luz, *Matthew 1–7: A Commentary*, trans. Wilhelm Lins (Edinburgh: T&T Clark, 1989), p. 379.

95 Barth, *The Christian Life*, p. 154.

96 Ibid., p. 160.

97 Colin Gunton, "Trinity, Ontology and Anthropology: Towards a Renewal of the Doctrine of the *Imago Dei*," in Colin Gunton and Christoph Schwöbel, eds., *Persons, Divine and Human* (Edinburgh: T&T Clark, 1991), p. 59.

98 The question of whether gift within the divine–human economy is unconditional, as Kathryn Tanner contends, or involves gift-exchange, as John Milbank argues, is an important feature of contemporary theological debates. However, as David Albertson suggests in his discussion of Patristic readings of the Lord's Prayer, one does not necessarily preclude the other. David Albertson, "On 'The Gift' in Tanner's Theology: A Patristic Parable," *Modern Theology* 21.1 (2005), 107–18.

99 John Inge, *A Christian Theology of Place* (Aldershot: Ashgate, 2003), p. 52.

100 See, for example, Gibney, *The Ethics and Politics of Asylum*, pp. 231–2; Walzer, *Spheres of Justice*, p. 33; and Dummett, *On Immigration and Refugees*, p. 69.

101 For a critical review of a range of theological readings of the parable in dialogue with Peter Singer's ethics and consonant with my own conception of Christian Cosmopolitan see Eric Gregory, "*Agape* and Special Relations in a Global Economy: Theological Sources," in Douglas Hicks and Mark Valeri, eds., *Global Neighbors: Christian Faith and Moral Obligation in Today's Economy* (Grand Rapids, MI: Eerdmans, 2008), pp. 16–42.

102 O'Donovan, *The Desire of the Nations*, p. 268.

103 Volf, *Exclusion and Embrace*, p. 67.

104 Volf's term for such hospitality is the less practice oriented one of "embrace."

105   By giving priority to deterrence over prevention, states refuse the possibility of creative engagement with the causes of refugeehood and settle for containment, a policy that is inherently fatalistic and refuses hope in a different future.

106   John Milbank, *Being Reconciled: Ontology and Pardon* (London: Routledge, 2003), pp. 92–7. *Homo sacer* is a suggestive analogy by which to frame the crucifixion. However, Milbank himself provides considerable qualifications to his own use of the analogy and he is right to do so. If pushed too far the analogy becomes doctrinally very problematic for a number of reasons. First, in relation to the Trinity and debates about patripassionism, it raises the question of in what way was the Son cast out of/excluded from the divine community? Second, the crucifixion itself involves maintaining certain cultic laws and is framed within much atonement theology in cultic and legal terms. So in what way can Jesus really be said to die outside the remit of the law? Third, in relation to Milbank's own reading of the atonement Jesus remains within his circle of friends and family, key members of which encircle him at his death. This raises the question of whether Jesus can really be said to die outside of or excluded from all human community. Lastly, an over-emphasis on Jesus as *homo sacer* can de-particularize Jesus, rendering him a universal archetype and thereby diminishing his historical personhood.

107   Denis Müller, "A Homeland for Transients: Towards an Ethic of Migrations," in Dietmar Mieth and Lisa Sowle Cahill, eds., *Migrants and Refugees* (London: Concilium/SCM Press, 1993), p. 143.

108   Morley, *Home Territories*, p. 230. See also Kibreab, "Revisiting the Debate on People, Place, Identity and Displacement," pp. 384–410.

109   See Ernst Lohmeyer, *The Lord's Prayer*, trans. John Bowden (London: Collins, 1965), pp. 79–87.

110   Bernd Wannenwetsch, "The Political Worship of the Church: A Critical and Empowering Practice," *Modern Theology* 12.3 (1996), 269–99. See also Reinhard Hütter, *Suffering Divine Things: Theology as Church Practice*, trans. Doug Scott (Grand Rapids, MI: Eerdmans, 2000), pp. 163–5.

111   See, for example, Eph. 2.19–22.

112   Wannenwetsch, *Political Worship*, p. 156.

113   For an example of this in relation to the hallowing of the suffering-dying, see the discussion of the hospice movement and how it contrasts with the practice of euthanasia in Bretherton, *Hospitality as Holiness*, pp. 160–89.

114   Hilary Cunningham, *God and Caesar at the Rio Grande: Sanctuary and the Politics of Religion* (Minneapolis, MN: University of Minneapolis Press, 1995), pp. 102–17. For an account of how involvement in the Sanctuary movement related North and Central Americans, in particular through accompaniment programs that sought to extend sanctuary beyond the borders of the USA, see Susan Bibler Coutin, *The Culture of Protest: Religious Activism and the US Sanctuary Movement* (Boulder, CO: Westview Press, 1993), pp. 45–62. The defining exception to the hospitality of these communities was political: in

being oriented to show hospitality to refugees they were hostile to advocates of the then Republican policy. As Cunningham puts it: "The Sanctuary communities are quick to embrace the class, race, gender, and denominational differences, but they do not easily absorb diverse 'political' orientations." Cunningham, *God and Caesar at the Rio Grande*, p. 132. This does not necessarily make it a party political or ideological movement. Rather, in welcoming the friendless stranger participants in the Sanctuary movement intrinsically placed themselves in opposition to those who would oppress these vulnerable others. On the dissident and prophetic nature of Christian hospitality see Bretherton, *Hospitality as Holiness*, pp. 141–2.

115 Cunningham, *God and Caesar at the Rio Grande*, p. 102.

116 Quoted in Coutin, *The Culture of Protest*, p. 120.

117 For an account of this inevitably conflictual process, the difficulty in overcoming paternalism, and the lack of openness to learning from refugees' experience of being helped in relation to the Sanctuary movement see Cunningham, *God and Caesar at the Rio Grande*, pp. 138–56.

118 This nostalgia can take the form of either a nationalist and imperialist longing to preserve an idealized past and vaunt one's own culture as intrinsically superior; or it can be manifested in an inverted snobbery whereby the culture of the other is valorized and naïvely idealized as representing an alternative to all that is wrong with one's own society. In the case of the latter, the nostalgia is projected on to the other. For example, the "West" is seen as individualistic, materialistic, and inauthentic in contrast to the sense of community, simplicity, and authenticity in Africa or Central America. Where these values are absent in such contexts the West is blamed without any equivalent critique of dynamics within those contexts that might be problematic.

119 Barth, *The Christian Life*, p. 172.

120 Coutin, *The Culture of Protest*, pp. 25–31. See also Ann Crittenden, *Sanctuary: A Story of American Conscience and the Law in Collision* (New York: Weidenfeld & Nicolson, 1988). There was a parallel recovery of sanctuary as a practice in the UK and the Netherlands during the mid-1980s that developed in response to changes in immigration law. For an account of these see Stephen Cherry, "Sanctuary: A Reflection on a Critical Praxis," *Theology* 93 (1990), 141–50.

121 Cunningham, *God and Caesar at the Rio Grande*, p. xiii.

122 Ibid., p. 25. In addition, the movement held services and vigils focusing on Central American issues, enabled undocumented refugees to testify publicly about their experiences, organized letter-writing campaigns to protest human rights abuses in Central America, lobbied Congress, provided social services to Central American refugee communities, sold and distributed Central American crafts and literature, organized press conferences, arranged visits and public presentations by visiting Central American activists and religious leaders, raised bail bond money for detained Central Americans, and helped detainees file for political asylum. Coutin, *The Culture of Protest*, p. 3.

123 Gibney, *The Ethics and Politics of Asylum*, pp. 146–54; Crittenden, *Sanctuary*, pp. 17–24.

124 For an account of the history of US immigration law concerning refugees and how its development relates to the work of the Sanctuary movement see Ignatius Bau, *This Ground Is Holy: Church Sanctuary and Central American Refugees* (New York: Paulist Press, 1985), pp. 38–123.

125 Crittenden, *Sanctuary*, pp. 25–58.

126 Cunningham, *God and Caesar at the Rio Grande*, p. 32; Coutin, *The Culture of Protest*, p. 30.

127 Coutin, *The Culture of Protest*, p. 164.

128 Coutin, *The Culture of Protest*, p. 143. For a full account of the trial see Crittenden, *Sanctuary*, pp. 195–340.

129 Coutin, *The Culture of Protest*, pp. 67–78. On the basis of her ethnographic study, Coutin notes the influence of Liberation theology in framing this process of listening. Participants understand themselves as reinterpreting the Bible from the perspective of the poor and re-read North American culture in the light of the Bible's call for justice. For example, one Tucson pastor she quotes states: "Where I find the conversion is people moving from viewing themselves and from reading the Bible from the point of view of North Americans, to reading the Bible from the point of view of Central Americans and of refugees." Ibid., p. 77.

130 Cunningham, *God and Caesar at the Rio Grande*, p. 33.

131 Quoted in Cunningham, *God and Caesar at the Rio Grande*, p. 112. See also Jim Corbett, *Goatwalking: A Guide to Wildland Living, a Quest for the Peaceable Kingdom* (New York: Viking, 1991).

132 Coutin, *The Culture of Protest*, p. 32.

133 Coutin, *The Culture of Protest*, pp. 37–41.

134 Coutin, *The Culture of Protest*, p. 34.

135 Quoted in ibid., p. 29.

136 Cunningham notes: "In resurrecting the tradition of ecclesial asylum, Sanctuary church groups attempted to frame their activities as a church–state conflict. This framework gave the religious groups involved a powerful set of cultural resources with which to combat the threat of government prosecution.... Because the issue of undocumented Central Americans was moved into a church – a cultural space and jurisdiction ostensibly protected from the arm of the State – Sanctuary severely limited the way in which the government could respond." Cunningham, *God and Caesar at the Rio Grande*, p. 35.

137 Quoted in Coutin, *The Culture of Protest*, p. 144. For a further example see the public declaration of sanctuary in a letter to the then Attorney General William French Smith. Crittenden, *Sanctuary*, p. 74.

138 There was a further division within the Tucson group itself in 1986 over criteria of selection of those to be helped. Cunningham, *God and Caesar at the Rio Grande*, pp. 169–75.

139 Ibid., p. 39.

140 Crittenden, *Sanctuary*, p. 88.

141 Cunningham, *God and Caesar at the Rio Grande*, p. 40; Coutin, *The Culture of Protest*, pp. 108–16. A measure of this is that the Tucson group enforced the legal distinction between deportable economic migrants and non-deportable refugees through the screening procedures they used to determine who to help cross the border. Ibid., p. 114.

142 Crittenden gives a particularly egregious and disturbing example of this. She details how the CRTF returned two teenage Mayan Indian refugees from Guatemala, who had been sent to Chicago for sanctuary, to Arizona because, as they put it, they were not politically useful. They were simply put on a bus by themselves. They never arrived. It was assumed that they had been deported. Crittenden, *Sanctuary*, pp. 90–1.

143 Quoted in Cunningham, *God and Caesar at the Rio Grande*, p. 41. See also the principles guiding the Tucson refugee support group: ibid., pp. 178–9.

144 Coutin, *The Culture of Protest*, pp. 192–5.

145 Evidence that the state authorities were aware that this was exactly the challenge the Sanctuary movement posed is given at the trial of eleven of the Tucson group for smuggling illegal aliens in 1984. As Cunningham notes, the Prosecutor filed a motion *in limine* to preclude the introduction of defenses that claimed: "(1) that the aliens being assisted were legitimate refugees entitled to live in the United States; (2) that the defendants' actions were justified on the basis of religious belief; and (3) that the defendants' actions were justified on the basis of good motives and beliefs that would negate criminal intent." The judge ruled in favor of the Prosecutor's motion and prohibited testimony and evidence that referred to: "(1) international law; (2) persecution and violence suffered by the aliens in their home countries; (3) comparative statistics pertaining to asylum policies for aliens from 'either communist-dominated countries and countries undergoing a socialist and communist revolution'; (4) comparative statistics regarding Central American aliens who have applied for or been granted asylum under the Refugee Act of 1980; and (5) religious convictions." Ibid., p. 54. At the trial, testimony about torture and persecution from the Central Americans helped was allowed only if the jury were absent. For a complementary account of the trial see also Coutin, *The Culture of Protest*, pp. 132–41.

146 A New Sanctuary Movement was initiated in January 2007 (see www.new sanctuarymovement.org, accessed May 22, 2008). However, this new movement differs in kind of the previous one in that it is focused on the situation of economic migrants in general rather than the plight of refugees in particular. Elements of the old Tucson sanctuary movement initiated Humane Borders (founded in 2000. See www.humaneborders.org, accessed May 22, 2008) which provides water stations as a humanitarian response to the needs of economic migrants traveling through the deserts on the US–Mexican border. Other related organizations are the Samaritans (www.samaritanpatrol.org, accessed May 22, 2008) and No More Deaths (founded in 2004. www.nomoredeaths.org,

accessed May 22, 2008) which have a more proactive role with patrols in the desert carrying food, medical supplies, and water. Unlike the New Sanctuary Movement they properly distinguish the political needs of refugees from the essentially economic and humanitarian needs of vulnerable economic migrants. They also advocate a "migrant centered immigration reform" equivalent to the "strangers into citizens" proposals advocated by London Citizens/Citizen Organising Foundation.

147   For a discussion of the different conceptions of sanctuary in the Old Testament see Bau, *This Ground Is Holy*, pp. 125–9.

148   William Ryan, "The Historical Case for the Right of Sanctuary," *Journal of Church and State* 29 (1987), pp. 213–16. Ryan argues for a direct legal continuity of practice and precedent between the ancient right of sanctuary as incorporated into English common law and the arguments for the provision of sanctuary by churches in the US Sanctuary movement as legal.

149   Trisha Olson, "Sanctuary and Penitential Rebirth in the Central Middle Ages," in *Boundaries of the Law: Geography, Gender and Jurisdiction in Mediaeval and Early Modern Europe*, ed. Anthony Musson (Aldershot: Ashgate, 2005), p. 40. While universal in aim, it was limited in practice. These limits varied with time and place. Some of those excluded in different times and places were Jews, heretics, serfs, traitors, those who committed felonies in a church, and public debtors (that is, those who embezzled the state).

150   "Letter 153: Augustine to Macedonius (413/414)," in *Augustine: Political Writings*, ed. E. M. Atkins and R. J. Dodaro (Cambridge: Cambridge University Press, 2001), p. 71–87. The contrast between Roman sanctuary and the sanctuary offered in the church is a crucial one in distinguishing the peace of the earthly city from the true and certain peace of the city of God. This is seen in Augustine's analysis of the sanctuary that Romulus offered to criminals at the foundation of Rome and how this contrasts with the sanctuary offered by Christians to their enemies. *City of God*, I, 34.

151   Ryan, "The Historical Case for the Right of Sanctuary," p. 214.

152   Gervase Rosser, "Sanctuary and Social Negotiation in Medieval England," in *The Cloister and the World*, eds. John Blair and Brian Golding (Oxford: Clarendon Press, 1996), pp. 61–2.

153   It is important to note that there were two basic forms of sanctuary: general and chartered. As William Chester Jordan summarizes it: "General sanctuary was the privilege that attached to churches to receive suspected felons for a fixed interval (the establishment of a time limit was not required under canon law), during which the government determined whether they were legally entitled to the church's protection. If they were and were willing to go into exile [abjuration], the Crown forwent capital punishment. A chartered or special sanctuary ... was characterized by a charter issued by a prince giving the institution in control of a church additional privileges beyond those understood to pertain to its asylum for suspected felons." Examples of such chartered sanctuaries in England include Westminster, Saint Martin-Le-Grand (London),

Durham, and Beverley. Chartered sanctuaries were geographically much larger and included protection for many lesser offenses, most notably for debtors. William Chester Jordan, "A Fresh Look at Medieval Sanctuary," in *Law and the Illicit in Medieval Europe*, eds. Ruth Mazo Karras, Joel Kaye, and E. Ann Matter (Philadelphia, PA: University of Philadelphia Press, 2008), p. 18. In providing a sanctuary for debtors these chartered sanctuaries were a vital check on the power of money to make people debt slaves. The most notable sanctuary in this respect was Saint Martin-Le-Grand, which stood on the border of the City of London before Henry VIII had it demolished in 1548.

154 Rosser, "Sanctuary and Social Negotiation in Medieval England," pp. 63–4. Rosser states: "The mechanism of sanctuary and abjuration therefore appears, from the perspective of the local community, to have operated as a means to resolve tensions, either by facilitating the negotiation of an immediate reconciliation before the church and altar, or by allowing one party in a dispute to remove himself, either permanently or for a certain period, from the neighborhood." Ibid., p. 69. For a particular striking account of just such an occasion see Olson, "Sanctuary and Penitential Rebirth in the Central Middle Ages," p. 38.

155 Olson, "Sanctuary and Penitential Rebirth in the Central Middle Ages," p. 39.

156 The use of contradiction is in keeping with how it is defined in Chapter 2. The practice of sanctuary was not a form of dissent or opposition to the crown. Indeed, the sovereign often reinforced and upheld the privilege of sanctuary, as the example of chartered sanctuaries indicates.

157 Rosser, "Sanctuary and Social Negotiation in Medieval England," pp. 64–79. The history and development of the right of sanctuary and its different forms in Europe is a complex one. For an overview of what the practice involved see J. Charles Cox, *The Sanctuaries and Sanctuary Seekers of Mediaeval England* (London: George Allen & Sons, 1911), pp. 1–33.

158 This is certainly the case in early and late medieval England. Evidence is less available for the rest of Europe where the practice of sanctuary has received very little scholarly attention. Jordan, "A Fresh Look at Medieval Sanctuary," pp. 18–20.

159 Jordan notes that the practice of sanctuary was not gradually eroded throughout the medieval period. Rather, it suffered a wholesale assault on it in the early modern period. Jordan, "A Fresh Look at Medieval Sanctuary," p. 30.

160 Ryan, "The Historical Case for the Right of Sanctuary," p. 225.

161 Rosser, "Sanctuary and Social Negotiation in Medieval England," p. 58. See, for example, the classic studies of the development and decline of sanctuary practices in England by Norman Trenholme, *The Right of Sanctuary in England: A Study in Institutional History* (Columbia, MO: University of Missouri Press, 1903); and Isobel Thornley, "The Destruction of Sanctuary," in *Tudor Studies*, ed. R. W. Seton-Watson (London: Longman, Green & Co., 1924), pp. 182–207.

162   It is of perhaps more than arcane concern to note that the development of a bill of rights emerges and becomes necessary at exactly the point at which the custom of sanctuary as a way of providing limits to the power of the state and of money is systematically dismantled. As noted in Chapter 1, it was in 1628 that the "Petition of Rights" was pressed on Charles I by Parliament. However, what is little remarked upon is that while the Petition of Rights sought to address the growing centralization of sovereign power, completely absent from it was any attempt to address the growing centralizing power of the merchants and bankers in the City of London.

163   Ryan, "The Historical Case for the Right of Sanctuary," p. 228.

164   Rosser notes that while the principle and practice of sanctuary underwent similar constrictions in the rest of Europe, it continued to be maintained into the modern period. Rosser, "Sanctuary and Social Negotiation in Medieval England," p. 59.

165   Ryan, "The Historical Case for the Right of Sanctuary," p. 229.

166   Olson, "Sanctuary and Penitential Rebirth in the Central Middle Ages," p. 43; Agamben, *Homo Sacer*, pp. 104–7.

167   Olson, "Sanctuary and Penitential Rebirth in the Central Middle Ages," pp. 43–4. As an aside, on Olson's reading, the proper metaphorical location of Anselm's satisfaction theory of atonement is not the law court but the sanctuary, such that Christ offers not a payment for wrong but the rejuvenation of relationship between God and man through a gift of remorse and anguish at the tearing asunder of proper relationship through sin. Conversely, in sanctuary practice, the aggrieved was expected to exercise grace.

168   Quoted in ibid., p. 44.

169   Cox, *The Sanctuaries and Sanctuary Seekers of Mediaeval England*, pp. 10–11. For an account of these conditions and the process of abjuration see Jordan, "A Fresh Look at Medieval Sanctuary," pp. 24–7.

170   Jordan, "A Fresh Look at Medieval Sanctuary," p. 31.

171   Cunningham, *God and Caesar at the Rio Grande*, p. 76.

172   For full details of the proposal and an account of how of the proposal follows the points set out here see: www.strangersintocitizens.org.uk, accessed May 22, 2008). I should declare my hand at this point and say that I was actively involved in helping to develop the COF proposal.

173   Even when the rights of refugees are respected, history suggests that this respect is highly contingent and owes more to the vagaries of foreign policy than it does to concern for humans qua humans. See, for example, Loescher on the early development of UNHCR: Loescher, *Beyond Charity*, pp. 55–74.

4

Global

Consumerism, Fair Trade, and the Politics of Ordinary Time

Introduction

So far the conditions and possibilities of faithful witness have been considered within a local and a national arena. This chapter shifts the focus to the context of globalization and the question of how to extend the bonds of friendship and justice to those who live beyond our immediate political community. While previous chapters have touched on the dynamics of commodification as it impacts Christian witness, economic life will be a central focus of this chapter, in particular, the possibilities of faithful witness under conditions of global capitalism.

As outlined in the Introduction there is a wide-ranging debate about the health and vibrancy of democratic life and patterns of civic association in Western liberal democracies. Some argue that what is seen is decline in political participation and the deracination of existing forms of public friendship that are central to maintaining social cohesion and political stability. Others argue that far from decline, what is occurring is the emergence of new forms of political participation and ways of acting together for the common good, ways that are more appropriate to contemporary political problems and patterns of life. Political consumerism is seen as one of the most significant examples of these emergent forms of political action.

Political consumerism involves the intentional pursuit of political ends through patterns of consumption and market-based transactions. According to Jørgen Goul Andersen and Mette Tobiason, "A political consumer is usually defined as a person who makes value considerations when buying or refraining from buying certain goods and products, in order to promote a political goal."[1] Michele Micheletti notes that although the phenomenon itself is not new, for example, the use of boycotts for political ends dates back to the eighteenth century, use of the term "political consumerism" originates in the mid-1990s.[2] Practically, churches are key catalysts and sponsors of emergent forms of political association, most notably political consumerism. The Fair Trade movement is but one of the most prominent examples of this. Theologically this is of particular interest because central to what shapes the contemporary forms of the earthly city are capitalism and consumerism. However, what theological analysis there is of the relationship between capitalism, consumerism, and Christian witness tends to be wholly negative and undermines any possibility of constructive forms of engagement such as political consumerism.[3]

The first section of this chapter defines political consumerism and contrasts it with consumerism as a particular way of structuring desire. I argue that political consumerism, when set within the wider practices of the Christian tradition, is a means by which to reform desire within existing patterns of consumption. The second part of the chapter sets out why political consumerism should be considered a necessary and legitimate response to the contemporary, globalized context by assessing how political consumerism enables, albeit in limited ways, ordinary political actors to express neighbor love and pursue a just and generous global good. The third part locates political consumerism within debates in Christian political thought and argues that, as a phenomenon, it is best understood as a form of "ordinary politics." In contrast to previous chapters, the focus of this chapter is less on the political witness of the church acting as a communal witness and more on the opportunities and responsibilities of individual Christians (who are, nevertheless, situated in and formed by their ecclesial context).

Defining Political Consumerism

Before analyzing the relationship between Christian witness and political consumerism further clarification of what is meant by the term "political consumerism" is needed. Political consumerism is an umbrella term for a range of activities that need further delineation. Political consumerism assumes a turn to the economy as an arena for effecting political change and has four interrelated foci it addresses in order to effect change. First, there is the attempt to change the structure, priorities, and organization of a particular arena of the market or of the global economy as a whole. Examples of where this focus is the primary emphasis are ethical investment schemes, subscription farming, or community-supported agriculture and farmers' markets. Second, there is a focus on production and the adaptation or invention of new ways of producing goods in a more just and environmentally responsible way. This is seen most clearly in organic farming and the development of technologies to produce energy by wind or solar power. Third, there is a focus on changing patterns of consumption: for example, labeling schemes. Fourth, it constitutes a form of civic activism and an expression of political voice through the mediating actions of interrelated organizations, coalitions, and campaigns that make claims on states, corporations, and international institutions.[4] For example, consumption of "green" or "environmentally friendly" products by citizen-consumers buttresses claims by advocacy groups about wide public concern for further political action on environmental issues. Fair Trade illustrates how each of these foci are integrated in a particular form of political consumerism: in relation to the first focus, Fair Trade seeks to establish a more equitable and direct relationship between consumers and producers, thereby contesting the dominant neoliberal logic of global capitalism that says market competition rather than a prior set of values or social relations should determine economic transactions. In relation to the second focus, Fair Trade organizations work with producers to establish environmentally sustainable means of production and cooperative ways of organizing themselves. In relation to the third focus, Fair Trade goods are a form of "buycott" that are marketed both as a means to change what products are consumed and to affect how consumers think about their patterns of consumption.[5] Lastly, Fair Trade organizations are enmeshed within and a catalytic part of a wider movement working for reform of international trading rules and practices to ensure "trade justice." Purchase of Fair Trade goods contributes to this movement and, as Nick Clarke et al. argue, it is often part of a repertoire of political action in support of this movement.[6] Through a case study of the Fair Trade organization Traidcraft, they argue that such an organization provides a pathway "through which relatively individualized actions are articulated with more collectivized modes of action and, in the process, help to shape new forms of public life and alternative visions of economic futures."[7] It is this last focus and the link between political action and political consumerism that are explored most directly in this chapter.

To understand how political consumerism constitutes a form of political action it is important to distinguish it from, on the one hand, *politicized consumption*, and on the other, *consumerized politics*. Political consumerism involves the intentional pursuit of political ends via patterns of consumption. By contrast, consumption itself can become highly politicized whether or not consumers consciously seek political ends through what they buy. For example, in the mid-1990s, the consumption of beef in Europe became highly politicized at the height of the controversy around bovine spongiform encephalopathy (BSE) or "mad cow disease." It is unlikely that consumers were intentionally pursuing political ends by not buying British beef; nevertheless, the consumption of beef was a politically charged issue.

However, not only is there a difference between political consumerism and politicized consumption, but also between political consumerism and consumerized politics. Like political consumerism, consumerized politics utilizes the processes of consumerism for political ends, but is not oriented toward changing any aspect of the market, or modes of production or patterns of consumption. Rather, it is using the processes of consumerism as a way of initiating, mediating, and sustaining change in the existing political system. The Make Poverty History/ONE Campaign is an example of consumerized politics in practice.[8] While its overall aim related to the structure of the global economy, unlike Fair Trade, its primary focus and objective is political change for political goals rather than using economic change to effect political goals. Some argue that party politics itself is becoming a form of consumerized politics.[9] Where political consumerism and consumerized politics overlap is that both adopt the vocabulary of consumerism, branding political messages and attaching political significance to lifestyle choices.

Use of the term political consumerism is highly problematic because of the negative associations with the term consumerism. Thus to assess how political consumerism can constitute a form of Christian political witness the term consumerism must be defined more closely and a contrast drawn between consumerism as a *habitus* or regime of life and political consumerism as a non-revolutionary attempt to restructure this regime by utilizing what is to hand. Calling political consumerism something different, such as market-based political action or simply political consumption, could circumvent the problematic association with consumerism. However, there is a pragmatic and polemical advantage to retaining the term. Pragmatically, the term political consumerism is a standard one used within debates in political science and sociology, thus its retention allows for common conversation about the same phenomenon. Polemically, the term political consumerism problematizes overly dismissive jeremiads against consumerism by calling for greater attention to what the precise issue is within the panoply of consumer activities that is being denounced.

Consumerism and the Formation of Desire

We cannot stay alive without consuming things, and all societies – ancient and modern – have practiced some form of conspicuous consumption, so why should our society be characterized as a consumer society? Zygmunt Bauman argues that our society engages its members primarily in their capacity as consumers.[10] Bauman states: "The way present-day society shapes up its members is dictated first and foremost by the need to play the role of the consumer, and the norm our society holds up to its members is that of the ability and willingness to play it."[11] Yet, as Bocock comments: "Consumption is founded on a *lack* – a desire always for something not there. Modern/post-modern consumers, therefore, will never be satisfied. The more they consume, the more they will desire to consume."[12] He goes on to say: "People living under the influence of post-modern capitalism's consumer culture will continue to desire the unattainable – that is the satiation of all their desires."[13] One could go even further and suggest that what is important now is not the satiation of desire, but the desire of desire: that is, the need to have one's desire constantly stimulated in order to feel alive when life itself is conceived in terms of the need to consume more. As Vincent Miller puts it: "[Consumerism] is about the joy of desiring itself, rather than possessing."[14] The fundamental moral issue is thus not the amount or the nature of what is consumed but how particular patterns of consumption, embedded within a wider set of practices, structure what and how we desire. On this reading, consumerism constitutes a *habitus* or regime of life that orients us to the world in a particular way. It is at this point that we find an affinity between Christianity and consumerism, both of which are ways of structuring desire.

For Daniel Bell there is, at precisely this point, an inherent opposition between how capitalism (and derivatively consumerism) structures and disciplines desire and how Christianity does so. He states: "At the heart of my argument is the assertion that the conflict between capitalism and Christianity is nothing less than a clash of opposing technologies of desire."[15] Capitalism captures, distorts, and disciplines human desire in sinful, unnatural directions. By contrast, Christianity is "about the healing or liberating of desire from sin. It is a therapy, a way of life that releases desire from its bondage ... so that desire may once again flow as it was created to do."[16] My account of political consumerism developed here is not fundamentally in opposition to Bell's argument. Rather, it problematizes the absolute opposition between capitalism and Christianity that Bell sets up by opening up crevices and fissures within capitalism that are amenable to loving relations. It also, in keeping with the Augustinian political vision set out in Chapter 2, disrupts the monolithic picture of the structure of relationships at work within global capitalism.[17] By resituating desire within a narrative of other or environmental concern and interpersonal relations, political consumerism constitutes a form of generative mimesis where what one longs for and invests in is redirected toward a common, global good, instead of being shaped either by rivalry with others, the immediate needs of one's family, one's own desire for self-fulfillment, or even the desire of desire itself.[18] Political consumerism can be a way of rendering oneself vulnerable to the presence of occluded others within the global economic and political system and cultivating dissatisfaction with the injustices of that system.

However, this is by no means automatic. A central argument of this chapter is that political consumerism acts in this way only when situated within a wider tradition of practices. Nevertheless, political consumerism should be seen, within the logic of Bell's own account of how Christianity constitutes a therapy for desire, as part of the repertoire by which Christians, within the contemporary context, can school themselves to desire and seek first the kingdom of God.[19] In Miller's terms, it provides a crucial means of "unveiling the commodity fetish" because it cultivates habits of being mindful of the origins of products by reconnecting products with a wider context.[20] Political consumerism thus constitutes a way of deepening one's agency through the formation of a reframed structure of pleasure, desire, and satisfaction that is "in but not of" the very forms of consumerism. It is thus a legitimate part of a process of deepening moral conversion, pointing as it does to an alternative logic of relationships to that set up by consumerism. It is my contention that acts of political consumerism can constitute a way of inhabiting a consumer culture so as to tentatively and precariously nourish creaturely, virtuous, and loving patterns of life within and through the prevailing hegemony.

Some historical examples of political consumerism in practice illustrate the difference between consumerism and political consumerism. One such example is the Indian independence movement's boycott of British goods and its promotion of *Swadeshi* goods. Here political consumerism was a means of articulating anti-Imperial and anti-modern sentiments and of forming a collective political identity among diverse groups in a context where few other avenues were available for widespread political participation.[21] Similarly, in Victorian Britain, consumers mobilized to seek cheaper and safer services and more accountable providers of such utilities as gas and water in urban contexts. These consumer cooperatives were focused on breaking the power of monopolies and contributed to the formation of an urban, civic political identity.[22] Contemporary political consumerism harks back to and reiterates this earlier moment in the history of the consumer, a reiteration that the churches have been key in enabling. From boycotts of corporations like Nestlé, to the initiation of the Fair Trade movement, to the development of ethical investment schemes we find that churches are key catalysts for and sponsors of political consumerism and the identification of patterns of consumption with pursuit of goods in common.[23]

Contrasting political consumerism with consumerism in the above way should not be read as saying that political consumerism is a self-sustaining means of reforming desire. Rather, it is by locating it within the broader practices of Christianity that political consumerism becomes a means for the reformation of desire. To say this is to go against much theorizing about consumerism that sees it as choice directed. An example of the emphasis on choice is Zygmunt Bauman who states: "To embrace the modality of the consumer means first and foremost falling in love with choice; only in the second, and not at all indispensable place, does it mean consuming more."[24] However, such critiques assume an intrinsic link between consumerism and an anthropology that posits an unsituated, autonomous, self-reflexive subject. Yet the choosing of consumer goods is only partially directed by choice. It is also directed by the need to sustain particular kinds of relationship and is located in particular kinds of practice. Reframing an understanding of consumerism as practice directed rather than choice directed unveils how patterns of consumption are shaped more by the practices they are embedded within than by self-generated choices or media-manipulated desires. For example, the activity of playing football or tennis directs the paraphernalia purchased more than any individual decision. Practices shape what is bought, how it is bought and put to use. Practices norm how and what is to be consumed.[25] Shopping is only ever a moment within a wider performance of particular practices, for example, cooking. Different virtues, skills, histories, resources, and contexts will inform what is bought and consumed and how it is consumed. As Alan Warde points out, by situating patterns of consumption within practices we attend less to individual choices and more to how consumerism is constitutive of good and bad regimes of everyday life.[26] Furthermore, much consumption is done as the background to supporting the basic patterns of everyday life (buying school lunches) and is embedded within infrastructures (transport, energy, water) over which consumers have little, if any control.[27] In short, the consumer is neither an autonomous chooser nor a gulled fool but an active and reflexive participant within normed, internally differentiated practices that are themselves part of wider constellations or traditions of practice that are directed to different visions of the good life. Empirical research on who is involved in political consumerism seems to affirm this, suggesting that it constitutes a deepening and extension of an existing practice such as cooking or parenting – two key stimuli for organic and environmentally responsible consumption.[28] As Clark et al. note in relation to Fair Trade:

> The development of fair-trade consumption in the United Kingdom does not aim to simply enrol people as consumers but rather addresses them as members of varied social networks with the aim of extending their [existing] commitments into their consumption habits and channelling their energies into recruiting friends, family, work colleagues, or fellow parishioners.[29]

Political Consumerism as Apprenticeship in the Virtues

To reinforce the importance of locating political consumerism within a wider account of Christian belief and practice, political consumerism can be envisaged as a way of cultivating virtue. Micheletti gives just such an account of how political consumerism enables the expression and reinforcement of the virtues. According to Micheletti, political consumerism seeks to embed the virtues of modesty, patience, honesty, trust, and prudence in market transactions via political agitation such as boycotts, thereby transforming both the individual involved and the political and economic structures.[30] The problem with Micheletti's account is that although she recognizes the need for prior forms of social capital for political consumerism to inculcate the virtues, she dislocates her account of the virtues from any thick tradition: that is, for Micheletti, virtues exist in a historical vacuum. Micheletti's account needs to be supplemented by something like MacIntyre's account of the relationship between the virtues and particular moral traditions. Virtues depend on particular traditions and communities of character formation that establish the *telos* of what is sought and a vision of what the common good consists of.[31] Christianity is just such a tradition and is thus able to initiate and sponsor different forms of political consumerism as prudential means of pursuing its vision of the common good. At the same time, the shape and ends of the political consumerism it sponsors have a symbiotic relationship with a range of other political and ecclesial practices within Christianity. Like the relationship between broad-based community organizing and Christianity, political consumerism as an emergent form of political action subsists on "archaic" forms of life.

An example of political consumerism in practice helps illustrate the symbiosis between tradition and political consumerism. The Montgomery bus boycott in 1955 that contributed to the American civil rights movement is a key example of political consumerism. The bus boycott was a form of individual political action in which the churches played a crucial coordinating role. Indeed, the success of the boycott depended on the prior organizational capacity, social networks, and patterns of association of the churches. The boycott itself represented a shift to grassroots direct action and the market as an arena of political action and away from the legal and regulatory focus organized by the National Association for the Advancement of Colored People. Women had a vital role and the shift to political consumerism opened a space to act for those previously excluded from politics.[32] However, political consumerism – as a form of tactical, subcultural resistance – was not enough by itself. Both the prior life of the churches involved and regulatory change and government action were required in order to consolidate real, strategic change.[33] Thus, as David Vogel argues in relation to the development of political consumerism in the USA, political consumerism does not substitute but complements other forms of political activity.[34] In effect the relationship is symbiotic, for in relation to the civil rights movement in the USA, in the first instance government proved unwilling or incapable of action – so political consumerism created the political conditions for the possibilities of state action or long-term political change. By implication, how Christianity shapes political consumerism will differ from how it is shaped and directed in other traditions and without such a connection, political consumerism is just as liable to refetishize commodities and remystify global capitalism.[35]

Political Consumerism as Neighbor Love

What I am trying to suggest is that even within capitalism and consumerism, there are means available for enabling and mediating concern and care for others and extending the bonds of friendship and pursuing justice. Older moral vocabularies help articulate how political consumerism mediates non-commercial and moral patterns of relationship. Boycotts, "buycotts," and other forms of political consumerism are a means of shunning or ostracism.[36] Political activities that deploy processes of shunning against a particular corporation or mode of production are not simply trying to diminish market share. Rather, they are trying to bring shame and dishonor upon those judged guilty. This is most apparent in media-focused and "culture jamming" campaigns that associate a particular brand or logo, for example, Nike or Gap, with negative practices, for example, sweatshop working conditions. Even when a corporation desists from its morally bad practice, consumers often continue to shun the products of that corporation both out of a sense of its continued shame and a sense that the corporation has not sufficiently repented of its sin.[37]

Locating political consumerism as a form of shunning helps identify its primary and catalytic significance. Many justifications for buying Fair Trade products or organic produce follow utilitarian lines. For example, Fair Trade is seen as a way of distributing resources to the poor and organic food is said to taste better and be healthier. Yet such grounds are questionable and highly contested.[38] They also miss the point. While the worth of buying Fair Trade or organic produce has a material dimension, its worth originates in its political and moral value. To buy such products is to register, at some inchoate level, disquiet with how the current economic system and means of production situate us in relation to other humans (in the case of Fair Trade) or animals and the environment (in relation to organic produce). Political consumerism is significant because, in the *first* instance, it is a moral and political gesture that contests the prevailing order of things. It is a form of critique; however, like Alinsky's approach to community organizing, the form its critique takes is not simply opposition or negation but contradiction. Political consumerism embodies in practice a different logic of relationship to that at work in the dominant economic order and thereby unveils the limits and contingency of that order. Such action may not be very efficient, effective, or even much of an alternative, but it is a way of denaturalizing and defetishizing economic relations, reframing consumption by embedding it within a moral framework and locating it within an alternative social and political imaginary. It thereby opens a space for new material alternatives to emerge.[39] It may be a small gesture – a micro-political one – but for those who know the significance of mustard seeds (Luke 13.18–19), there is no shame in this, especially when such small gestures are often the foundation of more fundamental structural changes. The history of the civil rights movement offers a parallel: the switch to political consumerism opened a space for more widespread engagement and thence more wholesale and meaningful political change over time.[40] Likewise, Fair Trade through small gestures looks forward to and opens space for more fundamental ameliorative change. As noted in Chapter 3, within an economy of grace, small steps can bear manifold fruit. In many ways, it is a concrete way in which hearts and minds may be prepared to pursue such change. In short, it is, as part of the repertoire by which we reform desire so as to desire first the kingdom of God, an act of both ecclesial and political *ascesis*.

Fair Trade as Contradiction

As an activity within the economy, political consumerism acts in recognition of the inherently social or "fraternal" nature of economic relations, denying capitalism's attempt to render economic relations asocial and atomistic. It is a way of re-forging economic relations as a form of what Gibson-Graham calls "economic being-in-common" that makes explicit the social and political connections within which economic relations are always already situated and dependent on.[41] As Karl Polanyi argued, prior to the nineteenth century, no market existed that was not embedded within or subservient to social and political relations.[42] Drawing on anthropological and historical research, Polanyi concludes that outside of the anomaly of a "free" market system humans neither pursue their individual interest in the possession of material goods nor produce for gain, but rather, an individual produces for use and acts "so as to safeguard his social standing, his social claims, and his social assets. He values material goods only in so far as they serve this end."[43] This may be an over-statement or not apply in every case, but the central point remains true: the ruling principle of society was not economic. Moreover, the formation of a global market system wherein social and political relations are organized around the demands of the market and the need to produce for gain rather than use is a historical and contingent phenomenon that depended on massive amounts of state intervention to impose it.[44] The result of this historical process was that, as Polanyi summarizes it: "Instead of economy being embedded in social relations, social relations are embedded in the economic system."[45] Polanyi argues that the formation of this market system inherently led to spontaneous counter-movements to re-embed market relations within social and political relations as populations and governments struggled to cope with the deleterious impact of an unregulated market on society and on nature.[46] Regulatory checks such as employment legislation and political movements such as trade unions operated at the level of the nation-state and are examples of the kind of counter-movement that Polanyi discusses. Such counter-movements can be examples of what I have called contradictions, as they may offer an alternative social, political, and economic logic to that which determines the status quo. One way to understand political consumerism in general, and Fair Trade in particular, is as a counter-movement that seeks to re-embed global economic relations. It does so in two ways.

i. Re-prioritizing the social

The first way Fair Trade constitutes a counter-movement is that it seeks to re-embed economic relations within social relations. Fair Trade constitutes an attempt to render the de facto interdependence of consumer and producer into an intentional moral relationship, which recognizes that my continued wellbeing is related to the wellbeing of all. Thus far it conforms to the logic of time–space compression, but does so in a way that humanizes the relationship by establishing a genuinely common world of action.[47] In seeking to pay a just price, for example, for coffee, as opposed to a price that the current economic system makes possible, I pay a price over and above what is necessary to purchase coffee. In doing so I am behaving hospitably by recognizing that I, as the consumer, and the producer exist in a common world. Thus, buying Fair Trade goods constitutes a means of recognizing the faceless producer as a person or as an end in and of themselves. Fair Trade operates in recognition of an inherent set of relations and duties denied by the dominant economic system. However, recognition of these relations and duties is not opposed to or antithetical to good economics. Contemporary economists increasingly note the importance of such relationships to economic growth and that a breakdown in social relations has an adverse economic impact.[48] This is reflected in the use of such categories as "wellbeing," "trust," "happiness," and "social capital" in relation to economics.[49] However, in Christian terms the ground of Fair Trade is not technological and economic developments but the hospitality we receive from Christ that establishes the grounds for friendship, just relations, and mutual sharing in a common world in a context of rupture and alienation.

ii. Reestablishing place

Second, Fair Trade seeks to re-embed economic relations within time and space by seeking to uphold the distinctness or otherness of the producer as someone situated within a particular place. Capitalism has a geography; not only is it dominated by Western-based and Western-owned corporations, but unjust employment practices in the Philippines or Guatemala are driven disproportionately by the feeding of consumerism in the West. Buying Fair Trade goods is an attempt to recognize this geography and that actions in one place affect another. As in the archaic societies analyzed by Marcel Mauss, the pattern of the exchange of gifts, goods, and services at work in Fair Trade are tokens by which a conscious sense of moral obligation and interdependence is built up and maintained.[50] Fair Trade helps foster a sense of obligation and empathy for those who are beyond my immediate field of care and who live in distant producer countries. However, unlike the implicitly paternalistic, magnanimous gift economy of international aid and the explicit paternalism of clientelistic gift economies on many plantations in the developing world, both of which serve to reinforce entrenched power relations, the gift economy at work in Fair Trade empowers producers to act independently – politically, economically, and socially – within their context.[51] Like broad-based community organizing, Fair Trade enables the poor and marginalized to forge a place from which to act on their own behalf.[52] Thus, while it is enfolded within the processes of global capitalism, Fair Trade does disrupt the homogenizing dynamics of post-Fordist global capitalism, which destabilize the local pursuit of a just and generous political order so that there may be no obstacle to the efficient and cost-effective flow of capital, commodities, and people.

Conversely, political consumerism is not simply about linking disparate, individual Western consumers with place-specific producers. As part of forming counter-geographies of globalization, Fair Trade can also help foster a stronger sense of place among consumers of Fair Trade produce. An example of this is the formation of "Fairtrade Towns," which entail "landscapes of consumption" becoming places of collective political mobilization and action by local political authorities.[53]

In Polanyi's terms, Fair Trade is a way, albeit a severely limited way, of re-embedding labor, land, and money within a wider social and political matrix, thereby inhibiting the destructive effects of commodification on place-based politics and social relations. As such, political consumerism is a defensive act and a contradiction that upholds or forges anew an institutional plurality that serves as a bulwark against the totalizing and liquefying thrust of modern forms of economic power by creating alternative patterns of socially and politically embedded economic relations. It is a political act because it is a form of judgment about the proper ordering of economic relations as they pertain to the common, global good.

Daniel Bell argues that the sin of capitalism is that it fractures friendship. He states:

> [C]apitalism is sin because it fractures the friendship of humanity in God. It disrupts the original, peaceable flow of desire that is charity; it ruptures the sociality of desire, which by nature seeks out new relations in the joyous conviviality that is love.[54]

This may well be true; however, this is different from saying that capitalism abolishes the possibility of friendship with one's neighbor and with God. What is important to consider are the ways in which capillaries of friendship and forms of faithful witness can be forged and sustained within any hegemonic system. My contention is that political consumerism is one means of forging and sustaining friendship, albeit a fragile and tentative one, within the hegemony of global capitalism.

Fair Trade, Globalization and the Emergence of Political Consumerism

The contemporary salience of political consumerism as a means of forging public friendships depends on its ability to facilitate political participation within the context of economic globalization and weak supranational and international political structures. However, to understand why this is the case it is important to understand in more detail why political consumerism constitutes an appropriate response to globalization.

Political action, in the context of globalization, necessarily takes the form of acting as consumer-producers via consumer-mediated modes of action and cultural production for three reasons. First, modes of political consumerism are constructive attempts to relate our local social and political identity to a global horizon of concern and recognize that we all exist within a single economic and social system. We are all both locally employed producers, subject to local political conditions, and consumers of global products, subject to the vagaries of global capitalism. To act as political animals we must act in our capacity as consumers because the global market is just as determinative of political life as the local political institutions of a particular state (and in some cases more so). We may wish it were otherwise, but we cannot ignore this condition of economic life. Second, the market is the primary and most readily available mode of mediation for ordinary political actors who seek to express public friendship and just relations with others living thousands of miles away, yet whose lives are intimately bound up with their everyday patterns of consumption. Finally, as discussed in the previous chapter, the weakness and nascent character of the international political system and the fact that national government are often unwilling to act on issues of global concern – for example, climate change – means that political consumerism is one of the few avenues available for ordinary political agency.[55] The example of Fair Trade illustrates this.[56]

In 2001 FINE defined Fair Trade as follows:

> Fair Trade is a trading partnership, based on dialogue, transparency and respect, that seeks greater equity in international trade. It contributes to sustainable development by offering better trading conditions to, and securing the rights of, marginalized producers and workers – especially in the South. Fair Trade organizations (backed by consumers) are engaged actively in supporting producers, awareness raising and in campaigning for changes in the rules and practice of conventional international trade.[57]

As already noted, a key catalyst for its development was the work of church-related groups; notable among these were the Mennonite Central Committee in the USA from the 1940s onward and that of Traidcraft in the UK from 1979 onward. Like the practice of sanctuary outlined in Chapter 3, the conceptualization behind Fair Trade draws on "archaic" Christian commitments, in this case, the notions of a just price and a just wage that informed medieval economic relations.[58]

As a political act that seeks just relations between consumers and producers, political consumerism is also remedial action necessary because of the feckless nature of national political authorities in relation to global capitalism. To illuminate the political dynamics at work in political consumerism one can draw an analogy with just war theory. In contradiction to global capitalism being postulated as necessarily an amoral and lawless arena of human activity, equivalent to war, political consumerism articulates the possibility of moral norms and practices governing even this most problematic area of human action. In short, political consumerism constitutes a way of acting in an ordered and moral way where the rule of law flows weakly and political authorities act arbitrarily. In the absence of the proper exercise of political authority to ensure a just judgment and a peaceable order governing the economy, ordinary political actors turn to the market as a means of bringing public accountability to economic relations. On this account, something like Fair Trade is by no means a panacea, neither does it offer a wholesale alternative to global capitalism; rather, as already stated, it is a contradiction pointing the way to the remedial improvement of an existing order.

The just war analogy can be developed further. Pacifists can be seen as equivalent to those who seek to model and uphold alternatives to consumerism, while those who pursue political consumerism by setting up Fair Trade companies, etc., are equivalent to those who argue for just war. Just as there is not a complete disjuncture between just war theorists and pacifists in relation to the legitimate use of force (for example, in relation to police actions), there is no necessary conflict or antagonism between the organic, locally oriented farmer and the purchaser of organic food in a supermarket.[59] Instead, they exist on a continuum. The implication of my overall argument is that deeper immersion in the practices of Christianity should lead more in the direction of the active support of such things as farmers' markets and away from what can be the use of organic or "ethical" produce as a marker of bourgeois social distinction. As with debates within just war theory, there are those who do not see capitalism as always and everywhere intrinsically corrupting, and so political consumerism may constitute a positive moral obligation, and those who see political consumerism as a lesser evil in comparison to a capitalism and consumerism without restraint.[60]

A full evaluation of political consumerism necessitates situating it within a broader theo-political vision. Any account of the Christian life has to reckon with the dual problematic of Christian political thought: that we are called to seek first the kingdom of God but also to seek the welfare of the city even though it be Babylon (Jer. 29.7). As outlined in Chapter 1, much contemporary Christian political thought has rightly affirmed the importance of seeking first the kingdom of God. However, what might be called the "ecclesial turn" in theological reflection upon political life has tended to downplay the significance of pursuing and maintaining the shadow of the peace of the city of God found in the earthly city. In keeping with previous chapters, what follows is an assessment of political consumerism as just such a means of pursuing this more shadowy, but no less legitimate peace.

Ordinary Politics and the Peace of Babylon

i. Political consumerism as penultimate politics

Following Bonhoeffer, political consumerism could be called a "penultimate" politics.[61] By emphasizing the penultimate character of attempts to seek the peace of Babylon faithfully, compromise or assimilation can be avoided, for penultimate politics lives in the light of its own contingency and the contingency of the prevailing hegemony and thereby resists all attempts to ontologize both injustice and historical forms of political relations. For Bonhoeffer, the penultimate is that which prepares the way for the ultimate. At the same time, as Bonhoeffer stressed, talk of the penultimate must recognize the givenness and goodness of the "natural" order. Thus, historical forms of political relations, although fallen, do matter for they are improvisations, through time, of the created order, and cannot simply be disregarded or abandoned as per much modern contractarian and revolutionary political thought. Bonhoeffer's account of the penultimate also emphasizes how God is hidden in the world and how following the crucified one demands an orientation to and responsibility for the world. However, while drawing on Bonhoeffer's conception of penultimate politics, framing political consumerism in terms of the penultimate is not how I will frame its theological character. Situating pursuit of the peace of Babylon as somehow penultimate places it outside the penumbra of directly ecclesial practices.[62]

ii.   *Political consumerism as* bricolage

Following the work of Stanley Hauerwas, another way of framing political consumerism theologically is to interpret it as a form of what Michel de Certeau calls *bricolage*: the creative use of the prevailing hegemony in order to divert and adapt it.[63] Hauerwas develops de Certeau's conception of *bricolage* as a framework for how to work within the given constraints of the dominant political order.[64] Hauerwas calls for discriminating engagement rather than either complete withdrawal or general involvement.[65] Following de Certeau, Hauerwas uses the term "tactic" to describe how the church is to operate in public life. A tactic makes no attempt to control a situation or claim a social space as its own, nor does it attempt to define the rules of engagement or develop a general strategy. Instead, it is an ad hoc circumstantial engagement that makes use of what is there.[66] As we saw in relation to Alinsky, such tricksterism can be a legitimate part of Christian witness. For Hauerwas, there will always be a tension between the church and its "host" society, the church always, in some way, constituting a contrast to the wider society.[67] It is from its position as a "contrast society" that the church has the critical distance to say "no" to the prevailing ideological legitimations of injustice, violence, and oppression but also to imagine and develop new ways of doing things.[68] Hauerwas's approach emphasizes how the church should never be over-identified with the world it is bearing witness to and brings to the fore the provisional, improvised, and circumstantial nature of the faithful pursuit of Babylon's peace. However, the problem with de Certeau and, by implication, Hauerwas is that political witness is reduced to a form of subcultural resistance. To view either political witness or political consumerism strictly in terms of de Certeau's account of *bricolage* is to see it as a form of pessimistic "making do" that evidences a chronic lack of commitment and concern for the salvation of Babylon. Or as John Howard Yoder puts it: "There is nothing in *bricolage* worth dying for."[69] As already noted in the Introduction, the missiological orientation of the church implies neither withdrawal nor subcultural resistance but, as exemplified in the stories of Joseph, Daniel, and Esther, it entails combining active investment in Babylon's wellbeing with faithful particularity and obedience to God.

In contrast to *bricolage*, a theological account of politics does not seek only to transgress the prevailing hegemony but acts in expectation of its transfiguration. The faithful pursuit of Babylon's peace expects the irruption of God's sovereign acts of grace in the midst of the earthly city. To borrow and adapt Alain Badiou's phrase, we might call such a politics a "politics of the event."[70] Such acts of grace, in contrast to both a penultimate politics and the eschatologically oriented, yet tradition-dependent politics of the *ekklesia*, surpass all that precedes them and change the terms and conditions of the politics and social life that follow them. The paradigm and definitive event is of course the resurrection of Jesus Christ, but just because Christ has come it does not mean that God ceases to act in human history. Precisely because Christ has come, the Spirit can break open in *sui generis* ways the kingdom of God among us, ways that are over and beyond human construction and the precedents of history and tradition. In short, "miracles do happen."[71] Any account of Christian political witness has to be open to the possibility of God's sovereign acts of grace in the world, while at the same time ordering its own, eschatologically oriented life in prudential, habitual, and tradition-specific ways.[72] To frame Christian political witness in terms of tactical subcultural resistance forecloses the possibility of the irruption of God's sovereign acts of grace in the midst of the earthly city.

There is a further, theological reason for not wholly aligning political consumerism with de Certeau's account of *bricolage*. In many ways de Certeau's conception of *bricolage*, and thence of the church as a kind of corporate trickster, is commensurate with a kenotic, cruciform vision of power. However, de Certeau (in contrast to Alinsky) has an intrinsically agonistic and violent understanding of the relationship between those forced to deploy tactics and the holders of strategic power. De Certeau's recourse to military metaphors and the work of Clausewitz is not incidental, for as he says himself, he is describing an "everyday art of war."[73] Such a conception of the relationship between the church and the world is theologically problematic for a number of reasons: first, it makes violence without end rather than an originary and hoped-for peace the true pattern of human relations (something that Hauerwas himself is avowedly opposed to); second, it leaves little room for those irruptions of the eschaton named earlier as miracles; and last, it cannot conceive of the peace of the earthly city as being of genuine value. In short, framing political consumerism wholly in terms of *bricolage* would be to establish a Manichean false dichotomy between church and world. Moreover, to conceive of the relationship between the church and the world solely in terms of *bricolage* is a refusal to take responsibility for how Christianity is itself, for better and for worse, partially constitutive of and congruent with the world as it is. Such a refusal undermines the need for both repentance and celebration and forecloses discerning how the prevailing hegemony is both graced and disgraced. By contrast, political consumerism, as a mode of political action, accords with an Augustinian political vision and reckons with the full ambiguity of political life before Christ's return.

iii.   Political consumerism as ordinary politics

In the light of the above, I turn now to the liturgical calendar, which provides a helpful rubric for framing a theo-political vision through which to interpret political consumerism. What follows extends and builds on analysis of the relationship between worship and political witness in Chapters 2 and 3.

Within the liturgical year there is a rhythm of fasting, feasting, and ordinary time, each of which reflects different moments in the Christian life. The seasons of fasting are when we embody the cruciform pattern of discipleship as those who hunger and thirst for righteousness and who cry out with John of Patmos, "Amen. Come, Lord Jesus!" (Rev. 22.20). These are seasons of lament for the continued sin and suffering we see around us and when we long for the ascended Lord's return. The Christian life also involves times of feasting. Such moments are anticipations of the messianic banquet and the healing and redemption of creation. They are times when we attend to how the Spirit breaks open the eschaton now and we can be ecstatically overwhelmed by the immanent presence of God. It is at the Eucharist that we remember our future and celebrate and liturgically embody such times. However, Christian witness tends to be collapsed into seasons of fasting and feasting, presence and absence, immanence and transcendence. Such divisions ignore the third season of the Christian life: ordinary time. Ordinary time is that period when we are called to focus on and live faithfully within the mundane, commonplace practices of everyday life; that is, within the ongoing life of the *saeculum*. It is ordinary time – the time in between fasting and feasting – that is the major key or predominant mode of the Christian life. For the most part, encounter with God and the bursting out of the new creation occur not in some special spiritual time or zone but through and amid the vicissitudes, conflicts, and contingency of our everyday life. The link between ordinary time and the accounts already given of listening to Scripture and to others is that ordinary time is the liturgical articulation and housing of life in the *saeculum* as that context when we listen to and try to make sense of Scripture in the company of strangers. Echoing the discussion of the relationship between Alinsky and Augustine in Chapter 2, ordinary time liturgically values what it means to be in between – in between two histories (the eschatological and the fallen, that together constitute the *saeculum*), in between God and world, in between *oikos* and *polis*, and in between resident and alien – as the primary location of the Christian life.

While much has been made of the link between worship, liturgy, sacraments, and the formation of a Christian theo-political vision, little attention has been given to the liturgical year within such discussions.[74] Yet to focus on liturgy and the sacraments is to emphasize the spatial at the expense of the temporal ordering of Christian witness. However, the spatially determined, place-dependent nature of the sacraments means that particularity is upheld seemingly at the expense of universality. Proper attention to the temporal dimensions of Christian witness better enables us to conceive how the belief and practices of Christianity are at once particular and universal. Over-attention to the spatial aspect of Christian witness tends to reduce it to a local manifestation, which if universalized is hegemonic. In contrast, situating the spatial within the temporal allows for a non-uniform universality or pluriformity where the particular embodiments of Christian witness are related synchronically and diachronically and together constitute the catholic – i.e., universal – witness of the church. The best analogy is with a piece of music that can have distinct moments and movements within it, yet whose wholeness and fullness is constituted through time.

Attention to the temporal ordering of Christian witness within the liturgical year helps us notice the spaces in between formal participation in either ecclesial or political life. That which seems peripheral can be revalued as a locus of divine–human relationship. We relate to God not only through direct presence or absence but also in oblique, circumlocutionary, contingent, and seemingly coincidental ways. This peripheral mode of divine address helps situate the non-institutional and emergent forms of contemporary politics outlined in this chapter that Christian political thought tends to ignore because it is so focused on the actions of either the church or the state. In relation to participation in politics the term ordinary denotes two things. First, it denotes ordinary forms of political action outside of formal political structures and institutions undertaken by people acting apart from their capacity as office holders or membership of an identifiable political body. It is a form of non-expert, non-specialist, and unofficial politics and as such accords with the primary emergent forms of political action in the contemporary context.[75] Second, drawing on the above discussion of "ordinary time," what I am calling "ordinary politics" encompasses the exercise of Christian freedom and responsibility by ordinary political actors within the informal politics of everyday life at home, at work, and in the marketplace. The implication of ordinary politics is not to politicize such arenas of everyday life. Rather, it is to recognize that on occasions actions within such arenas can, in limited circumstances, be engaged with in a directly political way, precisely with the aim of restoring to them a non-political, private character; that is, so that actions like shopping may once more be undertaken in such a way that they are not chiefly concerned with the public or common good. Rather, such private actions are freed by obedience to a prior act of political judgment that has established an arena of moral relations with respect to the activity undertaken, whether that is shopping or something else.

Ordinary politics, understood as part of faithful political witness within the *saeculum*, reinforces the continuity and coherence between worship and political life that has been so frequently undermined within the Christian tradition. A comparison of Ambrose's and Augustine's conception of the moral life will serve both to give an example of a false dichotomy between the church and the world and theologically locate my account of ordinary politics within an account of the relationship between asceticism and vocation. As an account of the relationship between asceticism and vocation it sketches the basis of a "mirror" of faithful citizenship and the intersections between citizenship and discipleship. Such an account moves beyond the strictly political nature of ordinary politics by locating it within a broader understanding of the moral life.

Ambrose established a distinction between "ordinary" moral duties (*media officia*) – which include following the Ten Commandments – and counsels of perfection (*perfecta officia*) – paradigmatically found in the Sermon on the Mount.[76] Ambrose's distinction between ordinary and perfect rests on a shift from a Ciceronian emphasis on different contexts for duty to a two-fold standard of Christian morality: one for a selective band of monks and clergy and another for everyone else.[77] There is a strong sense in Ambrose that the pursuit of mutual or reciprocal benefit is part of the virtuous life,[78] and that bodily practices such as how we speak, show hospitality, and conduct friendships may be a training ground or precursor for more intense embodiments of virtue.[79] However, the effect of his double standard is to delegitimize the ordinary as moral or honorable in any real sense: ordinary moral duties become implicitly equated with the pursuit of selfish gain.[80] Added to this, for Ambrose it is the spiritual elite who are truly Christian: clergy and monks replacing Cicero's sages as the truly virtuous.[81] While this new aristocracy is not based on blood or property but on ordination and vocation, Ambrose's division between the spiritual elite and ordinary Christians loses the Pauline emphasis on the possibility of moral excellence and wisdom as obtainable by anyone through Christ in the power of the Spirit. Moreover, inherent in Ambrose's division between ordinary and perfect – a division that becomes increasingly magnified throughout the medieval period – is a false conceptualization of the secular as that outside of ecclesial institutions and thence as not a domain of truly Christian witness.

Augustine came to reject Ambrose's division between ordinary and perfect.[82] As R. A. Markus notes, over and against the advocacy of a spiritual elite, Augustine vindicates "Christian mediocrity." Markus states that for Augustine:

> Mediocrity and perfection were no longer on opposite sides of a great divide that cut through the Christian community, creating a two-tier Church. ... For Augustine the ordinary Christian was no more remote from grace and salvation than the monk or ascetic. All are called to pursue perfection; none attain it here, but all are commanded to run so as to obtain the prize (1 Cor. 9.24; Phil. 3.12). Perfection is the distant goal, imperfection the inescapable condition – for monk and lay person alike.[83]

Augustine's attention to the needs of "ordinary" Christians can be seen most explicitly in his sermons and commentaries, in particular his commentary on the Psalms. Of all Scriptural texts, the Psalms in particular had come to be seen as medicine for the soul and there was a proliferation of commentaries on the Psalms in the fourth century.[84] Michael McCarthy notes that:

> Unlike most of these commentaries ... which seem to be directed at monastic communities, Augustine addresses his church as a whole: from those who have come to the basilica to avoid the temptation of games, circuses, and fights to the converted astrologer, from consecrated virgins to the married mother. In what comes down to us as his *Enarrationes in psalmos* ... Augustine speaks directly to a gross and complex populace whom he can hardly idealize.[85]

As discussed in Chapter 2, key for Augustine was the sense that Christians live in the *saeculum* – the time between the times – a condition that prohibits any sense of an over-realized eschatological purity. Following Augustine, ordinary politics can be envisaged as a contextually appropriate moment within the life of worship and as a form of response to God's address within the *saeculum*; that is, as a means of faithful witness, albeit one suffused with the need for penitential prayer and afflicted with unresolved tensions.

The theological conceptualization of the ordinary life as the primary domain of faithful witness is underlined and amplified through Irenaeus's understanding of the relationship between creation and eschatology. For Irenaeus there is a single creation (material creation is not a second or derivative creation from an originally spiritual one), yet creation is imperfect; that is to say, it does not arrive in full bloom, but must grow up and mature in order that it might then receive its perfection in Christ.[86] This need for growth and development applies in particular to humans.[87] The Fall constitutes a turn away from the path to maturity and results in humans walking backwards into chaos and nothingness. As Douglas Farrow puts it: "In the fall man is 'turned backwards.' He does not grow up in the love of God as he is intended to. The course of his time, his so-called progress, is set in the wrong direction."[88] Jesus Christ redeems creation by restoring creation to its original goodness and enabling creation, through the perfecting actions of the Spirit, to once more move into its fulfillment. There is no movement back to an original state, but a movement *forward* to perfection: a perfection that is inaugurated by Christ at the ascension wherein the material creation is taken into the life of God. In Irenaeus's eschatology the emphasis is not on *space* (that is, a move out and beyond creation) but on *time*: the advent of the kingdom of God involves a movement to a new time through the existing creation.[89] This is written into the very structure of *On the Apostolic Preaching*, which recounts the history of blessing and curse that culminates in the life, death, and resurrection of Jesus Christ. For Irenaeus, and as already suggested in Chapter 3 in the discussion of hallowing bare life, the eschatological fulfillment of creation involves a movement, via differentiation and development, through history. Without such a movement there can be no discrete identities that take up and play with creation in particular ways through history and so there can be no interplay of persons in communion. Based on his account of the relationship between creation and eschatology Irenaeus understood asceticism, or the spiritual life, not as an escape from or overcoming of the bodily life, but as the life of God lived in all dimensions of the body.[90] On this account, ascetism, like all good games from football to chess, is a form of disciplined or serious play, and not, as it was for Ambrose, a kind of restraining bolt upon our unruly passions.[91] The holy spiritual life for Irenaeus is the healed human life that anticipates its eschatological fulfillment now.[92] As Olivier Clément notes, commenting on Cyril of Alexandria and Irenaeus's understanding of deification:

> To be deified is therefore to become someone living with a life stronger than death, since the Word is life itself and the Spirit is the one who brings life. All human possibilities are brought into play. The structures of thought, feeling, friendship, creativity, while remaining only human structures, receive an infinite capacity for light and joy. ... Thus holiness is life in its fullness.[93]

The implication of this is that it is not only monks and other ascetics who are holy. As Clément points out, on this account, the mother who knows how to console her child and how to bring them to spiritual birth is as holy as the monk who prays all night.

This theme of the ordinary life as both a realm of ascetic discipline and the creative pursuit of virtue and faithful witness is of course reiterated and developed in manifold ways in Protestant theology from Luther and Calvin onward.[94] For example, Luther in his lectures on Genesis states that: "all our actions in domestic life are pleasing to God and that they are necessary for this life in which it becomes each one to serve the one God and Lord of all according to one's ability and vocation. ... Let them know that a woman suckling an infant or a maid sweeping a threshing floor with a broom is just as pleasing to God as an idle nun or a lazy Carthusian."[95] Crucially vocation is not about a "religious" vocation set apart from ordinary life or even about a particular office or role but about giving oneself to one's neighbor in loving service (which as argued in Chapter 2 can occur in any context) freed to love through salvation in Christ and empowered to serve by the Holy Spirit.[96] As noted in Chapter 2, family, work, and public life – that is, those contexts in which we take on particular roles or offices – are those distinct yet mutually constitutive and co-inhering spheres of communication and responsibility in which humans discover, respond to, and play with the different ways in which creation is an occasion for communion with God and others.[97] It is my contention that initiatives such as Fair Trade or community organizing are means of playing with creation within the *saeculum* in disciplined and generative ways, ways that seek to love one's neighbor and that are open to the healing and perfection of the *saeculum* in Christ. Following Irenaeus, the Christian life in ordinary time is life lived in the *saeculum* as that which is open to its healing and fulfillment in Christ.[98] It is within the context of ordinary time that the role of Christians acting as participants in the *saeculum* – that mutual ground between the earthly city and the city of God – is affirmed as part of the penumbra of the life of worship.

Contrary to classical conceptions of a division between the realm of necessity, located in the *oikos*, and a realm of freedom, located in the *polis*, in Christianity, the ordinary life of family and work can be a realm of freedom and meaningful action. In modern political thought, the restatement of this antinomy was developed most by Arendt, but it also features in Nietzsche. For both, public life is the only meaningful arena of action. A central cause for this emphasis in their work is that both are haunted by the problem of time and how to give value to a life within the flux of time. For Nietzsche it is a heroic will-to-power and for Arendt it is the ability to pass judgment on the great deed or political event that gives meaning to human life against the absurdity of human life in time and its endless repetition within the realm of necessity.[99] However, as Wolin recognized, the great gift of Christianity to politics is time.[100] Christians have time to hope and live in a time when change is possible and in which past and present are connected in the communion of saints.[101] A Christian vision of time as history and as open to redemption undergirds the possibility of meaningful participation not only in politics, but also in the family and in work as activities open to the fulfillment of time in Christ and so having significance beyond the immediate needs and vicissitudes of the moment. Within Christianity, the ordinary life is a realm of freedom and meaningful activity, and one where divisions between *oikos* and *polis*, freedom and necessity, are blurred and break down.

In the light of the above, political consumerism constitutes an instance of ordinary politics for three reasons. First, it enables ordinary political actors, within the mundane activities of their life, to take responsibility for the political impact of their economic actions under conditions of globalization where political authority is weak or nonexistent. Second, it incorporates awareness of one's duty of care for others, both near and far, and therefore, in contradiction of consumerism, it recognizes that in shopping we do not act alone or simply for ourselves. It thereby constitutes a modest form of what Bonhoeffer called "vicarious representative action": that is, taking action in the name of another through representing that other in one's own person; this includes taking on the consequences of that action on behalf of the other.[102] Third, like ordinary time, it upholds time and space as good, creaturely limits against those philosophical and technological detractors who see time, space, and finitude as limits to be overcome. Political consumerism brings to the fore how time and space (or less abstractly, tradition and place) matter and deterritorialization, detraditionalization, and time–space compression are neither absolute nor inevitable.

Summary

The argument set out here is that political consumerism is a prudential means of enacting Christian freedom and responsibility by ordinary political actors in a context of global political relationships and economic interdependence. Analysis of the phenomenon of political consumerism unveils the constructive possibilities available for sustaining and forming Christian witness in ordinary time under conditions of global capitalism. It is the use of the market as an arena of political action that distinguishes it from other forms of political action and from consumerism as a regime of life. As a form of political action it has neither the messianic pretensions of the prevailing political ideologies of the twentieth century nor the demonic despair of their postmodern aftermath. It is a modest form of ordinary politics that provisionally tries to humanize capitalism in a way that accords with a theological anthropology and brings accountability to global economic relationships by situating them within a wider moral and political order.

Notes

1 Jørgen Goul Andersen and Mette Tobiason, "Who Are These Political Consumers Anyway? Survey Evidence from Denmark," in Micheletti et al., eds., *Politics, Products, Markets: Exploring Political Consumerism Past and Present* (New Brunswick, NJ: Transaction, 2004), p. 203.

2 Michele Micheletti, *Political Virtue and Shopping: Individuals, Consumerism, and Collective Action* (New York: Palgrave MacMillan, 2003), p. x.

3 See, for example, William Cavanaugh, *Theopolitical Imagination: Discovering the Liturgy as a Political Act in an Age of Global Consumerism.* (Edinburgh: T&T Clark, 2002), pp. 97–122; Message of John Paul II for the World Day of Peace, January 1, 1999, para 2; Stephen Long, *Divine Economy: Theology and the Market* (London: Routledge, 2000), p. 237; and Eugene McCarraher, "The Enchantment of Mammon: Notes Toward a Theological History of Capitalism," *Modern Theology* 21.3 (2005), 429–61. More constructive and nuanced appraisals can be found in Vincent Miller, *Consuming Religion: Christian Faith and Practice in a Consumer Culture* (New York: Continuum, 2004) and Peter Sedgwick, *The Market Economy and Christian Ethics* (Cambridge: Cambridge University Press, 1999).

4 Nick Clarke et al., "The Political Rationalities of Fair-Trade Consumption in the United Kingdom," *Politics and Society*, 35.4 (2007), pp. 585–6.

5 I use the term "Fair Trade" to denote a particular way of structuring relations between consumers and producers as distinct from its usage as a proper name, notably for the Fairtrade Foundation in the UK and the Fairtrade Labelling

Organizations International, an umbrella organization for different Fair Trade labeling initiatives around the world. For an overview of how Fair Trade works see Alex Nicholls and Charlotte Opal, *Fair Trade: Market-Driven Ethical Consumption* (London: Sage, 2004) and Geoff Moore, "The Fair Trade Movement: Parameters, Issues and Future Research," *Journal of Business Ethics* 53.1 (2004), pp. 73–86. For a chronology of the Fairtrade Mark in the UK see www.fairtrade.org.uk/what_is_fairtrade/history.aspx.

6   Nick Clarke et al., "The Political Rationalities of Fair-Trade Consumption in the United Kingdom," pp. 583–607.

7   Ibid., p. 590–1.

8   See Douglas Hicks, "Global Poverty and Bono's Celebrity Activism: An Analysis of Moral Imagination and Motivation," in Douglas Hicks and Mark Valeri, eds., *Global Neighbors: Christian Faith and Moral Obligation in Today's Economy* (Grand Rapids, MI: Eerdmans, 2008), pp. 43–62.

9   John Corner and Dick Pels, *Media and the Restyling of Politics: Consumerism, Celebrity and Cynicism* (London: Sage, 2003).

10   Zygmunt Bauman, *Work, Consumerism and the New Poor* (Buckingham: Open University Press, 1998), p. 24.

11   Ibid.

12   Robert Bocock, *Consumption* (London: Routledge, 1993), p. 69.

13   Ibid.

14   Miller, *Consuming Religion*, p. 144.

15   Daniel Bell, *Liberation Theology after the End of History: The Refusal to Cease Suffering* (London: Routledge, 2001), p. 2.

16   Ibid., p. 3. For another example of this kind of approach see William Cavanaugh, *Being Consumed: Economics and Christian Desire* (Grand Rapids, MI: Eerdmans, 2008).

17   See also Michel de Certeau, *The Practice of Everyday Life*, trans. Steven Rendall (Berkeley, CA: University of California Press, 1988), p. 27. In addition, Gibson-Graham argue that a key moment in moving beyond capitalism is learning to see how it constitutes but one of a range of forms of production and consumption within the contemporary context, unveiling its contingency and thereby denaturalizing it. J. K. Gibson-Graham, *Postcapitalist Politics* (Minneapolis, MN: University of Minnesota Press, 2006), pp. 53–68. In terms of Christian witness, deconstructing and delegitimizing the theological frameworks that have shaped perceptions of capitalism is a vital part of this denaturalizing process. As John Milbank argues, envisaging capitalism as natural and inevitable owes much to the natural theology of Paley, Malthus, and others. John Milbank, "The Body of Love Possessed: Christianity and Late Capitalism in Britain," in *The Future of Love: Essays in Political Theology* (Eugene, OR: Cascade Books, 2009), pp. 80–3.

18   Use of the term "mimesis" draws directly on René Girard's account of the structure of desire, especially his often overlooked account of how mimesis can be a generative process. On this see Rebecca Adams, "Violence, Difference, and

Sacrifice: A Conversation with René Girard," *Religion and Literature* 25.2 (1993), pp. 9–33.

19 For Bell's account of how Christianity constitutes an ensemble of technologies of desire that stand against capitalist discipline see Bell, *Liberation Theology after the End of History*, pp. 87–96.

20 Miller, *Consuming Religion*, pp. 182–8.

21 Micheletti, *Political Virtue and Shopping*, pp. 40–2; Frank Trentmann, "The Modern Evolution of the Consumer: Meanings, Knowledge, and Identities before the Age of Affluence," *Cultures of Consumption, an ESRC–AHRB Research Programme Working Paper No. 10* (2004), p. 31.

22 Trentmann, "The Modern Evolution of the Consumer, pp. 19–24.

23 Micheletti, *Political Virtue and Shopping*, pp. 58–60, 104–5; Vogel, "Tracing the American Roots of the Political Consumerism Movement," in Micheletti et al., *Politics, Products, Markets*, pp. 87–8.

24 Zygmunt Bauman, *Work, Consumerism and the New Poor*, p. 30.

25 On this see Alan Warde, "Theories of Practice as an Approach to Consumption," *Cultures of Consumption, an ESRC–AHRB Research Programme, Working Paper No. 6*, March 18, 2004.

26 Ibid.

27 Clarke et al., "The Political Rationalities of Fair-Trade Consumption in the United Kingdom," p. 589.

28 Anderson and Tobiason, "Who Are These Political Consumers Anyway?" pp. 203–21; Micheletti, "Why More Women? Issues of Gender and Political Consumerism," in Micheletti et al., *Politics, Products, Markets*, pp. 245–64; and Anne Tallontire, Erdenechimeg Rentsendorj, and Mick Blowfield, *Ethical Consumers and Ethical Trade: A Review of Current Literature* (London: Natural Resources Institute, 2001).

29 Clarke et al., "The Political Rationalities of Fair-Trade Consumption in the United Kingdom," p. 593.

30 Micheletti, *Political Virtue and Shopping*, pp. 149–154.

31 On this see Bretherton, *Hospitality as Holiness*, pp. 9–30.

32 Micheletti, *Political Virtue and Shopping*, p. 54–7.

33 Vogel, "Tracing the American Roots of the Political Consumerism Movement," in *Politics, Products, Markets*, pp. 83–7.

34 Ibid., pp. 83–100.

35 Clarke et al. discuss the case of organic farming as a mode of ethical consumption. While noting how organic farming in California has come to serve oppressive labor practices and reinforce negative aspects of consumerism, their case study of Riverford Organic Vegetables points to how the move to larger-scale modes of production do not of necessity lead to unethical patterns of production. What they do not draw out from their research is how their case study represents an almost textbook example of MacIntyre's thesis: it is the commitment to the excellence of farming as a practice by key figures involved in Riverford that provides the moral vision and community of character that

enables it to remain an ethical enterprise. Nick Clarke et al., "The Spaces and Ethics of Organic Food," *Journal of Rural Studies* 24 (2008), 219–30. Their research underlines my claim that connection to some wider vision and tradition of practice is crucial for keeping political consumerism moral and resisting the processes of commodification of land and labor.

36   "Buycotts," ethical investment schemes, and labeling schemes have an element of shunning: one purchases certain goods and services in order to shame and shun other, non-ethical purveyors of related goods and services. For example, in purchasing Fair Trade coffee I am simultaneously actively shunning other non-Fair Trade products.

37   Monroe Friedman, "Using Consumer Boycotts to Stimulate Corporate Policy Changes: Marketplace, Media and Moral Considerations," in Micheletti et al., eds., *Politics, Products, Markets*, pp. 55–6.

38   Nicholls and Opal point out that for the most part, Fair Trade is an inefficient way of transferring money to poor farmers and that the primary benefits are external to the economics of Fair Trade. Nicholls and Opal, *Fair Trade*, pp. 47–52.

39   See, for example, Michael Goodman, "Reading Fair Trade: Political Ecological Imaginary and the Moral Economy of Fair Trade Foods," *Political Geography* 23(2004), 891–915.

40   The move away from the micro-political to an emphasis on the national and the structural can be read as leading to the corruption of the civil rights movement and implicated in its demise. For such an account see Charles Payne, *I've Got the Light of Freedom: The Organizing Tradition and the Mississippi Freedom Struggle* (Berkeley, CA: University of California Press, 1995).

41   Gibson-Graham, *Postcapitalist Politics*, p. 84.

42   Arguably, Polanyi is correct in his normative account of the embedded nature of markets but wrong in his assertion that no disembedded markets existed prior to the early modern period. As Maurice Glasman argues, Polanyi's analysis applies equally well to the impact of the disembedded ancient maritime economy upon the political and social fabric of Rome and Athens: it destabilized the embedded landed economy and political systems of these cities, leading to measures of social protection. Maurice Glasman, "Landed and Maritime Markets in Ancient Rome: The Polanyi Paradigm Reconsidered," unpublished paper.

43   Karl Polanyi, *The Great Transformation: The Political and Economic Origins of Our Time*, 2nd Beacon Paperback edn (Boston, MA: Beacon Press, 2002), p. 48.

44   Ibid., pp. 59–70.

45   Ibid., p. 60.

46   A recent example of exactly this ad hoc response was the Federal intervention in a number of banks such as Goldman Sachs and part-nationalization of various financial institutions, including the takeover of the Federal National Mortgage Association (Fannie Mae) and the Federal Home Mortgage Corporation (Freddie Mac) in 2008 by the then President George W. Bush despite his ideological

opposition to such a move. As the then Treasury Secretary Henry Paulson stated at the time: "Fannie Mae and Freddie Mac are so large and interwoven in our financial system that a failure of either of them would create great turmoil in financial markets here and around the globe." http://news.bbc.co.uk/1/hi/business/7602992.stm (accessed September 12, 2008). Whether or not this was the right course of action is another matter. Polanyi's point is simply that governments cannot be seen to be doing nothing and wider social and political movements develop as a response to the deleterious impact of the intensive commodification of ever more aspects of life.

47 A concrete example of how Fair Trade establishes a common world of action is the practice of 90 percent of International Federation of Alternative Trade members providing pre-finance or advance payments to producers, which provides crucial cash flow to producers at a vital stage in the production process. Nicholls and Opal, *Fair Trade*, pp. 110–16.

48 Joseph Stiglitz, "Foreword," in Polanyi, *The Great Transformation*, pp. x–xi.

49 For an extensive account of these developments see John Atherton, *Transfiguring Capitalism: An Enquiry into Religion and Global Change* (London: SCM-Canterbury, 2008).

50 Marcel Mauss, *The Gift: The Form and Reason for Exchange in Archaic Societies* (London: Routledge, 2002). For an assessment of Mauss's account of gift and how it contrasts with a divine economy of blessing see Bretherton, *Hospitality as Holiness*, p. 133. See also Polanyi, *The Great Transformation*, pp. 46–67 for an account of the sophisticated nature of gift economies and how market relations are embedded within them.

51 Nicholls and Opal note that in contrast to development projects which are often controlled by outsiders or Westerners and then evaluated on the basis of criteria set by the donor country, Fair Trade initiatives represent a direct transfer of money to the producer in the form of a social premium paid over and above the price of the goods. The decision on how to spend this premium is taken by the whole cooperative. Nicholls and Opal go on to note that the plantation owners often provide housing, transport, healthcare, and schooling on the basis of a gift economy unenforceable by contract. These gifts serve to reinforce the dependency of workers on the owners. By contrast, Fair Trade organizations seek to empower producers by working through and helping to establish cooperatives. Nicholls and Opal, *Fair Trade*, pp. 47–51. This is not to say that Fair Trade establishes equal relations between consumers and producers – it is still an asymmetric exchange, the power lying with the consumer not the producer and with both being dependent on the global market mechanisms of shipping, banking, supermarkets, etc., to mediate the relationship.

52 Critiques of the economics of Fair Trade miss its essentially political character.

53 On this see Nick Clarke et al., "Fairtrade Urbanism? The Politics of Place Beyond Place in the Bristol Fairtrade City Campaign," *International Journal of Urban and Regional Research* 31.3 (2007), pp. 633–45.

54 Bell, *Liberation Theology after the End of History*, p. 151.

55 Such agency is not futile. Micheletti's example of the "Good Environmental Choice" scheme in Sweden suggests how what she calls "soft laws" such as a labeling scheme, which depend on non-state actors and the market-chain itself for legitimacy, can operate as sources of authority and accountability in the absence of effective government control or regulation. Micheletti, *Political Virtue and Shopping*, pp. 119–47. On how political consumerism constitutes a form of "soft power" in a global context in which there are weak enforcement mechanisms see Andreas Follesdal, "Political Consumerism as Chance and Challenge," in *Politics, Products and Markets*, pp. 3–20.

56 The term Fair Trade is used here to denote the set of interconnected practices associated with the Fair Trade movement rather than the Fair Trade organization itself.

57 FINE was created in 1998 as an informal association of the four main Fair Trade networks based in Europe: IFAT (International Fair Trade Association), FLO (Fair Trade Labeling Organizations International), NEWS! (Network of European Worldshops), and EFTA (European Fair Trade Association). They issued a joint statement setting out an agreed definition of Fair Trade in December 2001. From: www.fairtrade-advocacy.org/documents/FAIRTRADEDEFINITIONnewlayout2. pdf (accessed July 8, 2008).

58 For a general discussion of the development of reflection on a just price and a just wage in medieval thought see Diane Wood, *Medieval Economic Thought* (Cambridge: Cambridge University Press, 2002), pp. 132–58. These notions have been revived in Roman Catholic social teaching from *Rerum Novarum* onward. See, for example, *The Catechism of the Catholic Church*, #2434.

59 The figure of the self-consciously locally oriented farmer is perhaps exemplified by Wendell Berry. However, such a figure raises the issue of vocation. Not everyone is called to be a farmer but all may actively support modes of production that emphasize environmental and ethical considerations in their production methods. For an example of Wendell Berry's work on related themes see *Sex, Economy, Freedom and Community: Eight Essays* (New York: Pantheon Books, 1993).

60 James Childress heuristically identifies two schools in contemporary just war thinking, the "Princeton School" which sees war as, on occasions, a moral duty and positive good and the "presumption against violence" school which identifies war as a necessary but tragic evil required in order to pursue justice. James Childress, " 'Nonviolent Resistance: Trust and Risk Taking' Twenty-Five Years Later," *Journal of Religious Ethics* 25.2 (1997), 213–20.

61 Bonhoeffer, *Ethics*, trans. Reinhard Krauss, et al., ed. Clifford Green. Vol. 6, *Dietrich Bonhoeffer Works* (Minneapolis, MN: Fortress Press, 2005), pp. 146–70.

62 This comes to the fore in Bonhoeffer's discussion of the "arcane disciplines" of the church and the need for a "religionless Christianity." There is a problematic ambiguity in Bonhoeffer about how the practices of the church relate to participation in the life of the world. It is this ambiguity that has given rise to such divergent interpretations of his phrase "religionless Christianity."

63 de Certeau, *The Practice of Everyday Life*, pp. 29–39.

64 While I focus on the work of Hauerwas, another account that explicitly draws on de Certeau's conception of tactics in order to frame a response specifically to consumerism is Vincent Miller. The critique of Hauerwas's use of de Certeau could equally apply to Miller. See especially, Miller, *Consuming Religion*, pp. 179–224.

65 Arne Rasmusson, *The Church as Polis: From Political Theology to Theological Politics as Exemplified by Jürgen Moltmann and Stanley Hauerwas* (Notre Dame, IN: University of Notre Dame Press, 1995), p. 227.

66 On this see Hauerwas, *After Christendom? How the Church Is to Behave If Freedom, Justice, and a Christian Nation Are Bad Ideas* (Nashville, TN: Abingdon Press, 1991), pp. 16–18.

67 Rasmusson, *The Church as Polis*, pp. 225–6.

68 However, as Reinhard Hütter argues, to conceptualize the church as a "contrast society" posits the church as a constituent within a wider comprehensive public or society which determines the church's own public or political life. Rather, as argued in Chapter 2, the church is constituted as a public through its relation to Christ, primarily in worship, and may or may not, at any given moment or in any given context, represent a contrast to a wider society. Hütter, *Suffering Divine Things*, pp. 170–1.

69 Yoder, *The Jewish–Christian Schism Revisited*, p. 194. Yoder develops a critique of Jeffrey Stout's use of the term of *bricolage*.

70 Alain Badiou, *Saint Paul: The Foundation of Universalism*, trans. Ray Brassier (Stanford, CA: Stanford University Press, 2003); Alain Badiou, *Being And Event*, trans. Oliver Feltham (London: Continuum, 2006).

71 This phrase is used by Slavoj Žižek to summarize the thought of Alain Badiou. Slavoj Žižek, *The Ticklish Subject: The Absent Centre of Political Ontology* (London: Verso, 1999), p. 135.

72 Being open to the sovereign acts of God is not an antinomian imperative that militates against ecclesial order. While such events may disrupt and overturn our prudential patterns of church order, such prudential patterns of life are the necessary condition for discerning and being open to the irruption of the ultimate: those who want to be ready for when the bridegroom arrives must keep awake with their wicks trimmed and their oil jars full (Matt 25.1–13). On this see Bonhoeffer, *Ethics*, pp. 161–4. In short, institution is not the enemy but the condition of Spirit-inspired spontaneity.

73 de Certeau, *The Practice of Everyday Life*, p. 39.

74 See, for example, *Blackwell Companion to Christian Ethics*, eds. Stanley Hauerwas and Samuel Wells (Oxford: Blackwell, 2004); Cavanaugh, *Theopolitical Imagination*; Geoffrey Wainwright, *Doxology: The Praise of God in Worship, Doctrine, and Life: A Systematic Theology* (London: Oxford University Press, 1980); and Bernd Wannenwetsch, *Political Worship: Ethics for Christian Citizens* (Oxford: Oxford University Press, 2004).

75 See Ulrich Beck, *The Reinvention of Politics: Rethinking Modernity in the Global Social Order*, trans. Mark Ritter (Oxford: Polity Press, 1997); Pippa

Norris, *Democratic Phoenix: Reinventing Political Activism* (Cambridge: Cambridge University Press, 2002); and Inglehart, "Postmodernization Erodes Respect for Authority, But Increases Support for Democracy," in Pippa Norris, ed., *Critical Citizens: Global Support for Democratic Government* (Oxford: Oxford University Press, 1999), pp. 236–56.

76   Ambrose, *On the Duties of the Christian Clergy*, in *Nicene and Post-Nicene Father, Second Series*, vol. X, trans. H. De Romestein, eds. Philip Schaff and Henry Wace (Edinburgh: T&T Clark, 1989), I, 11; I, 36–37.

77   Ivor Davidson, "Introduction," Ambrose, *De Officiis. Vol. 1: Introduction, Text and Translation*, trans. Ivor Davidson (Oxford: Oxford University Press, 2001), pp. 85–6.

78   See, for example, *On the Duties of the Christian Clergy*, I, 22–3.

79   Ibid., I, 2–5 (on speech); III, 22 (on friendship).

80   See, for example, *On the Duties of the Christian Clergy*, II, 7; III, 2. Ambrose reinterprets that which is useful as that which is truly virtuous.

81   Ambrose himself appears to have been an Alinsky-type figure working hard politically to ensure that Nicene orthodoxy rather than Arianism prevailed in Milan, uniting the church across Northern Italy and securing it from Imperial co-option. With the church across the Roman Empire underwriting an increasingly fragile civic life, Ambrose also became the most important civic leader and benefactor of Milan. Davidson comments: "The stereotypical image of Ambrose the spiritual giant reducing his opponents to silence and bringing emperors to their knees is only one dimension of the story; behind it lies the far more prosaic reality of a figure who had to labour against serious odds, to manoeuvre his way out of many a tight corner, and to improvise in the face of often significant opposition. Sanctity of character, intensity of conviction, and intellectual gifts all remain relevant categories in any summary of Ambrose's qualities, but political astuteness, an ability to work on popular emotions, and a genius for creating the impression that he was most in control when it was least true were also vital weapons in his arsenal." Ibid., p. 65. In short, Ambrose was a past master of "political jujitsu." On the relationship between ecclesial authority and the maintenance of civic life in late antiquity see Peter Brown, *The Rise of Western Christendom: Triumph and Diversity* AD 200–1000 (Oxford: Blackwell, 1997).

82   Augustine initially moderates, and then, through conflict with both Pelagians and Donatists, he moves beyond Ambrose's distinction between ordinary Christians and the spiritual elite. As R. A. Markus points out: "He had rejected Manichaean asceticism not only as an insult to the value of created nature, but because it implied too radical a dichotomy between the ordinary believer and a spiritual elite. ... His answer to both Donatist and Pelagian perfectionism was the same." R. A. Markus, *The End of Ancient Christianity* (Cambridge: Cambridge University Press, 1990), pp. 52–3.

83   Ibid., p. 65.

84 Michael McCarthy, "An Ecclesiology of Groaning: Augustine, the Psalms, and the Making of the Church," *Theological Studies* 66.1 (2005) p. 26.

85 Ibid.

86 Irenaeus, "Translation: Against Heresies," trans. Robert Grant, in Robert Grant, *Irenaeus of Lyons, The Early Church Fathers* (London: Routledge, 1997), p. 145–6 (IV.6.2, 11.2).

87 St Irenaeus of Lyons, *On the Apostolic Preaching*, trans. John Behr (Crestwood, NY: St Vladimir's Seminary Press, 1997), p. 47.

88 Douglas Farrow, "St Irenaeus of Lyons: The Church and the World," *Pro Ecclesia* 4.3 (1995), p. 348.

89 As I hope will be clear from the discussion of Augustine's conception of the relationship between eschatology and history in Chapter 2, there is no necessary conflict between Augustine and Irenaeus in their accounts of eschatology.

90 John Behr, *Asceticism and Anthropology in Irenaeus and Clement* (Oxford: Clarendon Press, 2000), p. 209.

91 Augustine is frequently criticized for having a negative view of passions and emotions, but as Eric Gregory argues, this is a misreading in that Augustine rejects a Stoic view of emotions and comes to understand emotions as central to the moral life (Gregory, *Politics and the Order of Love*, pp. 274–91). I contend that Augustine's understanding of Christian asceticism is much closer to that of Irenaeus than Ambrose in this respect.

92 See, for example, Irenaeus, "Translation: Against Heresies," in Robert Grant, *Irenaeus of Lyons, The Early Church Fathers* (London: Routledge, 1997), pp. 164–5 (V.2.2, 2.3).

93 Olivier Clément, *The Roots of Christian Mysticism: Text and Commentary*, trans. Theodore Berkeley, 4th edn (London: New City, 1997), pp. 264–5.

94 On the different ways in which vocation was developed in Reformation thought (and their implications for the related theo-political visions) see Paul Marshall, *A Kind of Life Imposed on Man: Vocation and Social Order from Tyndale to Locke* (Toronto: University of Toronto Press, 1996).

95 Martin Luther, "Lectures on Genesis," in *Luther's Works*, 55 vols., eds. Jaroslav Pelikan and Helmut Lehmann (Philadelphia and St. Louis: Fortress and Concordia, 1955–86), vol. 3, p. 218. In his critique of Wingren's seminal account of Luther's conception of vocation, Kenneth Hagen argues that the main thrust of Luther's doctrine of vocation is that "(1) all Christians are to serve God in their occupation, that (2) every occupation is equal in the sight of God, and that (3) the purpose of vocation is to serve the neighbor." Kenneth Hagen, "A Critique of Wingren on Luther on Vocation," *Lutheran Quarterly* 16 (2002), p. 249. Despite the many different ways in which vocation has been conceptualized, this theme of the common vocation to love one's neighbor as part of one's response to God's call, a vocation that transcends and frames all particular offices or roles, is central to much post-Reformation theology. In particular, this more holistic understanding of vocation (*Beruf*) and its relationship

to the call of God (*Berufung*) is developed by Karl Barth for whom vocation is to be understood as our particular response to the command of God that is lived out in relation to our "freedom in limitation" that includes such things as personal aptitude, historical context, and age. See, in particular, Barth, *Church Dogmatics: The Doctrine of Creation*. Vol. III, part 4, trans. A. T. Mackay et al. (Edinburgh: T&T Clark, 1961), pp. 595–646.

96 This loving service may on occasions be one-sided or altruistic or self-sacrificial owing to the incapacity of one's neighbor to respond (because of their sin or physical condition or finitude), and at other times truly loving one's neighbor will involve reciprocity, best exemplified and experienced in the mutual up-building and reciprocity of that constitutes the unity of the body of Christ (Eph. 4.1–16). Within Christianity there is no necessary tension between *agape* and *philia* since both are transfigured through the grace of God. Indeed, we may now be friends with God (John 15.15). Aquinas gives the most developed account of how *agape* and *philia* are reconfigured through *caritas*. On this see Jeanne Heffernan Schindler, "A Companionship of *Caritas*: Friendship in St Thomas Aquinas," in *Friendship and Politics: Essays in Political Thought*, eds. John Von Heyking and Richard Avramenko (Notre Dame, IN: University of Notre Dame Press, 2008), pp. 139–62.

97 As Bonhoeffer framed it, drawing on Luther, these areas of responsibility or "mandates" are not "determinate forms of being" but involve "divinely imposed tasks" through which we may live life freely in relation to God and others. *Ethics*, pp. 68–9. Unlike Bonhoeffer, I would not include "church" as a distinct sphere or mandate as this would go against the argument set out in Chapter 3 for a theological cosmopolitanism by conceptualizing the church as one task among many. As O'Donovan notes, such a demarcation undermines both the catholic and eschatological identity of the church. O'Donovan, *The Ways of Judgement*, p. 254.

98 It is just this dynamic that lies at the heart of the doctrine of the Incarnation. The matter from which the Spirit fashions a body for the Son is the same matter as that which constitutes the persons of other, fallen, human beings. And the perfect life of obedience to the Father that the Spirit enables the Son to live is a life lived within and through the fallen society of a particular social, political, and economic context and the sinful relations therein. But this perfect life is not overcome by sin or the principalities and powers of this age; instead, Jesus redeems all that opposes or excludes true, good, and beautiful life and enables, once more, the life directed to perfection to be lived again. The events, relationships, and conflicts of Jesus' life, death, and resurrection are part of the purifying, healing, and perfecting way in which God assumes our humanity. Thus, the assumption of our humanity involves time, contingency, and struggle with the sinful conditions of human existence.

99 On this see Ronald Beiner, "Interpretive Essay," in Hannah Arendt, *Lectures on Kant's Political Philosophy*, ed. Ronald Beiner (Chicago: Chicago University Press, 1982), pp. 144–56.

100 Wolin, *Politics and Vision*, pp. 111–15.
101 This is a point that Stanley Hauerwas draws out in "Democratic Time: Lessons Learned from Yoder and Wolin," in *The State of the University: Academic Knowledges and the Knowledge of God* (Oxford: Blackwell, 2007), pp. 147–64.
102 Bonhoeffer, *Ethics*, p. 257. Christ's atonement is the ultimate example of such action.

Conclusion
Toward a Politics of Hospitality and a Theology of Politics

Through an engagement with a number of paradigmatic case studies I have argued that churches – in their local, denominational, and catholic form – are public bodies a dimension of whose witness involves enabling just judgment in relation to political problems that confront a particular polity, extending the bonds of neighbor love, and forging an institutional plurality as a defense against the totalizing thrust of modern state and economic power and thereby upholding places for human flourishing. This threefold public work combines together both to seek the peace and prosperity of the earthly city and to witness to the eschatological fulfillment of all things in Jesus Christ. The public work of the church is thus to be an agent of healing and repair within the political, economic, and social order, contradicting the prideful, violent, and exclusionary logics at work in the *saeculum* and opening it out to its fulfillment in Christ. The case studies are paradigmatic because each of them represents attempts to respond faithfully, hopefully, and lovingly to the Western, religiously plural, liberal nation-state and answer one of the key questions of contemporary politics: namely, what is the value and limits of the nation-state? What is the value and limit of the market? And what can we do together that we cannot do alone (or what is the value and limit of particular communities in relation to other such groups)? Thus each study delineated a different aspect of the conditions and possibilities of faithful political witness within the contemporary context.

Through deliberation on the issues raised by the case studies an underlying framework has emerged for stipulating a consistent yet contextually responsive theological conception of political action. Such a conception is located within what I have called a Christian cosmopolitan vision. As set out in Chapter 3, this vision identifies the end of humanity as neither a return to an original state of blessing nor a movement beyond the materiality of creation. Instead it involves a dynamic movement, via differentiation and development through history, to an eschatological fulfillment of creation. Part of this movement is constituted by loving one's near and distant neighbors, within concentric circles of sociality, as one seeks to invite others to do, and anticipate now the gathering of all peoples to the messianic banquet that has already begun amid the fallen structures of the earthly city. Within this Christian cosmopolitan vision the particularity of humans is constituted by their place; that is, our social, economic, political, and historical location in creation. As anticipated in Christ's resurrection and ascension, this placefullness is taken up by the Spirit and fulfilled in the eschaton. Politics within this Christian cosmopolitan vision involves the formation of a common world of meaning and action within particular places. The formation of such a world entails, on the one hand, the breaking down of those structures and patterns of relationship that exclude vulnerable strangers from this common world and, on the other, the upholding of those structures and patterns of relationship that maintain this world as a common one. *Neighbor love is operative on both these poles as it may serve either to uphold patterns of relationship within a place or disrupt the exclusionary logic within those same patterns.* We grow up within concentric circles of relationship oriented toward the eschatological horizon of fulfillment. This horizon of fulfillment both draws in and constantly interrupts all attempts to make such places idolatrously self-sufficient or totally encompassing in terms of economic, political, and social relationships. As the parable of the Good Samaritan exemplifies, this disruption takes the concrete form of the call to love one's neighbor, whoever they may be and whatever their circumstances. As explored in Chapters 2 and 4 in relation to Irenaeus, Luther, and Wannenwetsch, this is the defining human vocation, a vocation that is discerned and worked out within the particular places and relations within which we providentially find ourselves. On this account, various forms of nationalism and identity politics overvalue the particularity of a place (be it cultural or geographic), while liberal cosmopolitan, global conceptions of citizenship, and the reductive universalism of capitalism undervalue it.

The Christian practice of hospitality best articulates what valuing a particular place, while making room for vulnerable strangers (through responding to the vocation to love our neighbor), entails. As I have argued extensively elsewhere, hospitality toward strangers constitutes part of the church's witness to the Christ-event and the hospitality that weak and sinful humans have received from God. We who bring nothing to our relationship with God echo this in our reception of others. Thus, within the Christian tradition there is a consistent and special concern for the weakest and most vulnerable: the poor, the sick, and the refugee. Moreover, the focus on the vulnerable stranger will, on occasion, mean that the church finds itself actively opposed by those who would be, by Christian criteria of evaluation, inhospitable to the vulnerable stranger. Thus the Christian practice of hospitality is often, because of its priorities, deeply prophetic, calling into question the prevailing political hegemony. At the same time, as reiterated in Chapter 3 in the discussion of what it means to hallow bare life, hospitality requires that we come from somewhere, that we have a place from which to be hospitable. As the Christian cosmopolitan vision makes clear, concentric circles of sociality are central to what constitutes creaturely personhood in the image of God. Therefore, while we are the same as all other creatures, we are more like some persons than others and we are also like no other person; each person is unique. Hospitality toward vulnerable strangers is grounded on the above threefold pattern of interpersonal relationships that simultaneously values the particular places we come from while recognizing that these places are only truly valued when what we value about them is understood to be fulfilled eschatologically.

In worship, different dimensions of which were explored in Chapters 2, 3, and 4, we enact a Christian cosmopolitan orientation to the world. For in worship we move from the local and particular to the universal, we turn out from self to God and thence to neighbor. In worship the Christian community is oriented beyond the ties of kinship, place, and polity, as well as the boundaries of possible action, to include all those in need of God's help and mercy. In worship the catholicity/universality of the body of Christ is articulated in a particular place and our particularity is located within both the catholicity of the church and the eschatological horizon of fulfillment. Constitutive of this catholicity is the communion of saints such that our contemporary practice is located eschatologically in relation to those whose faithful witness has gone before and those who are yet to come. This eschatological universality is witnessed in the relationship between past, present, and future action as evidenced in the case studies through their conservative-radical politics and the link between indwelling a tradition and the pursuit of right judgments and neighbor love. For example, the Sanctuary movement drew on the practice of medieval sanctuary, while the Fair Trade movement draws on practices related to a just wage and a just price. Within the Spirit's eschatological economy, paradigmatically experienced in the Eucharist, "archaic" practice is folded into contemporary action and contemporary action is unfolded through past practice as both past and present are oriented toward the coming kingdom of God. As outlined in the Introduction, a number of contemporary accounts of politics suggest there is a radical disjuncture between modern politics and older forms of political mobilization and practice. This disjuncture is then set within either a declension or ascension narrative. However, such accounts fail as ways of reading Christian political endeavors in which ancient and modern interweave and renew each other.

As set out in Chapter 4, the predominant moment within the rhythm of a worshipful life is ordinary time, the time of focusing on what faithful response to God's address entails within the *saeculum*. This liturgical time in between seasons of feasting and fasting situates the exercise of Christian freedom and responsibility by ordinary political actors within the informal politics of everyday life at home, at work, and in the marketplace within the life of worship. Thus, attention to ordinary time helps frame the vicissitudes and contingency of faithful witness within the *saeculum*; the *saeculum*, as set out in Chapter 2, being that time between the times when the eschaton and fallen history co-mingle and Christians and non-Christians may discern and share goods in common. As argued in Chapter 4, faithful political witness in ordinary time involves playing with creation within the *saeculum* in disciplined and generative ways, ways that seek to love one's neighbor and that are open to the healing and perfection of the *saeculum* in Christ. In addition, attention to ordinary time enables the valuation of the micropolitical as just as important for conceptualizing faithful political witness as the set-piece relationships between church and state, and the ordinary political actor as just as significant as "heroic" figures such as Martin Luther King. However, attention to ordinary time in no way diminishes the importance of the role of the church as a public body whose "publicity"[1] and "politicalness"[2] are constituted by its worship.

As discussed in Chapters 2 and 3, a church is constituted as a public body through listening to both God and the strangers among whom it lives. Through listening and responding to the Word of God a church is assembled as a public body out of the world. Yet through listening to strangers a church is able to discern who is the neighbor to be loved and what goods there may be in common with others and thus how it may contribute to the earthly peace of a particular place and uphold that place as a common world in which all may flourish. In the process, what it means to respond to the Word of God is understood more specifically and concretely. Listening to and waiting on God and those among whom we live are thus central to the formation of faithful political action. The assessment of community organizing in Chapter 2 and of the Sanctuary movement in Chapter 3 served as case studies in what it might mean in practice to listen to others in order to discern who is your neighbor, what goods you might have in common, and how you might encounter God in relation with them. In addition, a case was made for the symbiosis between listening to Scripture and listening to others. I want here to consider further the relationship between listening and faithful political action. The central thrust of the argument will be that listening to the voice of Christ in Scripture and encountering the other in political life through such endeavors as community organizing foster humility and penitence which in turn enable true virtue and faithful public witness in the *saeculum* constituted by the formation of neighbor love and just, though contextually contingent, judgments.

Listening is a way for churches to practice humility in their negotiation of political life, ensuring that they glorify God rather than glorifying themselves. In short, it is an antidote to self-glorification, idolatry, and regimes of control. To explain this further requires returning to Augustine's understanding of the relationship between the earthly city and the city of God. As explored in Chapter 2, for Augustine, there can be no true justice in the earthly city because it is oriented to pride rather than love of God. For Augustine, justice is a synonym for love, as one can only give another their due in a truly public way (as opposed to giving each their private interest) if we love God first and foremost and so are able to order one's own loves in relation to God and others and so give each their due. However, in order to truly love God, and thence love others, we must be justified in and through Christ as we cannot properly order our love of God and others without the grace of God. On this account, within the city of God, to be just is to know how to love one's neighbor. However, in the earthly city there is a disjuncture between justice and love. What is possible within the earthly city is not true justice – a perfect state of harmonious loving relations – but remedial acts of just judgment. These may be contingent and insecure, but nevertheless, they preserve the good of the creation order as recapitulated in Christ and create space for the proclamation of the eschatological order established in and through Christ. Faithful witness involves enabling just judgment and pointing to the coming eschatological order through acts of neighborliness which point to the common world established in Christ's reconciliation of all things. The church is empowered by the Spirit to anticipate this eschatological order but such anticipations are not the preserve of the church: the Spirit acts beyond the *ekklesia*.

Through listening to Scripture and others, so as to discern who is the neighbor to be loved, a sense of obedience to the Word is nurtured. Listening is a therapy for the self-love or pride that is the attempt to secure oneself outside of relationship with God and pursue illusions of self-sufficiency both in relation to God and neighbor. It inoculates the church against developing false securities because in listening one has to deal with the world as it is rather than acting on the basis of our projected fantasies or idolatrous means of escape. In listening one must take seriously who is before one and attend to the situation rather than predetermine what to do in accord with some prior agenda, ideology, or strategy of control. Against interest-group and identity politics and their agonistic rivalry, political action born out of listening acts in trust that the other, like the biblical figures of Ruth and the

Syro-Pheonician woman, may well be the bearer of the word of life, although this may be either a word of judgment or a word of encouragement. In sum, listening is vital to deepening one's moral conversion in relation to God and others and thus one's ability to reason rightly about what is the right or just judgment to be made with these people, at this time, in this place. In order to know what is just, the first task of loving judgment is to listen.

As a constitutive dimension of hospitality, listening trusts and gives space and time to those who are excluded from the determination of space and time by the existing hegemony. However, one cannot one hear others if the space is over-determined by a single voice – for example, that of either the state or the market – that drowns out all other voices or predetermines how they may speak and what they will say. The formation of complex space and an institutional plurality is thus part of what it means to listen in practice as it creates a place in which different voices may be heard, each in their own way. Neither can one attentively listen at a distance or if constantly mobile. For example, the drop-in, drop-off, and drop-out cycle that often character-izes the approach of suburban or professional Christian groups in relation to the poor operate outside of long-term, in-depth relational involvement. In such cases hospitality is replaced by a patron–client relationship that rein-forces the distance between giver and receiver and so militates against genu-inely listening. Instead, listening requires active involvement and commitment to a particular place and the formation of relationships in that place because building trusting and stable relationships takes time and personal presence. Non-pecuniary institutions that are not wholly subject to logics of instru-mentalization or commodification are key for creating spaces amidst politi-cal, economic, social, and technological pressures that militate against developing such relationships. These institutions represent a legal, organiza-tional, financial, and physical place to stand. Congregations represent insti-tutions of this kind and are places constituted by gathered and mobilized people who do not come together for either commercial or state-directed transactions, but who instead come together to worship and care for each other. Without such places there are few real places through which to resist the processes of commodification by the market and the processes of instru-mentalization by the state. In short, if we have nowhere to sit together free from governmental or commercial imperatives, we have no public spaces in which to take the time to listen to each other and develop mutual trust.

By upholding practices that enable listening, the church, whether inten-tionally or not, contributes to the condition and possibility of politics within the *saeculum*. Without listening there can be no politics, and politics is a condition of any earthly rule which enables a moderately peaceable order, one derived from the pursuit of goods in common and not the exclusion or oppression of others, particularly the weak and vulnerable. As Aristotle noted, politics, as that which entails self-restraint and the conciliation of different interests within a territorial unit under a common rule, is not the only way to provide order. Tyranny, oligarchy, plutocracy, totalitarianism, and what de Tocqueville called "democratic despotism" are more common ways to rule. These impose order by subverting or repressing all other interests under the interest of the one, the few, or the many. By contrast, as Bernard Crick notes:

> The political method of rule is to listen to … other groups so as to conciliate them as far as possible, and to give them legal position, a sense of security, some clear and reasonable safe means of articulation, by which these other groups can and will speak freely. Ideally politics draws all these groups into each other so that they each and together can make a positive contribution towards the general business of government and maintaining order.[3]

Under the pressure of processes of commodification, rights-based proceduralism and technocratic administration, what is under threat, especially in poor communities most intensely affected by these processes, is the possibility of politics.

This book has argued, in relation to scripture and Augustine, that the church, in seeking to be faithful to its own vocation, inherently seeks the welfare of the earthly city, and in seeking the welfare of the earthly city the church encounters God more deeply. If this is the case, then upholding the very possibility of politics, through its practices of listening, is a political action consequent upon the church acting as church. To say, following Barth, that the church must be the church in order that the world knows itself as the world is to say that the church being faithful to its vocation calls forth particular kinds of social and political life. This social and political life is fallen and finite and cannot be overvalued as the bearer of all that it means to be human, but neither can it be undervalued as irrelevant or without any value. It must understand itself as world; that is, a particular, historically contingent and fallen form of the *saeculum* within which God is active and present in innumerable ways. Faithful action enables the world to be itself and not mistake itself for the church nor dismiss itself as without any meaning at all.

Listening, however, should not be understood as excluding judgment and proclamation. To make a judgment about how and what to proclaim requires in the first instance an act of listening. It is in the interconnection between listening, judgment, and proclamation that the symbiosis between the church acting as a public body or *res publica*, the formation of an institutional plurality, and the extension of the bonds of neighbor love emerges.

The modern state, in attempting to overcome politics, through its resort to various forms of legal, bureaucratic, and market procedures, closes down the spaces for judgment and responsibility both by the rulers and the ruled. For Hannah Arendt, a pointed example of exactly this was the Nazi, Adolf Eichmann, who refused to exercise judgment in the name of conforming to legal and bureaucratic regulations and so aided and abetted the Holocaust. The impact of a prevailing proceduralism can be discerned in the very advocacy of democracy itself. As O'Donovan notes:

> Much advocacy of democracy confuses two quite different things: electing governments and consulting about policy. Election is an aggregative exercise, roping different points of view together to form a majority. Consultation is a discriminative exercise, which entails weighing up different points of view. For representative action to have moral depth, the representative needs a comprehensive sense of what the people at its best, i.e., at its most reflective and considerate, is concerned about.[4]

O'Donovan points out that folding the process of consultation into the process of electoral legitimacy closes down any real moment of listening and divorces politicians from engaging in real consultation and shared deliberation with those they govern. The emphasis on procedures of legitimation in democracy focuses on the formal relationship between rulers and ruled and leaves out any concern about substantive political relations. Such an emphasis is in effect another way in which politics is replaced by procedures; this time, electoral procedures. A practice such as community organizing reinserts consultation into democratic politics; is a means by which to regenerate the ability to make judgments together with others about the goods held in common; and regenerates a sense of responsibility for those common goods, both by those who govern and by the governed.

Common goods are not simply the aggregation of individual self-interests but goods in which the flourishing of each is dependent on the flourishing of all. Pursuit of common goods requires political judgment rather than letting a market mechanism, electoral process, or some other technocratic procedure determine the good by some system of aggregation. Such proceduralism constitutes a refusal to make judgments. Whether in a court or on the street, listening is a precondition of making right judgments. Practices that set up a contradiction and involve confrontation and conciliation regenerate the need for judgment and responsibility on the part of the dominant political and economic power holders and their attempts to circumvent politics and avoid accountability through legal, bureaucratic, and market-based mechanisms. Indeed, Alinsky's controversial rule thirteen, which states "Pick the target, freeze it, personalize it, and polarize it," contains a profound insight about the conditions of political judgment in the modern age: it refuses the temptation to blame, put on trial, or let others claim they are cogs either within "the system," or an "ism" such as capitalism or racism, or swept along by some abstract force such as "History" or the "material dialectic."[5] Rather, it calls for the recognition that it is nameable persons who must take responsibility and be held accountable for the right and wrong judgments they make or omit to make.

The only places in which to learn judgment and responsibility for goods in common and from which to contradict and so rouse just judgments by political authorities is within the kinds of non-pecuniary, tradition-situated institutions of which churches are the paradigmatic example in the West. As outlined in Chapter 3, churches, as tradition-embedded institutions, uphold and give form to a vision of the good in which the infinite value or dignity of the individual is hallowed. Thus, such institutions are the building blocks of a more complex space that inhibits the totalizing, monopolistic thrust of the modern market and state that seeks to instrumentalize and commodify persons and the relationships between them. In extending the bonds of neighbor love, the church upholds the importance of society and social relationships to human flourishing and refuses their subordination to the needs of the market or the state. At the same time, through extending the bonds of *neighbor* love, churches seek to ensure that the social life which emerges is one oriented beyond the immediate needs of kinship, place, and politics and so is able to properly value all three as having an intrinsic but relative value in relation to the eschatological horizon. And in extending the bonds of neighbor *love* churches seek to bear witness to that order of love that is the ground and end of the *saeculum* amid the seemingly all-pervasive yet ultimately insubstantial *libido dominandi* of the earthly city.

The O'Donovans, as outlined in Chapter 1, give an account of how, after Christ's reign over the cosmos is established, ecclesial and political authority share a joint responsibility for ordering society and offering judgment between good and bad, innocent and guilty. As noted in the Introduction, Oliver O'Donovan understands the proper exercise of judgment as having the double, simultaneous aspect of discrimination and decision. Right judgment has both a retrospective element (as an act of discrimination it pronounces upon an existent state of affairs) and as a decision it has a prospective dimension (it is effective in establishing or clearing a space for a common field of meaning and action in which moral relations are possible).[6] It has been my contention both that the church's political action seeks to summon right judgments from political authority and that the church itself exercises judgment; that is, it discriminates between right and wrong in relation to particular issues and establishes public contexts in which moral relations are possible. The examples of community organizing, the practice of sanctuary, and Fair Trade illustrate exactly this kind of judgment born out of political action. As should be clear from all the preceding chapters, to take responsibility for both summoning and offering right judgment need not be viewed as necessitating the attempt by the church to take control or determine the outcome of events. Rather, it can be understood in the more modest sense of seeking the welfare of Babylon even while remaining a pilgrim people within that same city. On the O'Donovans account the form the judgment of the church takes in seeking the welfare of Babylon is the proclamation of the Gospel – that is, the promulgation of God's merciful judgment in Christ – while the judgment of political authority is the limited arena of coercive human legal and political judgment. It is the suggestion of this book that the promulgation of God's merciful judgment in Christ necessarily involves constituting the possibility of politics against the totalizing and anti-political thrust of Babylonian rule. The O'Donovans have been charged with attempting to revalorize Establishment or "Constantinianism" but this is to misunderstand the implications of what they say.[7] Establishment constituted one possible form for structuring such joint jurisdiction that maintains the ecclesial and political forms of judgment – and thus the possibility of politics – after Christ. However, it depends on the majority of the population being Christian and the rulers of the day confessing the name of Christ. In a situation where this is not the case the public life and practices of the church (i.e., that which proclaims the Gospel) entail actions that forge anew or maintain a peaceable social order within the *saeculum* and enable right judgments to be made in relation to particular issues: that is, its proclamation enables the world to be the world.[8]

The threefold public work of pursuing goods in common with non-Christian others, fostering an institutional plurality and extending the bonds of neighbor love, a work exemplified in community organizing, the offering of sanctuary, and Fair Trade, is what this joint jurisdiction entails within a contested, multi-faith, liberal-democratic context. Such action can be conceptualized as taking two interrelated and symbiotic forms: a hospitable politics and a politics of the common good. Hospitable politics relates to those situations in which the church, for reasons of Establishment, doctrine, or simply providential accident, is the initiator and lead in generating common action. By contrast, a politics of the common good occurs when no single tradition of belief and practice sets the terms and conditions of such shared action, and common action is a negotiated, multilateral endeavor. However, there is no opposition between these two forms. More often than not, what begins as a form of hospitality grows into a politics of the common good, and a politics of the common good may involve forms of mutual hospitality. The example of community organizing illustrates this. It began life in the UK under the auspices of the Anglican church and received strategic funding from the Church Urban Fund and in America was hosted and largely funded by the Roman Catholic Church until it grew into the multilateral initiative it represents today. As outlined in Chapter 2, its contemporary form involves a guest–host dynamic wherein there is a process of mutual hospitality. The same dynamic can be seen in the both the Sanctuary and Fair Trade movements.

In both hospitable politics and a politics of the common good there is wide scope for an exploratory partnership with those committed to democratic politics. For Christianity and democratic citizenship entail the proposition that the best way to prevent the subordination of human flourishing and mutually responsible social relationships to the demands of the market and the state is not law or some other procedure but through power born out of associating for common action. The congregation and the *demos* are echoes of each other and neither is an *ochlos* or crowd whose disassociated and disorganized form leaves the individual utterly vulnerable to concerted action upon her by the state or the market. The Labor movement is a paradigm example of the power of congregating for common action and the early history of the movement illustrates the possibilities of partnership between Christianity and democratic citizenship. In the case of the Labor movement it was democratic accountability brought to bear upon economic rather than political decision making. It is not a necessary relationship but that does not make it an improper one.[9] Moreover, as already articulated, it is a partnership that can bring a mutual discipline to both the congregation and the *demos*. In joint action in pursuit of common goods, the congregation has to listen to and learn to love its neighbors. Conversely, the church, as a congregation listening to and proclaiming the Word of God, brings an opening horizon of reference and relationship to bear upon the immediate needs and demands of the *demos*. All the case studies examined here constitute examples of this kind of partnership for common action between Christianity and democratic citizenship.

It is joint action in pursuit of common goods that positively and practically maintains the dialectical relationship between coercive rule (with its use of unilateral power) and proclamation (with its use of relational, generative power) that together forms and maintains a social order that allows for human flourishing within the *saeculum*.[10] However, the greater the moral distance between ecclesial and political authority the sharper the contradiction between the two. This is a perennial dynamic. The contradiction between political and ecclesial authority may, under the rule of a Diocletian or a Stalin, take the form of a martyr's death, or it may involve, in the absence of any rule, as was the case in parts of Western Europe in late antiquity, the church undertaking many aspects of rule until such time as it can facilitate the emergence of a distinct political authority. In a liberal-democratic polity with a relativistic culture where the dynamics of competition, commodification, and co-option deny the possibility of a shared world of meaning and common action, the form this contradiction may take is the pursuit of goods in common with non-Christian "others," be they of another faith or no faith, and action that facilitates just judgments by political authorities as against the collapse of justice into what the strong demand. In doing so the church, simply by attempting to be itself, will help ferment a faithful worldly politics; that is, a process through which to maintain commonality and recognize and peaceably conciliate conflict with others in pursuit of shared goods.

Epilogue

In an effort to draw these reflections together it is possible, on the basis of what has been argued here, to draw out some criteria or rules of engagement for what faithful political action might entail within the contemporary context. For the sake of clarity but at the risk of being overly reductive and platitudinous, these rules may be put in the following way. First, such action begins with listening to Scripture and the various others amongst whom one lives in order to discern who is the neighbor to be loved and what goods in common need to be pursued. Second, such action is, in the first instance, place based, as distinct from national or global, envisaging the local and regional as the primary arenas of faithful Christian action. Third, such action is associational as distinct from an over-reliance on and immediate resort to legal, bureaucratic, or economic procedures that circumvent the need to develop interpersonal relationships. Fourth, such action involves the church as a legal, physical, and social institution within which worship is constitutive of its public life. Fifth, such action connects to and takes seriously the ordinary patterns of family, work, and civic life as occasions for neighbor love and part of the penumbra of worship. Sixth, such action is not simply humanitarian or pastoral in scope, but seeks to address broader structural issues. Seventh, such action embodies a generative contradiction rather than either saying "no" or "yes" to the status quo. Finally, such action does not look, in the first instance, to the state or the market to address issues of common concern within particular places but to modes of self-organization and mutual support. Like those of St Benedict and Alinsky, these rules are neither exhaustive nor immutable, rather they are a means of orientation that establish parameters within which faithful political action may emerge within the conditions and possibilities of the contemporary context.

Notes

1   Publicity is used here in its older meaning, denoting "The quality of being public; the condition or fact of being open to public observation or knowledge," *Oxford English Dictionary, On-line* (Oxford University Press, 2008).
2   Defined as the capacity for developing into beings who know and value what it means to participate in and be responsible for the care and improvement of our common life.
3   Bernard Crick, *In Defence of Politics*, 5th edn (London: Continuum, 2005), p. 4.
4   O'Donovan, *The Ways of Judgment*, p. 179.
5   This is an insight born out of reflection on Hannah Arendt's essay: "Personal Responsibility under Dictatorship," in *Responsibility and Judgment*, ed. Jerome Kohn (New York: Schocken Books, 2003), pp. 17–48.
6   See "Introduction," n. 71.
7   See, for example, Stanley Hauerwas, "Remaining in Babylon: Oliver O'Donovan's Defense of Christendom," in *Wilderness Wanderings: Probing Twentieth Century Theology and Philosophy* (Boulder, CO: Westview Press, 1997), pp. 199–224.
8   As part of the promulgation of God's merciful judgment in Christ, Christian charities, political initiatives, and social welfare organizations can be located as part of the penumbra of the church. Such organizations and initiatives, if they confess Christ as Lord, derive the authority for their work from Christ and are part of the spontaneous and untidy manifestation of the church as it seeks to bear faithful witness to the Lordship of Christ. Such organizations seem to exist on the cusp between civil society and the church and are probably best understood as a distinctively Christian part of the mediatory and representative structures of civil society. They are a mediating structure between church, society, and government that represent and embody the proclamation of the Gospel within particular contexts and in relation to particular issues; for example, homelessness, drug addiction, parenting, education, and the like. But, as suggested by the analysis in Chapters 1 and 2, outside of relation to the church, or as an alternative to the church and active worshiping communities, they become debased and either co-opted or parodies of ecclesial communities.
9   As Oliver O'Donovan notes: "The case for democracy is that it is specifically appropriate to Western society at this juncture. It is a moment in the western tradition; it has its own ecological *niche*. This allows us no universal claims of the 'best regime' kind, nor does it permit the imperialist view that the history of democracy is the history of progress. Yet within its own terms it allows us to

be positive about democracy's strengths. The best regime is precisely that regime that plays to the virtues and skills of those who are governed by it; and this one serves us well in demanding and developing certain virtues of bureaucratic and public discourse that the Western tradition has instilled. It is our tradition; we are bred in it; we can, if we are sensible about it, make it work." *The Ways of Judgment*, p. 178.

10 Articulating a proper distinction between the kinds of power exercised in coercive rule as against that proper to proclamation through the pursuit of goods in common and neighbor love must await development beyond the scope of this volume. However, the articulation of a theological account of the differences between relational power (power with) and unilateral power (power over) is a crucial point in the development of a theology of politics. Hannah Arendt sketches the beginning of an account of relational power in Hannah Arendt, "On Violence," in *Crises of the Republic* (Orlando, FL: Harcourt Brace & Co., 1972), pp. 105–98. For a fuller account that begins to explore some of the theological issues from the perspective of process theology see Bernard Loomer, "Two Conceptions of Power," *Process Studies* 6.1 (1976), pp. 5–32. Modern Christian political thought, like most modern political thought, with its emphasis on the nature of sovereign power, has focused almost exclusively on unilateral power. For a helpful overview of different conceptions of power see Steven Lukes , "Power and Authority," in *A History of Sociological Analysis*, ed. Tom Bottomore and Robert Nisbet (New York: Basic Books, 1978), pp. 633–76. Interestingly, while Lukes identifies the two conceptions of power outlined here, he fails to develop this distinction in his own account of power, thus conforming to the general emphasis on sovereign power already noted. See Steven Lukes, *Power: A Radical View*, 2nd edn (New York: Palgrave-MacMillan, 2005).

Bibliography

Ananda Abeysekara, *The Politics of Postsecular Religion: Mourning Secular Futures* (New York: Columbia University Press, 2008).

John Ackerman, "Co-governance for accountability: Beyond 'exit' and 'voice'," *World Development* 32.3 (2004), 447–463.

Rebecca Adams, "Violence, Difference, and Sacrifice: A Conversation with René Girard," *Religion and Literature* 25.2 (1993), 9–33.

Georgio Agamben, *Homo Sacer: Sovereign Power and Bare Life*, trans. Daniel Heller-Roazen (Stanford, CA: Stanford University Press, 1998).

Georgio Agamben, *Means Without End: Notes on Politics*, trans. Vincenzo Binetti and Cesare Casarino (Minneapolis, MN: University of Minnesota Press, 2000).

Ambrose, "On the Duties of the Clergy," in *Nicene and Post-Nicene Father, Second Series*, vol. X, trans. H. De Romestein, eds. Philip Schaff and Henry Wace (Edinburgh: T&T Clark, 1989), pp. 1–89.

Ambrose, *De Officiis. Vol. 1: Introduction, Text and Translation*, trans. Ivor Davidson (Oxford: Oxford University Press, 2001).

David Albertson, "On 'The Gift' in Tanner's Theology: A Patristic Parable," *Modern Theology* 21.1 (2005), 107–18.

Saul Alinsky, "Behind the Mask," in *American Child: Which Way Community Action Programs?* 47.4 (1965), 7–9.

Saul Alinsky, *Reveille for Radicals* (New York: Vintage Books, 1969).

Saul Alinsky, *Rules for Radicals: A Pragmatic Primer for Realistic Radicals* (New York: Vintage Books, 1989).

Hannah Arendt, *The Origins of Totalitarianism* (San Diego, CA: Harcourt Brace Jovanovich, 1951).

Hannah Arendt, *The Human Condition*, 2nd edn (Chicago, IL: University of Chicago Press, 1958).

Hannah Arendt, "On Violence," in *Crises of the Republic* (Orlando, FL: Harcourt Brace & Co, 1972), pp. 105–98.

Hannah Arendt, *Lectures on Kant's Political Philosophy*, ed. Ronald Beiner (Chicago, IL: Chicago University Press, 1982).

Hannah Arendt, "Personal Responsibility under Dictatorship," in *Responsibility and Judgment*, ed. Jerome Kohn (New York: Schocken Books, 2003), pp. 17–48.

John Atherton, *Transfiguring Capitalism: An Enquiry into Religion and Global Change* (London: SCM-Canterbury, 2008).

Robert Audi and Nicholas Wolterstorff, *Religion in the Public Square: The Place of Religious Convictions in Political Debate* (Lanham: Rowan & Littlefield, 1997).

Augustine, *The City of God Against the Pagans*, trans. R.W. Dyson (Cambridge: Cambridge University Press, 1998).

Augustine, *Augustine: Political Writings*, eds. E. M. Atkins and R. J. Dodaro (Cambridge: Cambridge University Press, 2001).

J. L. Austin, *How to Do Things with Words*, 2nd edn (Cambridge, MA: Harvard University Press, 1975).

Derek Bacon, "Revitalizing Civil Society through Social Capital Formation in Faith-Based Organizations: Reflections from Northern Ireland," *Social Development Issues* 26.1 (2004), 14–24.

Alain Badiou, *Saint Paul: The Foundation of Universalism*, trans. Ray Brassier (Stanford, CA: Stanford University Press, 2003).

Alain Badiou, *Being And Event*, trans. Oliver Feltham (London: Continuum, 2006).

Jerome Baggett, "Congregations and Civil Society: A Double-edged Connection," *Journal of Church and State* 44 (2002), 425–54.

Michael Banner, " 'Who Are My Mother and My Brothers?': Marx, Bonhoeffer and Benedict and the Redemption of the Family," in *Studies in Christian Ethics* 9.1 (1996), 1– 22.

Karl Barth, *Church Dogmatics: The Doctrine of Creation*. Vol. III, part 4, trans. A. T. Mackay et al. (Edinburgh: T&T Clark, 1961).

Karl Barth, *The Christian Life: Church Dogmatics IV, 4, Lecture Fragments*, trans. Geoffrey Bromiley (Grand Rapids, MI: Eerdmans, 1981).

Ignatius Bau, *This Ground Is Holy: Church Sanctuary and Central American Refugees* (New York: Paulist Press, 1985).

Richard Bauckham, *The Theology of the Book of Revelation* (Cambridge: Cambridge University Press, 1993).

Gerd Baumann, *The Multicultural Riddle: Rethinking National, Ethnic, and Religious Identities* (London: Routledge, 1999).

Gerd Baumann, *Contesting Culture: Discourse of Identity in Multicultural London* (Cambridge: Cambridge University Press, 1996).

Zygmunt Bauman, *Work, Consumerism and the New Poor* (Buckingham: Open University Press, 1998).

Ulrich Beck, *Risk Society: Towards a New Modernity*, trans. Mark Ritter (London: Sage, 1992).

Ulrich Beck, "The Reinvention of Politics: Towards a Theory of Reflexive Modernization" in Ulrich Beck, Anthony Giddens, and Scott Lash, *Reflexive*

Modernization: Politics, Tradition and Aesthetics in the Modern Social Order (Cambridge: Polity Press, 1994).

Ulrich Beck, *The Reinvention of Politics: Rethinking Modernity in the Global Social Order*, trans. Mark Ritter (Oxford: Polity Press, 1997).

Ulrich Beck, "World Risk Society as Cosmopolitan Society? Ecological Questions in a Framework of Manufactured Uncertainties," *World Risk Society* (Cambridge: Polity Press, 1999).

Catherine Bell, *Ritual: Perspectives and Dimensions* (Oxford: Oxford University Press, 1997).

Daniel Bell, *Liberation Theology after the End of History: The Refusal to Cease Suffering* (London: Routledge, 2001).

Seyla Benhabib, *The Rights of Others: Aliens, Residents and Citizens* (Cambridge: Cambridge University Press, 2004).

Peter Berger, *The Desecularisation of the World* (Washington, DC: Ethics and Public Policy Centre, 1999).

John Behr, *Asceticism and Anthropology in Irenaeus and Clement* (Oxford: Clarendon Press, 2000).

Isaiah Berlin, *Liberty*, ed. Henry Hardy (Oxford: Oxford University Press, 2002).

Harold Berman, *Law and Revolution II: The Impact of the Protestant Reformation on the Western Legal Tradition* (Cambridge, MA: Belknap Press, 2003).

Wendell Berry, *Sex, Economy, Freedom and Community: Eight Essays* (New York: Pantheon Books, 1993).

Nigel Biggar, "The Value of Limited Loyalty: Christianity, the Nation, and Territorial Boundaries," in David Millar and Sohail Hashimi, eds., *Boundaries and Justice: Diverse Ethics Perspectives* (Princeton, NJ: Princeton University Press, 2001), pp. 38–54.

Amy E. Black, Douglas L. Koopman, and David K. Ryden, *Of Little Faith: The Politics of George W. Bush's Faith-Based Initiatives* (Washington DC: Georgetown University Press, 2004).

Tony Blair, *The Third Way: New Politics for a New Society*, Fabian Pamphlet 588 (London: The Fabian Society, 1998).

Tony Blair, Speech to the Christian Socialist Movement, Westminster Central Hall, March 29, 2001.

Philip Blond, ed., *Post-secular Philosophy: Between Philosophy and Theology* (London: Routledge, 1998).

Augusto Boal, *Theatre of the Oppressed*, trans. Charles and Maria-Odila Leal McBride (London: Pluto Press, 1979).

Augusto Boal, *Legislative Theatre: Using Performance to Make Politics* (London: Routledge, 1998).

Robert Bocock, *Consumption* (London: Routledge, 1993).

Luc Boltanski and Eve Chiapello, *The New Spirit of Capitalism*, trans. Gregory Elliot (London: Verso, 2005).

Dietrich Bonhoeffer, *Ethics*, trans. Reinhard Krauss et al., ed. Clifford Green. Vol. 6: *Dietrich Bonhoeffer Works* (Minneapolis, MN: Fortress Press, 2005).

Dietrich Bonhoeffer, *Life Together*, ed. Geffrey Kelly, trans. Daniel Bloesch and James Burtness, *Dietrich Bonhoeffer Works, Vol. 5* (Minneapolis, MN: Fortress Press, 1996).

Harry C. Boyte, *Commonwealth: A Return to Citizen Politics* (New York: Free Press, 1989).

Harry C. Boyte, *Everyday Politics: Reconnecting Citizens and the Public Life* (Philadelphia, PA: University of Pennsylvania Press, 2004).

Bradford Race Review, *Community Pride Not Prejudice: Making Diversity Work in Bradford, Presented to Bradford Vision by Sir Herman Ouseley* (2001).

Luke Bretherton, *Hospitality as Holiness: Christian Witness amid Moral Diversity* (Aldershot: Ashgate, 2006).

Luke Bretherton, "Valuing the Nation: Nationalism and Cosmopolitanism in Theological Perspective," in Stephen Holmes, ed., *Public Theology in Cultural Engagement: God's Key to the Redemption of the World* (Milton Keynes: Paternoster, 2008), pp. 170–96.

Peter Brown, *The Rise of Western Christendom: Triumph and Diversity AD 200–1000* (Oxford: Blackwell, 1997).

Don Browning, *A Fundamental Practical Theology* (Minneapolis, MN: Fortress Press, 1996).

Steve Bruce, *Religion and Modernization: Sociologists and Historians Debate the Secularization Thesis* (Oxford: Clarendon Press, 1992).

Steve Bruce, *God Is Dead: Secularization in the West* (Oxford: Blackwell, 2002).

Walter Brueggemann, *Hopeful Imagination: Prophetic Voices in Exile* (Philadelphia, PA: Fortress Press, 1986).

Walter Brueggemann, *A Commentary of Jeremiah: Exile and Homecoming* (Grand Rapids, MI: Eerdmans, 1998).

Hedley Bull, *The Anarchical Society* (London: Macmillan, 1977).

John Burgess, *The East German Church and the End of Communism* (Oxford: Oxford University Press, 1997).

Barry Buzan, Ole Waever, and Jaap de Wilde, *Security: A New Framework for Analysis* (Boulder, CO: Lynne Rienner, 1997).

Jill M. Bystydzienski and Steven P. Schacht, eds., *Forging Radical Alliances Across Difference: Coalition Politics for the New Millennium* (New York: Rowman & Littlefield, 2001).

John Calvin, *Institutes of the Christian Religion*, trans. Henry Beveridge (Grand Rapids, MI: Eerdmans, 1983).

John Calvin, *Calvin's Commentary – Volume 10 – Jeremiah 20–47* (Grand Rapids, MI: Baker, 1999).

John D. Caputo, *The Prayers and Tears of Jacques Derrida: Religion without Religion* (Bloomington, IN: Indiana University Press, 1997).

John D. Caputo, *On Religion* (London: Routledge, 2001).

Joseph Carens, "Aliens and Citizens: The Case for Open Borders," *The Review of Politics* 49.2 (1987), pp. 251–73.

Joseph Carens, "A Reply to Meilaender: Reconsidering Open Borders," *International Migration Review* 33.4 (1999), pp. 1088–9.

Stanley Carlson-Thies, "Charitable Choice: Bringing Religion Back into American Welfare," *Journal of Policy History* 13 (2001), 109–32.

José Casanova, "Immigration and the New Religious Pluralism: A European Union/ United States Comparison," in Thomas Banchoff, ed., *Democracy and the New Religious Pluralism* (Oxford: Oxford University Press, 2007), pp. 59–83.

Manuel Castells, *The Rise of the Network Society* (Oxford: Blackwell, 1997).

William Cavanaugh, *Torture and Eucharist: Theology, Politics and the Body of Christ* (Oxford: Blackwell, 1998).

William Cavanaugh, *Theopolitical Imagination: Discovering the Liturgy as a Political Act in an Age of Global Consumerism* (Edinburgh: T&T Clark, 2002).

William Cavanaugh, "Killing for the Telephone Company: Why the Nation-State is Not the Keeper of the Common Good," in Patrick Miller and Dennis McCann, eds., *In Search of the Common Good* (London: T&T Clark, 2005), pp. 310–332.

William Cavanaugh, *Being Consumed: Economics and Christian Desire* (Grand Rapids, MI: Eerdmans, 2008).

Michel de Certeau, *The Practice of Everyday Life*, trans. Steven Rendall (Berkeley, CA: University of California Press, 1988).

Edward Chambers with Michael Cowan, *Roots for Radicals: Organizing for Power, Action and Justice* (New York: Continuum, 2004).

Simone Chambers and Will Kymlicka, *Alternative Conceptions of Civil Society* (Princeton, NJ: Princeton University Press, 2002).

Stephen Cherry, "Sanctuary: A Reflection on a Critical Praxis," *Theology* 93 (1990), 141–50.

James Childress, " 'Nonviolent Resistance: Trust and Risk Taking' Twenty-Five Years Later," *Journal of Religious Ethics* 25.2 (1997), 213–20.

B. S. Chimni, "Globalization, Humanitarianism, and the Erosion of Refugee Protection," *Journal of Refugee Studies* 13.3 (2000), 243–63.

Church Urban Fund, *Faithful Representation: Faith Representatives on Local Public Partnerships* (London: Church Urban Fund, 2006).

Gerard Clarke, "Faith Matters: Faith-Based Organisations, Civil Society and International Development," *Journal of International Development*, 18 (2006), 835–848.

Nick Clarke, Clive Barnett, Paul Cloke, and Alice Malpass, "The Political Rationalities of Fair-Trade Consumption in the United Kingdom," *Politics and Society*, 35.4 (2007), 583–607.

Nick Clarke, Clive Barnett, Paul Cloke, and Alice Malpass, "Fairtrade Urbanism? The Politics of Place Beyond Place in the Bristol Fairtrade City Campaign," *International Journal of Urban and Regional Research* 31.3 (2007), 633–45.

Nick Clarke, Clive Barnett, Paul Cloke, and Alice Malpass, "The Spaces and Ethics of Organic Food," *Journal of Rural Studies* 24 (2008), 219–230.

Olivier Clément, *The Roots of Christian Mysticism: Text and Commentary*, trans. Theodore Berkeley, 4th edn (London: New City, 1997).

Clarke Cochran, *Religion in Public and Private Life* (London: Routledge, 1990).

Romand Coles, *Rethinking Generosity: Critical Theory and the Politics of Caritas* (Ithaca, NY: Cornell University Press, 1997).

Romand Coles, *Beyond Gated Politics: Reflections for the Possibility of Democracy* (Minneapolis, MN: University of Minnesota Press, 2005).

Romand Coles, "Of Tensions and Tricksters: Grassroots Democracy between Theory and Practice," *Perspectives on Politics* 4.3 (2006), 547–61.

Romand Coles and Stanley Hauerwas, *Christianity, Democracy, and the Radical Ordinary: Conversations between a Radical Democrat and a Christian* (Eugene, OR: Cascade Books, 2007).

Community Cohesion Unit, *Community Cohesion: A Report of the Independent Review Team Chaired by Ted Cantle* (London: Home Office, 2003).

William Connolly, *Why I Am Not a Secularist* (Minneapolis, MN: University of Minnesota Press, 1999).

William Connolly, *Pluralism* (Durham, NC: Duke University Press, 2005).

Jim Corbett, *Goatwalking: A Guide to Wildland Living, a Quest for the Peaceable Kingdom* (New York: Viking, 1991).

D. Scott Cormode, "Does Institutional Isomorphism Imply Secularization? Churches and Secular Voluntary Associations in the Turn-of-the-Century City," in *Sacred Companies: Organizational Aspects of Religion and Religious Aspects of Organizations*, eds. N. J. Demerath, Peter Hall, Terry Schmitt, and Rhys Williams (Oxford: Oxford University Press, 1998), pp. 116–31.

John Corner and Dick Pels, *Media and the Restyling of Politics: Consumerism, Celebrity and Cynicism* (London: Sage, 2003).

Ernesto Cortes, "Reweaving the Fabric: The Iron Rule and the IAF Strategy for Power and Politics," in *Interwoven Destinies: Cities and the Nation*, ed. Henry Cisneros (New York: W. W. Norton, 1993), pp. 295–319.

Susan Bibler Coutin, *The Culture of Protest: Religious Activism and the U.S. Sanctuary Movement* (Boulder, CO: Westview Press, 1993).

J. Charles Cox, *The Sanctuaries and Sanctuary Seekers of Mediaeval England* (London: George Allen & Sons, 1911).

Bernard Crick, *In Defence of Politics*, 5th edn (London: Continuum, 2005).

Ann Crittenden, *Sanctuary: A Story of American Conscience and the Law in Collision* (New York: Weidenfeld & Nicolson, 1988).

Hilary Cunningham, *God and Caesar at the Rio Grande: Sanctuary and the Politics of Religion* (Minneapolis, MN: University of Minneapolis Press, 1995).

Charles Curran, *The Moral Theology of Pope John Paul II* (Washington, DC: Georgetown University Press, 2005).

Patrick Curry, *Ecological Ethics: An Introduction* (London: Polity Press, 2005).

Irving Cutler, *The Jews of Chicago: From Shtetl to Suburb* (Chicago, IL: University of Illinois Press, 1996).

Grace Davie, *Religion in Modern Europe: A Memory Mutates* (Oxford: Oxford University Press, 2000).

Department of Communities and Local Government, *Preventing Violent Extremism: Winning Hearts and Minds* (London: Department of Communities and Local Government, 2007).

Department of Communities and Local Government, *Face to Face and Side by Side: A Framework for Partnership in Our Multi Faith Society* (London: Department of Communities and Local Government, 2008).

Jacques Derrida, *Acts of Religion* (London: Routledge, 2002).

Paul J. DiMaggio and Walter W. Powell, "The Iron Cage Revisited: Institutional Isomorphism and Collective Rationality in Organizational Fields," *American Sociological Review* 48.2 (1983), 147–60.

Robert Dodaro, *Christ and the Just Society in the Thought of Augustine* (Cambridge: Cambridge University Press, 2004).

Bernard Doering, ed., *The Philosopher and the Provocateur: The Correspondence of Jacques Maritain and Saul Alinsky* (Notre Dame, IN: University of Notre Dame Press, 1994).

Mary Douglas, *Purity and Danger: An Analysis of the Concept of Pollution and Taboo* (London: Routledge, 1966).

Michael Dummett, *On Immigration and Refugees* (London: Routledge, 2001).

Helen Rose Ebaugh, Janet Chafetz, and Paula Pipes, "Where's the Faith in Faith-Based Organisations? Measures and Correlates of Religiosity in Faith-based Social Service Coalitions," *Social Forces* 84.4 (2006), 2259–72.

Shmuel Eisenstadt, "The Reconstruction of Religious Arenas in the Framework of 'Multiple Modernities'," *Millennium: Journal of International Studies* 29.3 (2000), 591–611.

Omri Elisha, "Moral Ambitions of Grace: The Paradox of Compassion and Accountability in Evangelical Faith-Based Activism," *Cultural Anthropology* 23.1 (2008), 154–89.

Sara M. Evans and Harry C. Boyte, *Free Spaces: The Sources of Democratic Change in America* (New York: Harper & Row, 1986).

Richard Farnell et al., *"Faith" in Urban Regeneration: Engaging Faith Communities in Urban Regeneration* (Bristol: Policy Press, 2003).

Douglas Farrow, "St Irenaeus of Lyons: The Church and the World," *Pro Ecclesia* 4.3 (1995), 333–55.

John Field, *Social Capital* (London: Routledge, 2003).

John Neville Figgis, *The Political Aspects of S. Augustine's "City of God"* (Gloucester, MA: Peter Smith, 1963).

Alan Finlayson, *Making Sense of New Labour* (London: Lawrence & Wishart, 2003).

David Ford and C. C. Pecknold, *The Promise of Scriptural Reasoning* (Oxford: Blackwell, 2006).

Samuel Freedman, *Upon This Rock: The Miracles of a Black Church* (New York: Harper Perennial, 1993).

Hans-Georg Gadamer, *Truth and Method* (London: Sheed & Ward, 1981).

William Galston, *Liberal Pluralism: The Implications of Value Pluralism for Political Theory and Practice* (Cambridge: Cambridge University Press, 2002).

Michael Gecan, *Going Public: An Organizer's Guide to Citizen Action* (New York: Anchor Books, 2002).

Michael Gecan, *Effective Organizing for Congregational Renewal* (Skokie, IL: Acta Publications, 2008).

Andrew Geddes, *The Politics of Migration and Immigration in Europe* (London: Sage, 2003).

Matthew Gibney, *The Ethics and Politics of Asylum: Liberal Democracy and the Response to Refugees* (Cambridge: Cambridge University Press, 2004).

Matthew Gibney, ed., *Open Borders? Closed Societies? The Ethics and Political Issues* (Westport, CT: Greenwood Press, 1988).

J. K. Gibson-Graham, *Postcapitalist Politics* (Minneapolis, MN: University of Minnesota Press, 2006).

Anthony Giddens, *Self and Society in the Late Modern Age* (Cambridge: Polity Press, 1991).

Anthony Giddens, *Beyond Left and Right – the Future of Radical Politics* (Cambridge: Polity Press, 1994).

Paul Gifford, *The Christian Churches and the Democratisation of Africa* (Leiden: E.J. Brill, 1995).

Langdom Gilkey, *On Neibuhr: A Theological Study* (Chicago: University of Chicago Press, 2001).

Maurice Glasman, *Unnecessary Suffering: Managing Market Utopia* (London: Verso, 1996).

Charles Glenn, *The Ambiguous Embrace: Government and Faith-Based Schools and Social Agencies* (Princeton, NJ: Princeton University Press, 2000).

Michael Goodman, "Reading Fair Trade: Political Ecological Imaginary and the Moral Economy of Fair Trade Foods," *Political Geography* 23 (2004), 891–915.

Fred Graham, *The Constructive Revolutionary: John Calvin and His Socio-Economic Impact* (East Lansing, MI: Michigan State University Press, 1987).

Robert Grant, *Irenaeus of Lyons, The Early Church Fathers* (London: Routledge, 1997).

John Gray, *Post-liberalism: Studies in Political Thought* (London: Routledge, 1996).

Eric Gregory, *Politics and the Order of Love: An Augustinian Ethic of Democratic Citizenship* (Chicago, IL: University of Chicago Press, 2008).

Eric Gregory, "*Agape* and Special Relations in a Global Economy: Theological Sources," in Douglas Hicks and Mark Valeri, eds., *Global Neighbors: Christian Faith and Moral Obligation in Today's Economy* (Grand Rapids, MI: Eerdmans, 2008), pp. 16–42.

John De Gruchy, *The Church Struggle in South Africa*, 2nd edn (Grand Rapids, MI: Eerdmans, 1986).

Colin Gunton, "Trinity, Ontology and Anthropology: Towards a Renewal of the Doctrine of the *Imago Dei*," in Colin Gunton and Christoph Schwöbel, eds., *Persons, Divine and Human* (Edinburgh: T&T Clark, 1991), pp. 47–61.

Jürgen Habermas, *Between Facts and Norms: Contributions to a Discourse Theory of Law and Democracy*, trans. William Rehg (Cambridge, MA: MIT Press, 1996).

Jürgen Habermas, "Religion in the Public Sphere," *European Journal of Philosophy* 14.1 (2006), 1–25.

Jürgen Habermas, "Notes on a Post-Secular Society," www.signandsight.com/features/1714.html.

Kenneth Hagen, "A Critique of Wingren on Luther on Vocation," *Lutheran Quarterly* 16 (2002), 249–73.

Stephen Hart, *Cultural Dilemmas of Progressive Politics: Styles of Engagement among Grassroots Activists* (Chicago, IL: University of Chicago Press, 2001).

Michael Hardt and Antonio Negri, *Multitude: War and Democracy in the Age of Empire* (London: Hamish Hamilton, 2005).

Stanley Hauerwas, *The Peaceable Kingdom: A Primer in Christian Ethics* (Notre Dame, IN: University of Notre Dame Press, 1983).

Stanley Hauerwas, "Will the Real Sectarian Please Stand Up," *Theology Today* 44.1 (1987), 87–94.

Stanley Hauerwas, *After Christendom? How the Church Is to Behave If Freedom, Justice, and a Christian Nation Are Bad Ideas* (Nashville, TN: Abingdon Press, 1991).

Stanley Hauerwas, "Remaining in Babylon: Oliver O'Donovan's Defence of Christendom," in *Wilderness Wanderings: Probing Twentieth Century Theology and Philosophy* (Boulder, CO: Westview Press, 1997), pp. 199–224.

Stanley Hauerwas, *With the Grain of the Universe: The Church's Witness and Natural Theology* (London: SCM Press, 2001).

Stanley Hauerwas, *The State of the University: Academic Knowledges and the Knowledge of God* (Oxford: Blackwell, 2007).

Stanley Hauerwas and Samuel Wells, eds., *Blackwell Companion to Christian Ethics* (Oxford: Blackwell, 2004).

Stefan Hauser, "The Cost of Citizenship: Disciple and Citizen in Bonhoeffer's Political Ethics," *Studies in Christian Ethics* 18.3 (2005), 49–69.

Teresa Hayton, *Open Borders: The Case against Immigration Control* (Sterling, VA: Pluto Press, 2000).

Nicholas Healy, *Church, World and the Christian Life: Practical-Prophetic Ecclesiology* (Cambridge: Cambridge University Press, 2000).

Nicholas Healy, "Ecclesiology and Communion," *Perspectives in Religious Studies* 31.3 (2004), 273–90.

Volker Heins, "Giorgio Agamben and the Current State of Affairs in Humanitarian Law and Human Rights Policy," *German Law Journal* 6.5 (2005), 845–60.

David Herbert, *Religion and Civil Society: Rethinking Public Religion in the Contemporary World* (Aldershot: Ashgate, 2003).

Christine Hepworth and Sean Stitt, "Social Capital and Faith-Based Organisations," *Heythrop Journal* XLVIII (2007), 895–910.

Douglas Hicks, "Global Poverty and Bono's Celebrity Activism: An Analysis of Moral Imagination and Motivation," in Douglas Hicks and Mark Valeri, eds., *Global Neighbors: Christian Faith and Moral Obligation in Today's Economy* (Grand Rapids, MI: Eerdmans, 2008), pp. 43–62.

Albert Hirschman, *Exit, Voice, and Loyalty: Responses to Decline in Firms, Organizations, and States* (Cambridge, MA: Harvard University Press, 1970).

Home Office, *Working Together: Cooperation between Government and Faith Communities* (London: Home Office, 2004).

Home Office, Pursue Prevent Protect Prepare: The United Kingdom's Strategy for Countering International Terrorism (London: Home Office, 2009).

Sanford D. Horwitt, *Let Them Call Me Rebel: Saul Alinsky – His Life and Legacy* (New York: Alfred Knopf, 1989).

Wayne Hudson, "Postsecular Civil Society," in *Civil Society, Religion and Global Governance: Paradigms of Power and Persuasion*, ed. Helen James (London: Routledge, 2007), pp. 149–57.

Reinhard Hütter, *Suffering Divine Things: Theology as Church Practice*, trans. Doug Scott (Grand Rapids, MI: Eerdmans, 2000).

John Inge, *A Christian Theology of Place* (Aldershot: Ashgate, 2003).

Ronald Inglehart, *Modernization and Postmodernization* (Princeton, NJ: Princeton University Press, 1997).

Ronald Inglehart, "Postmodernization Erodes Respect for Authority, But Increases Support for Democracy," in Pippa Norris, ed., *Critical Citizens: Global Support for Democratic Government* (Oxford: Oxford University Press, 1999), pp. 236–56.

Christopher Insole, *The Politics of Human Frailty: A Theological Defense of Political Liberalism* (London: SCM Press, 2004).

St Irenaeus of Lyons, *On the Apostolic Preaching*, trans. John Behr (Crestwood, NY: St Vladimir's Seminary Press, 1997).

Jeffrey Isaac, *Democracy in Dark Times* (Ithaca, NY: Cornell University Press, 1998).

Dennis A. Jacobsen, *Doing Justice: Congregations and Community Organizing* (Minneapolis, MN: Augsburg Fortress, 2001).

Thomas Jeavons, "Identifying Characteristics of 'Religious' Organizations: An Exploratory Proposal," in *Sacred Companies: Organizational Aspects of Religion and Religious Aspects of Organizations*, eds. N. J. Demerath, Peter Hall, Terry Schmitt, and Rhys Williams (Oxford: Oxford University Press, 1998), pp. 79–95.

Derek Jeffreys, *Defending Human Dignity: John Paul II and Political Realism* (Grand Rapids, MI: Brazos Press, 2004).

Kristen Deede Johnson, *Theology, Political Theory, and Pluralism: Beyond Tolerance and Difference* (Cambridge: Cambridge University Press, 2007).

William Chester Jordan, "A Fresh Look at Medieval Sanctuary," in *Law and the Illicit in Medieval Europe*, eds. Ruth Mazo Karras, Joel Kaye, and E. Ann Matter (Philadelphia, PA: University of Philadelphia Press, 2008), pp. 17–32.

Charles Kegley and Rober Bretall, eds., *Reinhold Neibuhr: His Religious, Social and Political Thought* (New York: MacMillan, 1956).

Sigrun Kahl, "The Religious Roots of Modern Poverty Policy: Catholic, Lutheran, and Reformed Protestant Traditions Compared," *European Journal of Sociology* 46.1 (2005), 91–126.

Sheila Suess Kennedy and Wolfgang Bielefeld, *Charitable Choice at Work* (Washington, DC: Georgetown University Press, 2006).

Mary M. Keys, *Aquinas, Aristotle, and the Promise of the Common Good* (Cambridge: Cambridge University Press, 2006).

Gaim Kibreab, "Revisiting the Debate on People, Place, Identity and Displacement," *Journal of Refugee Studies* 12.4 (1999), 384–428.

Kim Knott, *The Location of Religion: A Spatial Analysis* (London: Equinox, 2005).

Robert Lambert, "Empowering Salafis and Islamists against Al-Qaeda: A London Counter-terrorism Case Study," *Political Science (PS) Online* January (2008), 31–5.

Jacqueline Lapsley, " 'When Mercy Seasons Justice': Jonah and the Common Good," in *In Search of the Common Good*, eds. Patrick Miller and Dennis McCann (London: T&T Clark, 2005), pp. 41–57.

Jon D. Levenson, "The Universal Horizon of Biblical Particularism," in Mark Brett, ed., *Ethnicity and the Bible* (Leiden: E. J. Brill, 1996), pp. 143–69.

Local Government Association, *Faith and Community: A Good Practice Guide for Local Authorities* (London: Local Government Association, 2002).

Gil Loescher, *Beyond Charity: International Cooperation and the Global Refugee Crises* (Oxford: Oxford University Press, 1993).

Ernst Lohmeyer, *The Lord's Prayer*, trans. John Bowden (London: Collins, 1965).

Stephen Long, *Divine Economy: Theology and the Market* (London: Routledge, 2000).

Bernard Loomer, "Two Conceptions of Power," *Process Studies* 6.1 (1976), pp. 5–32.

Vivien Lowndes and Adam Dinham, "Religion, Resources and Representation: Three Narratives of Faith Engagement in British Urban Governance," *Urban Affairs Review* 43.6 (2008), 817–45.

Steven Lukes, "Power and Authority," in *A History of Sociological Analysis*, ed. Tom Bottomore and Robert Nisbet (New York: Basic Books, 1978), pp. 633–76.

Priya Lukka and Michael Locke, *Faith and Voluntary Action: Community, Values and Resources* (London: Institute for Volunteering Research & University of East London, 2003).

Martin Luther, *Luther's Works*, 55 vols., ed. Jaroslav Pelikan and Helmut Lehmann (Philadelphia, PA and St. Louis, MO: Fortress and Concordia, 1955–1986), vol. 3.

Ulrich Luz, *Matthew 1–7: A Commentary*, trans. Wilhelm Lins (Edinburgh: T&T Clark, 1989).

David Lyon, *Jesus in Disneyland: Religion in Postmodern Times* (Oxford: Polity Press, 2000).

Jay MacLeod, *Community Organising: A Practical and Theological Appraisal* (London: Church Action, 1993).

Alasdair MacIntyre, "Community, Law and the Idiom and Rhetoric of Rights," *Listening* 26 (1991), 96–110.

Alasdair MacIntyre, *After Virtue: A Study in Moral Theory*, 2nd edn (London: Duckworth, 1994).

Alasdair MacIntyre, "Politics, Philosophy and the Common Good," in *The Macintyre Reader*, ed. Kelvin Knight (London: Polity Press, 1998), pp. 235–66.

Alasdair MacIntyre, *Dependent Rational Animals: Why Human Beings Need the Virtues* (London: Duckworth, 1999).

Jacques Maritain, *Christianity and Democracy*, trans. Doris C. Anson (London: Geoffrey Bles, 1945).

Jacques Maritain, *Man and the State* (Washington, DC: Catholic University of America Press, 1998).

Jacques Maritain, *Integral Humanism: Temporal and Spiritual Problems of the New Christendom*, trans. Joseph Evans (New York: Charles Scribner's Sons, 1968).

Robert A. Markus, *Saeculum: History and Society in the Theology of St Augustine* (Cambridge: Cambridge University Press, 1970).

Robert A. Markus, *The End of Ancient Christianity* (Cambridge: Cambridge University Press, 1990).

Robert A. Markus, *Christianity and the Secular* (Notre Dame, IN: University of Notre Dame Press, 2006).

Katherine Marshall and Marisa Van Saanen, *Development and Faith: Where Mind, Heart and Soul Work Together* (Washington, DC: World Bank, 2007).

Paul Marshall, *A Kind of Life Imposed on Man: Vocation and Social Order From Tyndale to Locke* (Toronto: University of Toronto Press, 1996).

David Martin, *A General Theory of Secularization* (New York: Harper & Row, 1979).

Charles Mathewes, "Faith, Hope, and Agony: Christian Political Participation Beyond Liberalism," *Annual of the Society of Christian Ethics* 21 (2001), 125–50.

Charles Mathewes, *A Theology of Public Life* (Cambridge: Cambridge University Press, 2007).

Marcel Mauss, *The Gift: The Form and Reason for Exchange in Archaic Societies* (London: Routledge, 2002).

Eugene McCarraher, "The Enchantment of Mammon: Notes Toward a Theological History of Capitalism," *Modern Theology* 21.3 (2005), 429–61.

Michael McCarthy, "An Ecclesiology of Groaning: Augustine, the Psalms, and the Making of the Church," *Theological Studies* 66.1 (2005), 23–48.

Andrew Mein, *Ezekiel and the Ethics of Exile* (Oxford: Oxford University Press, 2001).

Michele Micheletti, *Political Virtue and Shopping: Individuals, Consumerism, and Collective Action* (New York: Palgrave MacMillan, 2003).

Michele Micheletti, Andreas Follesdal, and Dietlind Stolle, eds., *Politics, Products, Markets: Exploring Political Consumerism Past and Present* (New Brunswick, NJ: Transaction, 2004).

John Milbank, "Enclaves, or Where is the Church?" *New Blackfriars* 73.861 (1992), 341–52.

John Milbank, *Theology and Social Theory: Beyond Secular Reason* (Oxford: Blackwell, 1993).

John Milbank, *The Word Made Strange: Theory, Language, Culture* (Oxford: Blackwell, 1997).

John Milbank, *Being Reconciled: Ontology and Pardon* (London: Routledge, 2003).

John Milbank, *The Future of Love: Essays in Political Theology* (Eugene, OR: Cascade Books, 2009).

Vincent Miller, *Consuming Religion: Christian Faith and Practice in a Consumer Culture* (New York: Continuum, 2004).

Stephen Monsma and J. Christopher Soper, *Faith, Hope and Jobs: Welfare-to Work in Los Angeles* (Washington, DC: Georgetown University Press, 2007).

Geoff Moore, "The Fair Trade Movement: Parameters, Issues and Future Research," *Journal of Business Ethics* 53.1 (2004), 73–86.

Caroline Moorehead, *Human Cargo: A Journey among Refugees* (London: Vintage, 2006).

David Morley, *Home Territories: Media, Mobility and Identity* (London: Routledge, 2000).

Chantal Mouffe, *The Democratic Paradox* (London: Verso, 2000).

Rachel Muers, *Keeping God's Silence* (Oxford: Blackwell, 2004).

Denis Müller, "A Homeland for Transients: Towards an Ethic of Migrations," in Dietmar Mieth and Lisa Sowle Cahill, eds., *Migrants and Refugees* (London: Concilium/SCM Press, 1993), pp. 130–147.

Alexander-Kenneth Nagel, "Charitable Choice: The Religious Component of the US Welfare Reform – Theoretical and Methodological Reflections on 'Faith-Based-Organizations' as Social Service Agencies," *Numen* 53 (2006), 78–111.

Alex Nicholls and Charlotte Opal, *Fair Trade: Market-Driven Ethical Consumption* (London: Sage, 2004).

Reinhold Niebuhr, *Moral Man and Immoral Society: A Study in Ethics and Politics* (New York: Scribner, 1932).

Reinhold Niebuhr, *The Nature and Destiny of Man: A Christian Interpretation*, 2 vols. (New York: Scribner & Sons, 1941–43).

Reinhold Niebuhr, *The Children of Light and the Children of Darkness* (London: Nisbet & Co., 1945).

Reinhold Niebuhr, *Christian Realism and Political Problems* (London: Faber & Faber, 1953).

Pippa Norris, *Democratic Phoenix: Reinventing Political Activism* (Cambridge: Cambridge University Press, 2002).

Martha Nussbaum, "Patriotism and Cosmopolitanism," in *For the Love of Country: Debating the Limits of Patriotism*, ed. Joshua Cohen (Boston, MA: Beacon Press, 1996), pp. 12–17.

Joan Lockwood O'Donovan, "The Church of England and the Anglican Communion: A Timely Engagement with the National Church Tradition?" *Scottish Journal of Theology* 57.3 (2004), 313–37.

Oliver O'Donovan, *The Desire of the Nations: Rediscovering the Roots of Political Theory* (Cambridge: Cambridge University Press, 1996).

Oliver O'Donovan, *The Ways of Judgment* (Grand Rapids, MI: Eerdmans, 2005).

Oliver O'Donovan, "What Kind of Community is the Church?" *Ecclesiology* 3.2 (2007), 171–93.

Oliver O'Donovan and Joan Lockwood O'Donovan, *From Irenaeus to Grotius: A Sourcebook in Christian Political Thought 100–1625* (Grand Rapids, MI: Eerdmans, 1999).

Oliver O'Donovan and Joan Lockwood O'Donovan, *Bonds of Imperfection: Christian Politics, Past and Present* (Grand Rapids, MI: Eerdmans, 2004).

Marvin Olasky, *The Tragedy of American Compassion* (Washington, DC: Regnery Publishing, 1992).

Trisha Olson, "Sanctuary and Penitential Rebirth in the Central Middle Ages," in *Boundaries of the Law: Geography, Gender and Jurisdiction in Mediaeval and Early Modern Europe*, ed. Anthony Musson (Aldershot: Ashgate, 2005), pp. 38–52.

Marion Orr, ed., *Transforming the City: Community Organizing and the Challenges of Political Change* (Lawrence, KS: University of Kansas Press, 2007).

Wolfhart Pannenberg, *Ethics*, trans. Keith Crim (Philadelphia, PA: Westminster Press, 1981).

John Paul II, *Evangelium Vitae* (London: Catholic Truth Society, 1995).

Charles Payne, *I've Got the Light of Freedom: The Organizing Tradition and the Mississippi Freedom Struggle* (Berkeley, CA: University of California Press, 1995).

Leo Penta, "Islands of Democratic Practice: Organizing for Local and Regional Power in the USA," Paper presented at the Biannual European Conference of the Inter-University Consortium for International Social Development in Cracow, Poland, September 24, 1999.

Karl Polanyi, *The Great Transformation: The Political and Economic Origins of Our Time*, 2nd Beacon Paperback edn (Boston, MA: Beacon Press, 2002).

Pontifical Council for Justice and Peace, *Compendium of the Social Doctrine of the Church* (London: Continuum, 2004).

Frank Prochaska, *Christianity and Social Service in Modern Britain: The Disinherited Spirit* (Oxford: Oxford University Press, 2006).

Robert Putnam, *Bowling Alone: The Collapse and Revival of American Community* (New York: Simon & Schuster, 2000).

Robert Putnam, "*E Pluribus Unum:* Diversity and Community in the Twenty-first Century. The 2006 Johan Skytte Prize Lecture," *Scandinavian Political Studies* 30.2 (2007), 137–74.

Ben Quash, " 'Deep Calls To Deep': Reading Scripture in a Multi-Faith Society," in Andrew Walker and Luke Bretherton, eds., *Remembering our Future: Explorations in Deep Church* (Milton Keynes: Paternoster Press, 2007), pp. 114–17.

Roy Rappaport, *Ritual and Religion in the Making of Humanity* (Cambridge: Cambridge University Press, 1999).

Arne Rasmusson, *The Church as Polis: From Political Theology to Theological Politics as Exemplified by Jürgen Moltmann and Stanley Hauerwas* (Notre Dame, IN: University of Notre Dame Press, 1995).

John Rawls, *Political Liberalism* (New York: Columbia University Press, 1996).

John Rawls, *The Law of Peoples* (Cambridge, MA: Harvard University Press, 2001).

David Rieff, *A Bed for the Night: Humanitarianism in Crises* (London: Vintage, 2002).

Richard Rorty, "Religion as a Conversation-Stopper," *Common Knowledge* 3.1 (1994), 1–6.

John Rist, *Augustine: Ancient Thought Baptized* (Cambridge: Cambridge University Press, 1994).

Stephen C. Rose, "Saul Alinsky and His Critics," in *Citizen Participation in Urban Development. Vol. 1: Concept and Issues*, ed. Hans B. C. Spiegel (Washington, DC: NTL Institute for Applied Behavioural Science, 1968), pp. 162–83.

Gervase Rosser, "Sanctuary and Social Negotiation in Medieval England," in *The Cloister and the World*, eds. John Blair and Brian Golding (Oxford: Clarendon Press, 1996), pp. 57–79.

William Ryan, "The Historical Case for the Right of Sanctuary," *Journal of Church and State* 29 (1987), 209–32.

Lamin Sanneh, *Translating the Message: The Missionary Impact on Culture* (Maryknoll, NY: Orbis Books, 1989).

Jeanne H. Schindler, "A Companionship of *Caritas*: Friendship in St Thomas Aquinas," *Friendship and Politics: Essays in Political Thought*, eds. John Von Heyking and Richard Avramenko (Notre Dame, IN: University of Notre Dame Press, 2008), pp. 139–62.

Thomas Schlereth, *The Cosmopolitan Ideal* (Notre Dame, IN: University of Notre Dame, 1977).

Christoph Schwöbel, "Particularity, Universality, and the Religions: Towards a Christian Theology of Religions," in *Christian Uniqueness Reconsidered: The Myth of a Pluralistic Theology of Religions*, ed. Gavin D'Costa (Maryknoll, NY: Orbis Books, 1996), pp. 30–46.

Peter Sedgwick, *The Market Economy and Christian Ethics* (Cambridge: Cambridge University Press, 1999).

Christopher Seitz, *Theology in Conflict: Reactions to the Exile in the Book of Jeremiah* (Berlin: Walter de Gruyter, 1989).

Amartya Sen, *Poverty and Famines* (Oxford: Clarendon Press, 1981).

Andrew Shacknove, "Who is a refugee?" *Ethics* 95.2 (1985), 274–84.

Ronald Sider, "Typology of Religious Characteristics of Social Service and Educational Organizations and Programs," *Nonprofit and Voluntary Sector Quarterly* 33.1 (2004), 109–34.

Georg Simmel, *The Sociology of Georg Simmel*, trans. Kurt H. Wolff (New York: Free Press, 1950).

Theda Skocpol, *Diminished Democracy: From Membership to Management in American Civic Life* (Norman, OK: University of Oklahoma Press, 2004).

Daniel Smith, "Jeremiah as Prophet of Nonviolence," *Journal for the Study of the Old Testament* 13.43 (1989), p. 97.

Daniel Smith-Christopher, *A Biblical Theology of Exile* (Minneapolis, MN: Augsberg Fortress, 2002).

Greg Smith, "Religion as a source of social capital in the regeneration of East London," *Rising East* 4.3 (2001), 128–57.

Greg Smith, "Faith in Community and Communities of Faith? Government Rhetoric and Religious Identity in Urban Britain," *Journal of Contemporary Religion* 19.2 (2004), 185–204.

James K. A. Smith, *Introducing Radical Orthodoxy: Mapping a Post-secular Theology* (Grand Rapids, MI: Baker Academic, 2004).

Steven Smith and Michael Sosin, "The Varieties of Faith-Related Agencies," *Public Administration Review* 61.6 (2001), 651–70.

Lewis D. Solomon, *In God we trust? Faith-based Organizations and the Quest to Solve America's Social Ills* (Lanham, MD: Lexington Books, 2003).

Robert Song, *Christianity and Liberal Society* (Oxford: Clarendon, 1997).

Basia Spalek, Salwa El Awa, and Laura McDonald, *Police–Muslim Engagement and Partnerships for the Purpose of Counter-Terrorism: An Examination, Summary Report* (Arts and Humanities Research Council/University of Birmingham, 2008).

Paul Statham, "Understanding Anti-Asylum Rhetoric: Restrictive Politics or Racist Publics?" in Sarah Spencer, ed., *The Politics of Migration: Managing Opportunity, Conflict and Change* (Oxford: Blackwell, 2003), pp. 163–77.

Rodney Stark, "Secularisation, R.I.P.," *Sociology of Religion* 60.3 (1999), 249–273.

Gerry Stoker, *Transforming Local Governance: from Thatcherism to New Labour* (London: Palgrave Macmillan 2004).

Jeffrey Stout, *Democracy and Tradition* (Princeton, NJ: Princeton University Press, 2004).

Anne Tallontire, Erdenechimeg Rentsendorj, and Mick Blowfield, *Ethical Consumers and Ethical Trade: A Review of Current Literature* (London: Natural Resources Institute, 2001).

Charles Taylor, "Multiculturalism and the 'Politics of Recognition,' " in *Multiculturalism and the "Politics of Recognition." An Essay by Charles Taylor*, ed. Amy Gutmann, (Princeton, NJ: Princeton University Press, 1992), pp. 25–73.

Charles Taylor, "Invoking Civil Society," in *Contemporary Political Philosophy: An Anthology* (Oxford: Blackwell, 1997), pp. 66–77.

Charles Taylor, *A Secular Age* (Cambridge, MA: Harvard University Press, 2007).

Jenny Taylor, "There's Life in Establishment – But Not as We Know It," *Political Theology* 5.3 (2004), 329–349.

The Participation of Catholics in Political Life (Vatican Congregation for the Doctrine of the Faith, 2002).

Isobel Thornley, "The Destruction of Sanctuary," in *Tudor Studies*, ed. R. W. Seton-Watson (London: Longman, Green & Co., 1924), pp. 182–207.

Norman Trenholme, *The Right of Sanctuary in England: A Study in Institutional History* (Columbia, MO: University of Missouri Press, 1903).

Frank Trentmann, "The Modern Evolution of the Consumer: Meanings, Knowledge, and Identities Before the Age of Affluence," *Cultures of Consumption, an ESRC–AHRB Research Programme Working Paper No. 10* (2004), pp. 1–46.

Miroslav Volf, *Exclusion and Embrace: A Theological Exploration of Identity, Otherness, and Reconciliation* (Nashville, TN: Abingdon Press, 1996).

Hent de Vries and Lawrence E. Sullivan, *Political Theologies: Public Religions in a Post-Secular World* (New York: Fordham University Press, 2006).

Geoffrey Wainwright, *Doxology: The Praise of God in Worship, Doctrine, and Life: A Systematic Theology* (London: Oxford University Press, 1980).

Jeremy Waldron, "Cultural Identity and Civic Responsibility," in *Citizenship in Diverse Societies*, eds. Will Kymlicka and Wayne Norman (Oxford: Oxford University Press, 2000), pp. 155–174.

Jeremy Waldron, *Law and Disagreement* (Oxford: Clarendon Press, 1999).

Andrew Walls, *The Missionary Movement in Christian History* (Edinburgh: T&T Clark, 1996).

Michael Walzer, *Spheres of Justice: A Defence of Pluralism and Equality* (New York: Basic Books, 1983).

Michael Walzer, "The Civil Society Argument," *Theorizing Citizenship*, ed. R. Beiner (New York: SUNY Press, 1995), pp. 153–74.

Bernd Wannenwetsch, "The Political Worship of the Church: A Critical and Empowering Practice," *Modern Theology* 12.3 (1996), 269–99.

Bernd Wannenwetsch, *Political Worship: Ethics for Christian Citizens* (Oxford: Oxford University Press, 2004).

Graham Ward, "Questioning God," in *Questioning God*, eds. John D. Caputo, Michael Scanlon, and Mark Dooley (Bloomington, IN: Indiana University Press, 2001).

Graham Ward, *True Religion* (Oxford: Wiley-Blackwell, 2003).

Alan Warde, "Theories of Practice as an Approach to Consumption," *Cultures of Consumption, an ESRC–AHRB Research Programme, Working Paper No. 6*, March 18, 2004.

A. Warde, G. Tampubolon, M. Tomlinson, K. Ray, B. Longhurst, and M. Savage, "Trends in Social Capital: Membership of Associations in Great Britain, 1991–98," *British Journal of Political Science* 33.3 (2003), 515–25.

Mark R. Warren, *Dry Bones Rattling: Community Building to Revitalize American Democracy* (Princeton, NJ: Princeton University Press, 2001).

Myron Weiner, *The Global Migration Crises: Challenges to States and to Human Rights* (New York: HarperCollins College Publishers, 1995).

George Weigel, "John Paul II and the Priority of Culture," *First Things* 80 (1998), 19–25.

Paul Weitham, "Introduction: Religion and the Liberalism of Reasoned Respect," in *Religion and Contemporary Liberalism*, ed. Paul Weitham (Notre Dame, IN: University of Notre Dame Press, 1997), pp. 1–37.

White Paper, *Communities in Control: Real People, Real Power* (London: Department for Communities and Local Government, 2008).

Bryan Wilson, *Religion in Sociological Perspective* (Oxford: Oxford University Press, 1982).

John Witte, *The Reformation of Rights: Law, Religion and Human Rights in Early Modern Calvinism* (Cambridge: Cambridge University Press, 2008).

Sheldon Wolin, "Contract and Birthright," *Political Theory* 14.2 (1986), 179–193.

Sheldon Wolin, *The Presence of the Past: Essays on the State and Constitution* (Baltimore, MD: John Hopkins University Press, 1989).

Sheldon Wolin, *Politics and Vision: Continuity and Innovation in Western Political Thought*, exp. edn (Princeton, NJ: Princeton University Press, 2004).

Diane Wood, *Medieval Economic Thought* (Cambridge: Cambridge University Press, 2002).

Richard Wood, *Faith in Action: Religion, Race, and Democratic Organizing in America* (Chicago, IL: University of Chicago Press, 2002).

Linda Woodhead, ed., *Peter Berger and the Study of Religion* (London: Routledge, 2001).

Robert Wuthnow, *Saving America? Faith-based Services and the Future of Civil Society* (Princeton, NJ: Princeton University Press, 2004).

John Howard Yoder, "How H. Richard Niebuhr Reasoned: A Critique of *Christ and Culture*," in *Authentic Transformation: A New Vision of Christ and Culture*, eds. Glen Stassen et al. (Nashville, TN: Abingdon, 1996), pp. 31–90.

John Howard Yoder, "The Christian Case for Democracy," in *The Priestly Kingdom: Social Ethics as Gospel* (Notre Dame, IN: University of Notre Dame Press, 1984), pp. 151–171.

John Howard Yoder, *The Politics of Jesus*, 2nd edn (Grand Rapids, MI: Eerdmans, 1994).

John Howard Yoder, *The Jewish–Christian Schism Revisited*, eds. Michael Cartwright and Peter Ochs (Grand Rapids, MI: Eerdmans, 2003).

Iris Marion Young, *Justice and the Politics of Difference* (Princeton, NJ: Princeton University Press, 1990).

Iris Marion Young, "Communication and the Other: Beyond Deliberative Democracy," in *Democracy and Difference*, ed. Seyla Benhabib (Princeton, NJ: Princeton University Press, 1996).

Slavoj Žižek, *The Ticklish Subject: The Absent Centre of Political Ontology* (London: Verso, 1999).

Index